# Learning from Young Children in the Classroom

## The ART and SCIENCE of TEACHER RESEARCH

## Daniel R. Meier
## and Barbara Henderson
### Foreword by Lilian G. Katz

# Learning from Young Children in the Classroom

## The Art & Science of Teacher Research

Daniel R. Meier
Barbara Henderson

*Foreword by*
*Lilian G. Katz*

Teachers College, Columbia University
New York and London

Published by Teachers College Press, 1234 Amsterdam Avenue, New York, NY 10027

"Just Looking," from *Word from the (415): Poems and stories by youth of San Francisco* (San Francisco: WritersCorps, 1996), reprinted by permission of WritersCorps Books.

Poems on pp. 56 and 82 reprinted by permission from Eric Chock, ed., *Small kid time Hawaii* (Honolulu, HI: Bamboo Ridge Press, 1981).

*Library of Congress Cataloging-in-Publication Data*

Meier, Daniel R.
    Learning from young children in the classroom : the art and science of teacher research / Daniel R. Meier ; Barbara Henderson ; foreword by Lilian Katz.
        p. cm.
    Includes bibliographical references and index.
    ISBN-13: 978-0-8077-4768-1 (alk. paper)
    ISBN-10: 0-8077-4768-8 (alk. paper)
    ISBN-13: 978-0-8077-4767-4 (pbk. : alk. paper)
    ISBN-10: 0-8077-4767-X (pbk. : alk. paper)
    1. Action research in education—United States.  2. Early childhood education—United States.  I. Henderson, Barbara.  II. Title.
    LB1028.24. M465 2006
    370.7'2—dc22                                                                2006037629

ISBN 13: 978-0-8077-4767-4 (paper)
ISBN 13: 978-0-8077-4768-1 (cloth)

Printed on acid-free paper

Manufactured in the United States of America

14  13  12  11  10  09  08  07        8  7  6  5  4  3  2  1

*For Toby*

Daniel R. Meier


*For Signe and Ingrid*

Barbara Henderson

# Contents

# Foreword

The term *research* implies an effort to search again, to undertake careful and assiduous inquiry about the nature of a particular event or phenomenon in need of deeper understanding. The researcher is focused on establishing basic and reliable facts and operating principles that can serve as a basis for improving the phenomena under investigation. Most educators are accustomed to such research being conducted by specialists who are not usually "in the trenches" themselves. Indeed, in recent times educators have been strongly urged to rely on research that meets strong scientific criteria that include random assignments of subjects to the processes being studied among many other standard research procedures intended to assure objectivity and reliability of the evidence; and so it has become a cliché to make claims for "evidence-based" research and practice.

In this book, Daniel Meier and Barbara Henderson offer us a detailed guide to another kind of research that is likely to assist educators in their work as much as—if not more than—the traditional experimental scientific research. The authors share with us a rich body of evidence produced by teachers conducting research in their own classes and programs, and many clear indications of how their experience of gathering evidence both enlighten their practices and benefit the children they serve. The examples of teachers' own data gathering address a very wide range of developmental and learning issues. The age range included in their discussion includes children up to 8 years old, and includes many aspects of teachers' research on the relationships of teaching to the learning of young children, as well as relationships of their own teaching to their own learning.

The comprehensive scope of this book provides a background of the historical context in which our teachers of young children are now working. It also offers readers guiding questions to help teachers launch their own patterns of research on their practices. Additionally, it includes good examples of how teachers can share with each other their work and the insights it yields; in this way they not only assist each other in teaching practices, but inspire each other as well.

The ultimate goal of all types of educational research is to improve practice so that it is increasingly effective in influencing children's growth, development, and learning. The kind of research that teachers can do, as so clearly shown in the pages that follow, does justice to the complex contexts in which teachers of young children work. The ideas, examples, stories, and suggestions and guidelines included here offer real promise for the improvements that we all strive for so intensely.

—*Lilian G. Katz*

# Acknowledgments

We wish to thank Brian Ellerbeck of Teachers College Press for his initial interest in this book and his support in waiting for the arrival of the book at the press. We also wish to thank Marie Ellen Larcada, who helped shepard the book through its final phase, and Lori Tate for the speedy production schedule.

Daniel would like to thank Barbara for helping conceptualize the idea for the book and writing the first two chapters. It was a pleasure to extend our work to writing and publication. I wish to thank the young child poets who gave their permission for the poems that appear in all chapters. I also thank all of the devoted teacher researchers featured in my chapters: Alvina Cheah, Cary Crawford, Evangeline Espiritu, Michael Escamilla, Jessica Fickle, Lukas Frei, Connie Jubb, Susan Kraus, Mary Lin, Kelly Lopez, Aaron Neimark, Ivy Ng, Jacqueline Paras-Frei, Norma Villazana-Price, Stacia Stribling, Pat Sullivan, Margaret Thrupp, Julie Vazquez-Torres, Sivinee Traiprakong, Nathan Weber, and Manuel Kichi Wong. Finally, a big big hug to Hazelle, Kaili, and Toby—without their patience and humor no book can be written in our household.

Barbara would like to thank Daniel, who remained supportive, optimistic, and forward looking throughout the long process of planning and writing this book. Writing this book allowed us to deepen our understanding of teacher research and draw on the wisdom of our students over the years to show what works. I also would like to thank my graduate students over the years, who have undertaken a huge range of teacher research projects both in coursework and as culminating field studies for their Master of Arts degrees. In particular, I thank the following former students and colleagues whose inquiries provided me with examples of teacher research undertaken in current early childhood settings: Carlyn Jue, Anne Markevich, Leanne Foley, Dale Richardson, Lynn Juarez, Cathy Greene, Susan Stevenson, Shelly Swanegan, Christine Olsen, Ivy Ng, Vivian Alipio, Ashley Kasperczyk, Patricia Sullivan, Ana Fisher, Amy Cheng, Lori McGaughey, Chae Ornelas, Roxanne Latif, Holly Andrews, Jessica Fickle, Jing-Tyng Shyu, Laura Miles-Banta, Jennifer Day, Cathy Richardson, Katya Alvarado, Michael Escamilla, and Jeanne Soulé. I also thank my family, near and far, for their patience and support.

# Introduction

Just Looking

*To me I see an eagle.*
*I'm just looking straight up.*
*Blue, just blue.*
*Maybe God.*
*hmm. Maybe*

*During the night it's much easier*
*because you see all the other things*
*—like UFOs.*

*I do wonder what's in the blue,*
*what's above it.*
*—Holy shoots!*
*Looks like a volcano right there!*
*An explosion just happened!*
*Oh—I'm seeing something!*
*George Washington? What's he doing there?*
*I can see the cloud moving.*
*I don't know. Just moving around.*
*I wonder how long it takes to get to the cloud . . .*
*All those clouds were shattering into pieces.*
*Now they're all together.*

—Kalani Lua, age 10
From *Word From the (415): Poems and*
*Stories by Youth of San Francisco,* 1996

Teaching and learning with young children often seems like Kalani's poem. For example, as we observe children trying to spell a word in their journals, or scan a circle of faces as we pose a question about a book, or look at two children building a block tower, we are looking just like Kalani's narrator in the poem. As the narrator "looks straight up" and sees "blue, just blue," sometimes in our early childhood work it's hard to tell how effective our teaching

1

and caregiving are. In other words, it just seems all "blue, just blue." And so to strengthen our teaching and caregiving, we wonder "what's in the blue, what's above it." Just as the narrator wonders about "the sky" and "the blue" and "what's above it," we as early childhood practitioners wonder what's going on for our children during the many small moments of teaching, and what's going on "above" the scene we are experiencing together.

Taking a cue from Kalani's poem on the value of looking more deeply at human experience, this book is about how teacher research and inquiry help us see what's going on ("see the blue") in our work with children and understand conceptually and practically how we can improve our teaching and caregiving ("I do wonder what's in the blue, what's above it"). Teacher research is a form of professional experience that deepens our teaching and learning experiences with children.

As Lilian Katz says about project-based work, "It is important for both children and educators to foster an intellectual disposition for a deeper and more accurate sense of experience. And a good way to start is not to ask, 'What do you want to know?' but 'What do you want to find out?'" (personal communication, July 20, 2006). This question is more concrete, more tied to experience for both children and educators, and a more fruitful direction for staying close to the world of young children. Teacher research and inquiry, then, help us better understand *what* it is that children are doing, and *how* and *why* they learn to talk, make friends, dance, play games, draw, hypothesize, collaborate, solve disputes, make sculptures. In this way, too, teacher research has the potential to serve as a model for ongoing professional support, collaboration, and growth. Teacher inquiry is also about educational change, a bottom-up or grass-roots framework for rethinking and redoing our work with children, families, and colleagues. Again, according to Lilian Katz, long-term work and inquiry with children lead to a "passion about discovery" and collaborative "work with a purpose."

As early childhood educators, we actually undertake research every day in our work, although we rarely realize it. We observe our children, we wonder what they are doing, and we make plans to help them to learn and get along better together. While we do this both consciously and unconsciously, we often do not think of it as research or as inquiry. The purpose and value of teacher research is to make this process more conscious, more deliberate, and more a part of our daily work as professionals. In the spirit of inquiry and problem solving, teacher research adds a sense of self-consciousness to our teaching through careful observation, documentation, analysis, reflective writing and representation, collaboration with colleagues, and sharing of what we've learned.

This book offers background and examples for early childhood practitioners to gain knowledge and skills for undertaking teacher research either in a college or university course or as part of their own professional inquiry and growth in an early childhood setting. As a book for educators who teach across the 0 to 8 age span, it presents a broad picture of teacher research ideas and principles across this developmental continuum. The book is also of interest to early childhood administrators, researchers, policymakers, and parents—all those interested in seeking new models for strengthening inquiry and change for young children, their families, and educators.

Chapter 1, "Framing Inquiry—And Staying Close to Children," is written by Barbara and provides an overview of the most important contributions of teacher research, showing in particular how it can help those of us working in early childhood. The chapter offers a description of central terminology in the field and provides a brief historical overview of central ideas, goals, and strategies in teacher research.

Chapter 2, "The Process of Inquiry—The Art of Doing Teacher Research," is written by Barbara and discusses ways to document children's learning and development across varied learning environments. The use of graphic documentation, such as photographs, children's drawings, and text captions, can provide useful and holistic assessments of children's learning and our teaching effectiveness.

Daniel wrote the remaining chapters. Chapter 3, "Using Teacher Research to Understand and Promote Children's Play and Interaction," looks at how teacher research helps us understand and strengthen children's social interactions and play. The examples from actual teacher research projects focus on effective ways that teacher researchers have conceptualized and carried out projects on children's social interactions and play.

Chapter 4, "Teacher Research and Understanding Children's Language Development," discusses the role of teacher research in understanding and improving young children's oral and nonverbal communication. Through examples of teacher research projects, both short- and long-term, the chapter presents practical ways to envision and carry out projects on language across the 0–8 age span.

Chapter 5, "Teacher Research and Children's Projects and Literacy Learning," helps us understand effective ways to design and carry out teacher research projects on children's project-based work, writing, dictation, reading, and literacy environments. Examples are drawn from both short- and long-term projects in multilingual early childhood settings.

Chapter 6, "Forms of Writing and Disseminating Teacher Research," addresses how teacher researchers can use writing and other forms of visual representation to reflect, understand, and disseminate our work. The chapter also offers ideas and strategies for strengthening our writing as we share our work with colleagues and the early childhood education field (ECE).

Chapter 7, "Future Directions for Teacher Research in Early Childhood Education," concludes the book by highlighting the essential elements of the value of doing teacher research in early childhood education. The chapter also discusses future directions that teacher research can take for ECE practitioners, administrators, families, researchers, policymakers, and teacher educators.

Just as the 10-year-old author Kalani does in his poem—"I do wonder what's in the blue"—teacher research helps us look more closely at what's "in the clouds," what's "in the blue," and what's "above it." We hope you find our ideas and strategies for teacher research to be valuable for you as well as your colleagues.

# CHAPTER 1

# Framing Inquiry— And Staying Close to Children

Ode to the Creek

*Ode to the creek that is part of a difficult puzzle,*
*Ode to the creek that is a piece of art,*
*Ode to the creek that chirps on top of the willow tree,*
*Ode to the creek that nourishes the deer and antelope,*
*Ode to the creek that is undercovered by earth,*
*Ode to the creek that holds my soul.*

—Mehrnush Golriz, age 10

Guiding Questions

1. What is teacher research?
2. What is its value for early childhood education and practitioners?
3. What are current influential models for teacher research in early childhood education?
4. What are different kinds of early childhood teacher research?
5. How can teacher research complement and strengthen popular curricular models and frameworks in early childhood?

## TEACHER RESEARCH AND EARLY CHILDHOOD PRACTICE

As in Mehrnush's poem, teacher research can be a "puzzle" that both "nourishes" us and holds our "soul." It is a journey of discovery and learning that is not always clear or easy. Since it is a relatively new endeavor in early childhood practice, educators have strong opinions about both its value and its potential challenges.

- "If I did research on my own teaching, who would believe me? After all, I'd be talking about myself."
- "Teachers should have a voice in educational research. We have an insiders' view into teaching and learning that university researchers and policymakers can never have."
- "I can't really do research myself; I don't know statistics."
- "I want to learn methods to do research on questions that matter to me in my daily teaching life."
- "How can teachers have time to do research? It is not realistic to the way our work lives are structured."

Teacher research in education in general is a practice with a long tradition, and over the past 15 years, there has been a resurgence of interest in the legitimacy of the research methodologies of teacher research. Teacher research is inquiry done by educators based on their own work in schools and other early childhood settings. Among early childhood educators, teacher research is uncommon, yet our practices and our working conditions provide us with great potential for sustained inquiry. And we do have a tradition; other teachers working with young children have written reflectively about their practice, most famously Vivian Paley and Sylvia Ashton Warner.

Research is a word that puts many of us off. A central goal of this book is to explain how teacher research is practical work, and work sorely needed in our profession today, as we face both an increasing push for standards-based curricula and a move toward requiring higher educational standards for early childhood teachers. Teacher research makes sense and adds value when incorporated within normal teaching practice. Teacher research is also a self-regulating activity, meaning that it begins with teachers themselves. It can enhance daily practice to improve our teaching, transform early childhood educators' professional lives, and affect educational policy. As ECE caregivers, teachers, and administrators reconceptualize themselves as professionals with unique knowledge to share, they become more effective advocates whose inquiry can change policy that concerns children and families.

How does teacher research connect naturally to normal teaching practice? Good teachers already ask questions of their practice, collect evidence from their students' behavior and performance, try out fixes, see what happens, and then adjust as needed. Therefore, the teaching cycle can be seen as a form of research based on taking practical action. Yet teachers are isolated in their classrooms, and so need ways to test out and verify their findings.

Teachers also need accountability structures and human support to help them be consistent and systematic about inquiry. Exchanging ideas with other teachers can extend teachers' work beyond the daily responses they gather from young students. Teacher research provides ECE professionals with a pathway, a set of methods, and a language to reach these goals.

When early childhood educators have knowledge of teacher research, and see it as a valid domain of study, they provide themselves with a framework for beginning this work, a sense of history on the teacher research movement, and a way to talk about what they do in classrooms as a part of a tradition of inquiry. Once early childhood educators see inquiry as key to teaching, they can find ways to sharpen that process of questioning and generating new knowledge. Teachers who undertake inquiry—by asking questions, documenting results, analyzing what they have found, and then presenting their findings—demonstrate to themselves, the families they serve, their administrators, and their colleagues that they, as ECE practitioners, understand and act upon the trust placed in them to support children's learning and development.

## Defining Teacher Research

Teacher research is the study of the self, focused on teachers' and caregivers' daily interactions with children, families, and teaching colleagues. Inquiries are informed by the quest to improve daily practice, often with the express goal of improving equity and access to quality schooling or nurturing group care. What then, makes such work "research" and not just teaching, or simply living? Stenhouse (1981) defines research as systematic, critical inquiry made public. Teachers' professional lives can become teacher research when teachers pay special attention to what they do. The process begins when teachers frame the challenges in their work as a starting point for inquiry and set out purposefully in search of better answers. This book also will demonstrate how teacher research need not demand more time from teachers. Instead, it presents ways for teachers to select different ways to use their time and energy in the classroom and during preparation periods.

In daily work as teachers and administrators, ECE professionals will always meet challenges to which they must respond. Teaching-as-research prompts the practitioner not simply to be reactive to events, but to take initiative to frame questions and propose solutions. Framing one's professional life as a set of questions is, therefore, the first step. The second step is for teachers to undertake a planned search for evidence that will help them understand their questions more deeply. In teaching each day, teachers collect relevant data about how children learn, where they struggle, how they develop, and what provides support. In doing research on their teaching practice, teachers can make plans about what they will collect, how they will catalogue it, and how they can analyze it to turn it into evidence for their claims to knowledge.

According to Stenhouse's definition, research must be made public to complete the cycle. Therefore, doing teacher research is also about learning to value the results of one's study enough to share findings with others. Doing inquiry modifies what teachers know, how they teach, and even the questions they ask about teaching, learning, and the institution of school itself. In preparing to enact their performance of findings (whether that performance is written, oral, graphic, or in another mode), teacher researchers clarify their thinking about what they've found and why it matters. Furthermore, they influence a small circle of educators by their example and their discoveries. At the same time, colleagues' responses to findings validate conclusions and further influence the meanings teachers take away from their research.

For many teachers, much about this process of response feels natural as these same steps are embedded in teaching itself. Each day in their daily normal practice, teachers inquire (e.g., What approach works best to teach this material? How should I set up the room for the children to be more productive?) and collect data (e.g., observing children at work and play, gathering work samples). They also communicate their findings, as they seek ways to connect with their students, talk to families, or collaborate with colleagues. With teacher research, teachers find ways to make these actions conscious and focused. As an approach, teacher research provides a set of tools and habits of mind that help teachers to stop reacting, and begin to see that by just looking, and then telling others what they see, they begin to deepen and clarify the professionalism of their role as early childhood educators.

Undertaking research focused on the practical teaching decisions that swirl around teachers daily allows them to take a self-regulated and powerful stance toward their teaching lives. Teacher research shows teachers how they can identify the most pressing issue within a competing mass of inputs, then frame a question, collect relevant data, and implement an action plan that helps them reach their goals. In this way, teacher researchers professionalize themselves as they become experts on the self-defined issues that most impact their teaching. As ECE practitioners begin to take charge of the environments where they work, the teaching climate changes and teacher researchers' initiatives for change become policy at their school sites.

Thus, research is a performance of original knowledge recently gained through planned study. The public sharing of teacher research is not limited to academic journals or formal conference presentations. Instead, to be alive and practical in early childhood settings, teacher research also must be created and used in local and informal ways, for example, through conversations or sharing of display panels. Teacher research is also a call to teachers to join the ranks of educational researchers and to contribute to broad-scale changes in educational research.

Currently, educational research is populated almost entirely by those who work at the university level. As professors, educational researchers teach courses to graduate or college-level students. They are, then, in some way teachers, but "teacher" is not a high-status identity within the academy and teaching is not the subject of most published work. Therefore, most educational researchers identify primarily with their training in a discipline such as psychology, linguistics, anthropology, sociology, economics, history, or philosophy. In early childhood education, our connections to developmental psychology have kept us closest to psychology, which was also the dominant paradigm for educational research in general from the 1950s until the early 1980s. Furthermore, traditional educational research does not draw from teacher knowledge as a primary source of new knowledge in the field. Instead, educational researchers intentionally embrace the role of outsiders in classrooms and schools, looking in to measure children's knowledge or evaluate teachers' approaches. The title of an influential early book on teacher research, *Inside/Outside: Teacher Research and Knowledge* (Cochran-Smith & Lytle, 1993) plays on this metaphor.

The result of this split within the field is that for teachers working daily with children, most educational research feels removed and irrelevant. Teachers often do not read the journals of educational research, and even teacher training programs make relatively little use of this work, opting instead for a focus on more practical aspects of curriculum and classroom management. Teacher research is, then, a move to bring the process of inquiry about classrooms and children back to teachers. The teacher research movement sees teachers as legitimate sources of knowledge about their own practice and about the processes of children's learning and development.

But can teachers undertake research in the midst of everything else they do? And why would they bother? When we undertake self-study of our teaching practices, we find ways to improve our teaching from the ordinary data of our teaching lives. Teacher research also gives us an arena to ask hard questions about our teaching, the institutions in which we work, and our students. For example: Why do certain activities work while others do not? How can we know whether and how well our approaches work? For whom do they work, and for whom do they fail? What is our own role in these successes and failures, and how can we do it differently next time? What are the roles of the institution, the power structures that it supports, and the inequities of the broader society?

Another way that teacher research stretches us as thinkers is that it gives us means and motivation to reach out to other educators to collaborate on ideas, share insights about teaching, and continue to learn and grow as professionals. People surround us as we teach; yet paradoxically, teaching is often an isolating profession. Teacher research provides a door to step outside of our normal educational setting and reflect more critically on the children and the school structures that surround us each day.

Isolation within teaching practices is common at the ECE level, in elementary, middle, and high schools, and even at universities. Most of us teach in our classrooms with closed doors, registering only to ourselves what is going on, and even then dimly. How much are we even conscious of? How much simply washes over us? Even when teachers share the teaching floor with assistants, we seldom make time to talk about what is going on and how we feel about it. In part, teachers tend not to collaborate with their assistant teachers because the hierarchical relationship and scheduling make a collaborative process hard. But this need not be the case. The goals of this book are to describe how teacher research gives practitioners in ECE a model, a format, and a set of tools that can help teachers to enhance their way of being with children and with teaching colleagues.

## What Can We Do with Teacher Research?

Teacher research serves a range of related purposes for teachers and administrators. As a form of inquiry, teacher research is open to many ways of looking at children, schools, and society. Teacher research can look inwards as well, and be primarily a study of the self as teacher or an act of artistic expression. For a teacher just beginning to consider teacher research, understanding the breadth of questions it can address might feel overwhelming. Yet there is freedom in this scope. Because teacher research can encompass many kinds of studies, teacher researchers should ask questions that matter most to them. As an illustration, here are 10 of the most common ways teacher research projects are framed.

1. Child study (a case study of a child)
2. Self-study (a case study of oneself)
3. Artistic expression (e.g., poetry, photography, sculpture, collage)
4. Teaching (e.g., an outcome measure of an instructional approach)
5. Learning and child development (an outcome measure of student change)
6. Development or implementation of curriculum
7. Classroom or school-wide environment
8. Building collaboration (e.g., among teachers, with families)
9. Professional development (e.g., an outcome measure of staff change)
10. Political and institutional critique

Child studies, self-studies, and artistic expression by the teacher are some of the most interior types of studies. These inquiries begin in the classroom with the teacher looking at a particular child or at him- or herself as teacher. Questions in these categories that our teacher researchers have asked include:

*Case study*: "How can I work effectively to guide a child who has difficulty with the transition from free play to a structured routine?" (Latif, 2005)

*Self-study*: "How did my growing-up environment in a homogeneous suburban community affect my art of teaching in a diverse urban setting?" (Kasperzyk, 2005)

*Artistic expression*: "What do the photographic portraits I take of my students show me about the attachment relationships I form with these toddlers I care for, and about the overall quality of my teaching?" (Fickle, 2003)

Although these studies begin with a distinctive focus on an individual, each of them goes beyond immediate, local concerns when the writing (and visual art) is persuasive, detailed, and believable enough that other teachers can transfer the message and experience to their own situations. These studies examine the particular to create new knowledge from an honest and critical examination of the course of events. The particular, then, stands as a key example of the phenomenon or concept, and through the eyes of the interpretive audience, generalizes to other settings.

Next are types of inquiry that address questions of teaching, learning, and children's development. Many teacher researchers choose to address teaching and learning as their research question because the goals of this research naturally coincide with the goals of schooling to teach content and skills. Our teacher researchers have asked such questions as:

*Learning and development*: "How can I, as a non-native speaker of English, be most effective using book reading with infants to promote children's English language development?" (Shyu, 2005)

*Teaching and learning*: "How do I, an experienced preschool teacher, develop classroom community among a group of transitional kindergartners when several have special needs in social and emotional development that require a good deal of my attention?" (Miles-Banta, 2004)

*Teaching and learning*: "How can I effectively teach science to my preschoolers, even though I lack confidence in my own knowledge in the discipline?" (Alvarado, 2006)

As these categories show, such questions, set in a teaching environment, make it hard to sort out a question primarily about teaching from a question primarily about learning and development. For a teacher researcher, it is fine to begin with a question that could go either way and then gradually develops through the process of collecting and analyzing the data. With these three examples, the first and second studies ended up primarily about children's learning and development, as influenced by the teacher's strengths; the study of classroom community focused mostly on teaching, as influenced by the composition of that particular classroom of learners. The third study, on science teaching, moved back and forth between teaching and learning through use of memoir, child observations, and reflections on the effectiveness of lessons and the classroom environment.

In contrast to these broader, discipline-based ways to focus on teaching, learning, and development, other teachers make a particular project-based or curricular tool the focus of their research. A curriculum-centered approach provides a more concrete way to look at questions of teaching, learning, and development, as it provides a set of materials, lessons, and a timeline across the unit to measure results. Some of our teacher researchers have asked the following curricular questions:

> *Curriculum assessment*: "How does the Open Court Reading program function in this preschool, and how does this contrast with my experience with Open Court as an elementary school teacher? (Jue, 2005)
>
> *Curriculum development*: "What lessons and activities most effectively engage my preschoolers with mathematical concepts?" (Markevich, 2006)
>
> *Curriculum Implementation*: "How can I use a long-term project on novel sensory experiences to build the confidence and ability to experiment with materials among our 2-year-olds?" (Markevich, personal communication)

The next layer is the educational environment—either the classroom or the whole school. Studies at this level often use multiple case studies to look contrastively across groups of children and see how different children react to changes in the environment. Studies that involve a whole school or center are most successful when they have a number of teachers collaborating to trace how the broader changes affect different teachers and children of different ages. For example, a teacher researcher looking at the teaching environment might ask:

> *Classroom environment*: "How can I change the math/science area to encourage my transitional kindergartners to engage in complex cooperative play, as they do in the art blocks areas?" (Soulé, 2004)

*School-wide environment*: "How does the teachers' coordinated use of
the conflict resolution program *Second Step®* (Committee for Children, 2002) affect the behavior and learning outcomes of children
at this urban elementary school? (D. Richardson, 2002)

*Outdoor environment*: "How can we change the play yard so that it promotes teaching and learning beyond the traditional borders of the
classroom doors?" (Juarez, personal communication)

Again, the focus of these studies is teachers' understanding of their local
environment. The knowledge generated becomes useful to others when accounts are trustworthy and the evidence provides a way for others to envision their own situations.

Next are studies that look primarily at the community of people touched
by the research through the lens of collaboration. A teacher research study
focused around such a question might look at the process as a group seeks
to build collaboration within a teaching staff, between a teacher and the
families served, or with a teacher co-researching a question with his or her
students. Such studies focus on the process of collaboration over content and
often problematize the normal course of events in schools that privileges one
group as experts (say, the teachers relative to the students, the teachers relative to the parents, or the administration relative to the teachers), while the
other group is subordinate. Teacher research works well as a methodology
to look at collaboration, because it is, at heart, a form of collaborative inquiry that seeks to equalize access to knowledge creation. Our teacher researchers have asked questions such as:

*Collaboration among teachers*: "How can the teachers working at our
early childhood center use shared conversations about their teaching to build a learning community?" (Greene, 2003)

*Collaboration among teachers and with administration*: "How can I
bring greater collaboration and a sense of a learning community to
my leadership to help retain my best teachers?" (Stevenson, 2003)

*Collaboration with families*: How can I draw upon my students' families' values to engage my kindergartners in a culturally appropriate
character development curriculum? (Swanegan, 2001)

At the outermost layer of types of teacher research are those that address
professional development and those making institutional and political critiques of schooling. These are two quite different ways of envisioning change.
Professional development works within existing systems. This kind of teacher
research serves as a kind of platform or pier for making changes supported
by current structures. For example, schools might use teacher research to help

their teachers better address accountability standards. In this vein, teacher researchers have asked:

> *Professional development of preservice teachers*: "How can I make the teacher preparation program at my college's Lab School provide my teacher candidates with experiences of thinking about schooling in learner-centered ways that will 'stick' once they are out working in the community?" (Olsen, 2001)
>
> *Self-directed professional development*: "How can I effectively teach early literacy skills to Chinese bilingual preschoolers, so they will perform well on the district assessment?" (Ng, 2006)
>
> *Professional development of a teaching demographic*: "How do early childhood teachers born and educated outside the United States experience their assimilation working in ECE centers in the United States, and what kinds of supports would these international teachers need to be effective in their work?" (Alipio, 2004)

In contrast, institutional critiques look at systemic factors in the society that create inequality and oppression within early care and schools. Such teacher research might ask how accountability standards differentially affect children within the system, say, as based on income levels, home language, or race. These kinds of critical inquiries are the most political and least likely to result in solutions that can be wholly successful without shifting economic, political, or discriminatory features of the broader society. Several teacher researchers have asked:

> *Political critique/self-study*: "How can my deeper understanding of race and identity impact the way I teach my family day care's literacy curriculum and my relationship to my students' families?" (Sullivan, 2005)
>
> *Institutional critique*: "How do Latino families perceive bilingualism and does the district program serve these children and families effectively?" (Fisher, 2004)
>
> *Institutional critique*: "How well are Chinese-bilingual children served by the transition from bilingual preschool to the district kindergartens?" (Cheng, 2004)

It is more common for schools and school leaders, especially within larger systems, to embrace teacher research as part of professional development. In comparison, it is more likely that teachers doing grassroots teacher research will embrace more radical and critical perspectives. Notably, forms of teacher research have stretched to accommodate both ways of approaching inquiry.

## The Teacher Research Tradition

> research: Diligent inquiry or examination in seeking facts or principles; laborious or continued search after truth; as, researches of human wisdom. *Syn*: Investigation; examination; inquiry; scrutiny. (*Webster's Unabridged Dictionary*, 1998)

Teacher research is a viable and critical example of educational research. At the same time, it also serves as an instrument of teachers' professional development and educational reform. Teacher research comes from a tradition of qualitative practitioner-based inquiry with roots in the United States, England, Australia, New Zealand, and Canada. Some key approaches for teacher research in our work have been articulated by Marilyn Cochran-Smith and Susan Lytle (1993, 1999), the Brookline Teacher Research Seminar (2003), Dixie Goswami and Peter Stillman (1987), Cindy Ballenger (1999), bell hooks (1994), and Vivian Paley (e.g., 1981, 1984). Within the breadth of traditions that teacher research makes claims to, a common defining quality is that the practitioner—meaning the professional who works directly with clients—completes such studies. For educators, these "clients" can include students, families, or teaching staff. These traditions also involve inquiry made in connection with the professional's normal daily practice and nearly always involve qualitative analyses. Qualitative analysis means that the studies are interpretive and linguistic rather than number driven. Most also involve:

1. Systematic collection of data;
2. Analysis of these data to determine evidence for claims;
3. Interpretation of findings where personal experience and the teacher's subjective perspective are valued, yet pertinent to a broader audience through relevant literature or to current political and social issues; and
4. Sharing of the researcher's findings with a relevant public.

## TEACHER RESEARCH AND EARLY CHILDHOOD CURRICULA AND PHILOSOPHIES

From these roots, many spreading branches have developed, 12 of which I consider here. Because of the intersection between teaching and research, I consider two kinds of traditions here. Some, such as Montessori and the project-based approach, are more practice-based and are not intended to result in public sharing of research results. Others come out of the research tradition and seek to involve practitioners in all phases of the production and sharing of new knowledge. These 12 related inquiry movements include:

1. Dewey and the progressive movement
2. Constructivist approaches, including High/Scope and developmentally appropriate practice (DAP)
3. Montessori educational practice
4. Action research
5. Reflective practice
6. The project-based approach
7. Reggio-inspired documentation
8. Teacher research (or teacher-as-researcher)
9. Narrative inquiry and teacher memoir
10. Japanese Lesson Study
11. Self-study of teaching practices
12. Descriptive Review

Within most of these traditions, except perhaps for the smaller ones such as Japanese lesson study or Reggio-inspired documentation, there are a range of philosophical orientations, and therefore no singular agreement on the definition or central purpose of the inquiry practice. I take each of the traditions in turn, considering in particular the work done in North America.

## Roots of Teacher Research in the Philosophy of John Dewey

Teacher research in the United States traces its immediate history to the work of John Dewey (1938, 1902/1959). Of particular importance to teacher research was Dewey's work between 1896 and 1904 when he ran the Laboratory School at the University of Chicago. His work there was based in classrooms with visionary teachers, including Ella Flagg Young, his wife, Alice C. Dewey, Lucy Sprague Mitchell, Katherine Camp Mayhew, and Anna Camp Edwards. Laura Tanner provides an excellent history of this time period in *Dewey's Laboratory School: Lessons for Today* (1997). The book is particularly relevant to early childhood educators because it describes the school as a social community that nurtures children's development within a play and project-based curriculum.

Teachers at the Lab School were specialists in their subject fields and taught material that was cutting edge at the time and relevant to then-current practices. Being specialists allowed the teachers to see the connections between the questions the children asked and the big questions within the disciplines. Teaching and learning came from experience, but became educative only with the benefits of a well-organized curriculum and structured engagement in problem solving. To create this curriculum, and to test its effectiveness, the teachers collaborated with one another and with the university faculty. The collaboration included teachers presenting their findings orally and in written reports, which appeared in the University of Chicago journal, *Elementary School Record.*

In Dewey's vision of educational research, teachers were naturally at the center because they came to inquiry on teaching and learning from their own teaching experience, and with the daily habits of monitoring and guiding student learning. To develop education as a discipline in its own right, Dewey believed that teachers' work needed to include inquiry on their practice. In this way, knowledge about teaching and learning came to teachers from a systematic study of their experiences. Experience was, for Dewey, the source of knowledge, although he also discussed widely that not any experience would do. Instead, learners needed to develop habits of being systematic and willing to ask tough questions. Dewey supported these habits in his teachers so that the teachers both modeled and supported the same approach among their students. The people who taught at the Lab School, primarily women, greatly influenced Dewey's developing educational philosophy, a view of education that was reflected throughout his philosophical writings (Grinberg, 2002; Tanner, 1997).

But Dewey's theoretical work in education, and his progressive approach to teacher education, were not mainstream. Most schools at the start of the 20th century operated firmly with teacher-centered, top-down curricula emphasizing recitation and memorization—an approach that left little room for creativity from teachers or students. Teachers were technicians who administered curricula, not professionals. Then sadly, when Dewey's ideas were embraced, as in the work of James Kilpatrick, proponents emphasized any type of experience and mistakenly omitted the reflective rigor Dewey described as key to making an experience educative. A neighbor of ours, Richard MacIntosh, born in Berkeley, California, in 1926, told us of attending the local public elementary school during the early 1930s. He said they spent lots of time in classes on weaving, pottery, and wood carving, and recalls getting in serious trouble one day because he was found under a table reading a reference book. Gerald Grant (2001) describes Dewey's reaction to the failure of school reforms ostensibly based on his philosophy, but undertaken in shoddy ways.

> After 40 years of watching the distortion of his ideals, Dewey despaired over schools where children spent the day making nut bread but could not read. He scolded followers who let pupils respond to things "according to their own desires" without the intelligent guidance of teachers. "Now such a method is really stupid," said Dewey, in perhaps the clearest sentence he ever wrote. (n.p.)

Progressive education embraces the philosophy that learning should be fun, active, practical, and responsive to the interests of the children; but balancing these interests, the progressive teacher must be responsible for guiding children to rigorous learning of content and skills that spring from these experiences. Strong thinkers don't create and converse in cutting-edge ideas simply by having any sort of experience. Instead, the structures of schooling and the routines of scientific inquiry were Dewey's reason for involving the children in practical activities. That is, teachers at the Lab School facilitated practical activities with the goal of promoting children's engagement as theory makers.

*The Rise of Positivism.* During the late 1910s and early 1920s, soon after Dewey's work at the University of Chicago Laboratory School came to a close, a different movement, often called positivism or empiricism, took center stage in U.S. educational research. While Dewey's writings had been primarily philosophical, and the research methods of his teachers reflective, inductive, and qualitative, the competing positivist approach sought empirically to measure human intelligence (IQ), emphasized quantitative assessment, and valued the objective view of the outside researcher. Most influential in the United States was the work of Lewis Terman and his colleagues at Stanford University, who revised and adapted the intelligence tests of Swiss psychologist Alfred Binet. (Interestingly, Piaget had worked with Binet just before he began his own theorizing on human development.) As compared with Dewey's work, the IQ movement in U.S. education represented an opposing view on assumptions made about the nature of human intelligence, on the purposes for schooling, and on the role of the teacher, as either technician or professional.

Dewey's vision of education promoted critical thinking and moral development focused around the individual's responsibility to community. His philosophy is called progressivism because it assumes that humans, and human society as a whole, can improve (progress) to higher and better ways of being. Dewey's primary goal for public education was, then, to educate citizens so they would be prepared to take active roles in a participatory democracy. In contrast, a system based around intelligence testing proposes that humans have a fixed "general intelligence." Within this model, schools were seen as places where the technical transmission of skills could take place efficiently. Therefore, a primary role of the schools would be to sort different kinds of learners so that each could be provided with a track appropriate to his or her fixed abilities. Incidentally, the United States military also adopted this methodology during enlistment for World War I. The Army Intelligence Test, based on the IQ measures, sorted recruits into trench digging through officer tracks. These contrasting views on the role of education and the role of teachers within the educational enterprise demonstrate how teacher research makes sense and in fact is central to teaching and learning in the progressive paradigm. At the same time, teacher research has been seen as of no importance within Terman's framework of positivism. In an often-quoted statement, educational historian Ellen Lagemann (2000) notes that the history of American educational research cannot be understood without seeing that Terman won and Dewey lost. With this defeat, teachers lost the early promise Dewey had extended to them of equal footing with professors of education, teachers serving as the practical field-based research-ers most knowledgeable about pedagogy.

*Bulwarks of Progressivism in Colleges of Education.* Even as most public schools either maintained or returned to traditional teacher-centered approaches, which set goals that students memorize given facts and master limited skills, progressive, or transformative, approaches to education spread throughout North American colleges of education. For example, one of the key teachers at the Lab School, Lucy Sprague Mitchell, went on in the 1930s to found the Bank Street School of Education. Bank Street extended Dewey's progressive, learner-centered approach into the training of teachers (Grinberg, 2002). Novice teachers learned how to teach first through reflection on their own learning experiences, which instructors guided in the teacher prepara-tion classroom. The goal of this approach to teacher preparation was to show teachers that even as novices, their insights about teaching and learning mattered. From the progressive perspective, teaching must begin with teachers understanding their own thinking, with all its glitches, stops, and starts. Experiencing and working through a problem from "Huh?" to "Aha!" is presumed to allow teachers the reflective capacity to understand and respond to the complexities of their students' thinking processes.

Bank Street instructors taught their teaching candidates to understand how students learned by undertaking careful observations, which the teacher candidates documented and then shared with their colleagues. The intent of a cycle of teaching, observing, reflecting, and sharing was that teaching would become a self-renewing act. In progressive schools, input from students in the daily world of the classroom was to be balanced by input from profes-sional colleagues who were both audience and critical respondents to one another's work. Following the path that Dewey had set out on 30 years be-fore, Bank Street–educated teachers undertook discovery-oriented curricula, used cutting-edge content, and created most materials themselves. In this way, teachers could be maximally responsive to the needs and interests of their students, and their reflective practice stance was similar to teacher research.

## Constructivism—The Influence of Piagetian Views

In the 1960s, progressive educators embraced the work of Piaget (e.g., 1950, Piaget & Inhelder, 1969) as another theorist who demonstrated that learning was led by the child's own developmental readiness to explore and ask good questions. In this view, children learn by "constructing" knowledge. Like a follower of Dewey, a constructivist teacher observes students to see what prior knowledge (e.g., mental schemes or operations) they bring to a lesson, provides materials and questions that prompt discovery, and promotes group inquiry among students, so that working together as peers, children can test the validity of their theories about phenomena. At Harvard, for example, teacher educators embraced a constructivist view, as typified by the work of Eleanor Duckworth (1996).

Duckworth's perspective grows from her work as a graduate student of Piaget. She then struggled in her work educating teachers in how to make Piaget's findings relevant for daily use in the classroom. She decided the structural (or stage-based) part of his theory was less helpful to teachers. Duckworth argues that, for two important reasons, knowing the stage a child is in does not have daily relevance. First, it would be impossible in normal classroom practice to assess stages, given the range of development in a classroom and the fact that children are not static within stages. Furthermore, due to the stage-like shifts Piaget predicted in development, if a teacher chose a logical concept as a focus for direct teaching, children would be either too young to get it or too old to need it. In contrast, the functional part of Piagetian theory—the part that provides an understanding of how people adapt to novel situations because they are internally motivated to learn— shows that learning is based on prior knowledge, and that people, rather than learning through primarily social transmission (or teaching as telling), instead must internally construct new skills and concepts for themselves. People learn based on interactions among active experience, social input, and the mechanisms of accommodation and assimilation, which leads to cycles of disequilibrium followed by equilibrium at a higher level, and back again.

Therefore, like the teacher educators at Bank Street, Duckworth embraces a pedagogy of observing her inservice and preservice teachers engaged in struggling with challenging problems so that they learn to observe and critique themselves and their peers as learners, all to better understand the teaching–learning process. What follows from her stance is that excellent teaching must be a form of research on the nature of the teaching process. The final essay of her 1996 book is entitled "Teaching as Research," and read in combination with the classic first essay, "The Having of Wonderful Ideas," does an excellent job of laying out the relationship between a constructivist stance and the move from teacher to teacher researcher.

In the same track, but specifically within early childhood education, the work of Constance Kamii (1982, 1989) helped us apply the work of Piaget to young children's learning in mathematics and physical knowledge. Kamii's later books (e.g., Kamii & Housman, 1999) also include the voices of the teachers she worked with, similar to how Duckworth embraced the idea that teachers who closely observe and record children's thinking to enhance their teaching also are developing new knowledge about the nature of learning and development.

The National Association for the Education of Young Children (NAEYC), the major ECE organization in the United States, has standards for developmentally appropriate practice (Bredekamp & Copple, 1997) that are constructivist in nature. Overall, constructivist and progressive philosophies of education require that teachers systematically observe children so that they can make pedagogical responses that allow students to construct their own theories about the world. This process requires a flexible awareness of children's needs and interests, such that the child and the teacher become co-researchers of the curriculum at hand—an approach that is not directly described as teacher research, but flows from the same stream.

The view of the teacher as a professional who responds to students flexibly, based on a systematic examination of classroom data, arises in several educational approaches relevant to early childhood. These include Montessori teaching, project-based curriculum, Reggio Emilia, High/Scope, and developmentally appropriate practice (DAP). Another connection between teacher research and the work of early childhood educators is the links to Piagetian- and Vygotskian-inspired curricula in sync with DAP and High/Scope. Both of these models rely on an engaged teaching style that requires the teacher to be a strong observer and facilitator of children's initiative. Environments and topics of study are to be tuned to the child's response to ideas, objects, and the need for movement and exploration. The child is seen as an active inquirer after knowledge and skills, and the teacher needs to provide situations that are emotionally nurturing, physically interactive, and cognitively challenging. Teachers need to converse with their students, valuing what students have to say and finding ways to ask questions that prompt children's further inquiry, in particular by helping children become more aware of their own thinking. In these conversations, the teachers model engagement with and curiosity about the world. Within High/Scope there are suggestions for teachers about how to record their observations of children at work, including "mental 'snapshots' of children's actions and words" (Hohmann & Weikart, 1995, p. 222), photos, and brief notes taken during the school day. These data are collected with the intent that teachers will meet to discuss and analyze the day's events to improve planning.

## Montessori—Follow the Child

Coming from a different source than positivism or constructivism, although sharing similar orientations toward the role of the teacher as observer and guide, is the work of Maria Montessori (1870–1953). Montessori stressed the importance of teachers being good observers who systematically gather evidence on the learning of their young students to effectively prepare the learning environment. One of the primary Montessori dictums is "follow the child." To follow the child with accuracy, teachers must look, record, and adjust. Montessori teachers are taught to keep regular anecdotal notes on all of their students to record how they are progressing with the Montessori materials that teachers make available. For example, teachers note the duration of work, the kind of focus the child puts forth to organize and persist with the job, and the nature of the child's successes and challenges with the task. From this collected data, Montessori teachers prepare larger assessment documents and, more important, use these to continually adjust the materials available in their classrooms, always letting careful observation of the child be the engine for change.

In this way, the Montessori model of teaching is related to teacher research because the teacher consciously asks a discrete question (e.g., "How is Raji doing with the lacing job?"), then collects relevant data, analyzes them, and takes action based on the findings. From week to week and year to year, there are similarities in the structure and setting of this kind of Montessori classroom, but there are differences too, because the children and their needs and interests are never exactly the same.

## Action Research

In this section, I turn away from the above practical approaches, and back to the history of the academy's view toward field-based research. Teacher research is not the first or only movement in which people working in the field made inquiry based on their professional practice. In the 1940s, social psychologist Kurt Lewin undertook a type of practical and political research he called action research (see, for example, Lewin, 1938, 1946, 1948). At the same time, John Collier, who served as the Commissioner for the U.S. Bureau of Indian Affairs from 1933 to 1945—throughout the Roosevelt presidency—created a similar approach (Collier, 1945). In the action research literature, Lewin is widely cited as the originator of the approach, but by some accounts (e.g., Cooke, 2002) Collier was more likely to have coined the term and originated the methodology. Both Lewin and Collier developed action research to promote equality of access to the resources of society and to expand democracy, especially with respect to racial conflicts. Collier and Lewin worked primarily at a policy level and within governmental organizations, although in one paper Lewin also turned his attention directly to the schools (Lewin & Lewin, 1942).

Action research is a broad field, in fact, wider in scope than teacher research because it spans multiple professions, including organizational development, public health, social services, and education. Action research typically focuses on the ethical impact of inquiry by addressing how the research can be undertaken in direct collaboration with participants. In this way, action research values the same expansion of democratic rights and responsibilities as found in the work of Dewey. Inquiry within action research traces a spiral from the framing of a problem or inequality, to the collection of data that can provide evidence of the problem. Next the action researcher enacts a plan that changes the situation, then collects a second round of data to identify whether there is evidence of change, and finally reports the findings to a relevant audience. In action research, those involved in the changes are themselves participants in the research.

Some forms of action research (e.g., McNiff, Lomax, & Whitehead, 1996) wrestle with the centrality of self within the research. These action research inquiries begin with the general framework, "How can I . . . ?" For example, in an educational setting, a teacher might ask, "How can I be more effective at involving the families with our project-based curriculum?" or, "How can I help the children to improve the quality of their community in my preschool classroom?" Common among the definitions for action research is the link between effective social action and an applied research base. Cooke (2002) cites Lewin as using an aphorism, "no action without research, no research without action" (p. 5), meaning that all interventions or policy actions made by an organization should be informed by research, and conversely, "research should not be for its own sake, but to lead to organizational change" (p. 5).

*Comparisons Between Action Research and Teacher Research.* Some practitioners and academicians working in teacher research choose the term "teacher action research" (Burnaford, Fischer, & Hobson, 2001). However, the relationship between teacher research and action research does not form an identity: Not all action research is teacher research, and not all teacher research is action research. Neither can be fully defined as a subset of the other. For example, some teacher research can be in the form of artistic expression, or may be written as a purely reflective piece. Nonetheless, most teacher research is action-based, as teachers share the goal of taking action to improve professional practices. Unlike teacher research, action research does not focus solely on teacher knowledge, looking instead to the dynamic and collaborative process of the broader research cycle. Furthermore, not all teacher research fits the definition of action research because action research focuses on changing behavior within organizations through the participation of those involved. Influential writers within the recent action research tradition (Carr & Kemmis, 1986; Elliott, 1991) describe action research as a form of "liberatory" or "emancipatory" research intended to create a more just and democratic society.

This social justice stance often is found in teacher research prompted by political or institutional critiques, but teacher research also can focus more narrowly, for example, on the effectiveness of an adopted curriculum. Such teacher research tends to be more conservative or apolitical, and occurs particularly when it is supported directly by school systems.

Like teacher research, most action research is undertaken by those working in the field. Unlike teacher research, outsiders, such as policymakers, union organizers, or university researchers, also can undertake action research in the field. Such outsider research becomes action research through the principal investigator's collaboration with those served by the action. Because of the emphasis on participation of those studied or affected by the actions of the inquiry, this form of research sometimes is called "participatory research" or community-based partnership research. Indeed, within teacher research a similar argument sometimes is made, so that studies by university researchers with the teacher acting as a co-researcher—or otherwise participating actively—may be labeled teacher research. Yet other teacher researchers prefer that the ideas and the insights of work called teacher research come either singularly or primarily from those in the classroom.

*Challenges to Action Research.* As described earlier, the movement known as positivism grew within the social sciences so that by the 1950s it was the dominant paradigm. Positivism is the belief that research is a scientific undertaking and should be conducted in formal and objective ways, typically using large quantitative data sets. Within the framework of positivism, social science research follows the experimental models of research in the hard sciences such as physics: Objective (meaning external) researchers frame a testable hypothesis (If . . . , then . . .) and show evidence for their claims through statistical methods. Statistical studies require large data sets, specialized knowledge of statistical methodologies, and the use of statistical software to analyze findings.

Positivism pushed out the qualitative, practitioner-based methods and the politically driven questions of action research. The decline of action-based methods throughout the 1950s and 1960s continued the trend, which had begun 30 years previously with Terman's assessments of human intelligence, and educational psychology continued to claim the role of the central discipline in education. Within this framework, schools serve not as sites for inquiry, but as locations that provide ready pools of similar-aged children for comparative analysis of constructs like intelligence, motivation, and achievement.

Because of the specialized techniques of statistical methodology and the emphasis on objectivity, practitioners are effectively shut out of undertaking their own studies. The zeitgeist of the times between the 1950s and the early 1980s was that the only real way to study human learning and development was through the quantitative measurement of behavior. With "evidence-based scientific research," the beat of the current drum in educational research, we are back to the same old story. Yet the questions external educational researchers have asked about teaching and learning rarely make it to caregivers and teachers. Furthermore, the pursuit of a single kind of research design can net only part of the truth about the complex processes of human learning in the institution of schooling.

Given this current hostile backdrop, at least on the national stage, to the goals and practices of teacher research, teacher researchers must not try to out-science the scientists. There, we will fail. Instead, teacher researchers should maintain an informed conversation around teaching practice, based on systematic, evidence-based claims for knowledge drawn from primarily qualitative, small-scale, insider studies—the kind of studies that teachers can do well. Teacher research can and does affect local teaching, and also can reach out to change educational policy. The strength of teacher research is in what teachers, as daily participants in children's learning, know about classroom practices, children's learning, and institutional benefits and constraints. Inasmuch as the major educational debates try to exclude teacher research, working on the margins may be where teachers are the strongest, and it is far from unanimous among educational researchers, broadly taken, that only experimental designs have merit.

## Reflective Practice

Positivism, too, has had powerful critics over the years. The disjuncture between educational theory and practice, as noted above, has been a major source of this critique. Positivism comes from a philosophy also known as "technical rationalism," which focuses on the ability of experts to create master plans that allow for maximum efficiency. However, technical rationality has only limited ways to talk about practice, and these do not tap into artistic or intuitive ways of knowing. In contrast, professionals report that a good deal of their in-the-moment decision making while working with clients rests upon intuition (Schön, 1983). This angle on "teaching as art" relates to teacher research and most often is known as reflective practice.

Donald Schön's influential book, *The Reflective Practitioner* (1983), was about how professionals engage in "reflection-in-action." Schön said that to improve professional practice, professionals had to find ways to frame, examine, and learn from the events of their professional lives. The book was written using a narrative case study model—a form that speaks to the storied lives that teachers lead in their classrooms, where teaching is embedded within the relationship with students.

In teacher education, Kenneth Zeichner, Susan Noffke, and others of their colleagues at Wisconsin State University wrote about the power of reflective practice for teacher training at the elementary and high school levels (Noffke & Stevenson, 1995; Noffke & Zeichner, 1987). Their goal was to create new teachers who would be able to respond in productive and dynamic ways to the changing conditions of teaching.

## Project-Based Curricula

Another link from ECE to teacher research, and back again to constructivism, is the project-based approach of Katz and Chard (1989). They define project work as "curriculum that encourages children to apply their emerging skills in informal, open-ended activities that are intended to improve their understanding of the world they live in" (p. xii). Project work is centered on a theme and develops in a purposeful, yet child-centered, manner to answer key questions the children have posed for themselves. As projects unfold, the teacher helps the class to select topics that are at the right level of focus, then takes on roles such as facilitator, scribe, and resource gatherer. To keep children interested in the development of these long-term projects, effective project-based teachers must conduct a kind of ongoing inquiry on their practice.

In the United States, some ECE professionals have adopted the use of documentation panels to make "authentic assessments" of children's learning within inquiry-oriented curricula. Authentic assessment, such as the work sampling system (Meisels, Jablon, Marsden, Dichtelmiller & Dorfman, 1994), provides a range of evidence gathered from natural teaching events and stands as an alternative to a standardized testing approach (Helm, Beneke, & Steinheimer, 1998). These authors link their work most strongly to the work of Vygotsky (1978, 1986), showing how if teachers are to remain within the zone most ripe for teaching (or Vygotsky's zone of proximal development—the ZPD), they must remain in conscious interchange with their students. Developmentally appropriate practice as measured by the ZPD cannot be demonstrated through standardized measures, but instead must be taken from naturalistic observations of children who are fully engaged in and motivated by the work before them. It follows, then, that "through documentation, the teacher can make it possible for others to 'see' the learning that takes place when developmentally appropriate teaching occurs" (Helm, Beneke, & Steinheimer, 1998, p. 15).

## Reggio-Inspired Documentation

The city of Reggio Emilia in northern Italy supports a municipal preschool program that uses a project-based approach to curriculum, which emphasizes the visual arts. Early childhood teachers in the United States have become familiar with the Reggio program through a number of influential books (Cadwell, 1997; Edwards, Gandini, & Foreman, 1998), as well as a traveling museum display called "The Hundred Languages of Children" and workshops that accompany the display or can be found at conferences such as those sponsored by NAEYC. The Reggio curriculum is based around relationships among the children, the children with the teachers, and the teachers with the parents. Like the project-based work embraced in Dewey's Lab school and as described by Katz and Chard (1989), the curriculum is enacted through long-term projects, or *progettazione*, on topics initiated by the children. As with other progressive educational approaches, the teachers are active in flexible and inquiry-driven ways to craft topic choices and activities, which are then supported through strategic use of the school environment. The Reggio schools view the children as competent, creative theory makers. Reggio teachers call this concept "the image of the child" and consider it a key aspect of their philosophy.

Over the past 10 to 15 years in the United States, a number of early childhood programs have modeled themselves directly after the Reggio schools, while many more programs take some inspiration from the approach. Within Reggio practice, teachers make ongoing records of the children's work and speech. These materials are displayed and discussed in a number of ways, including though documentation panels. The documentation panels are graphic displays that show the progress of a unit of study and seek to capture a range of perspectives through a variety of media. For example, panels will include the words of the children, the words and thoughts of the teacher, and examples of the children's work, including both products and photos of process.

Documentation panels serve three audiences: (1) the children, as a tool for memory and as a source of pride in their work, both of which help them to extend a project; (2) the teachers, as a way to understand what they are doing in the classroom around a project, that is, what is working and what needs tuning up; and (3) the broader school community, to understand what is happening in the classroom with respect to children's learning and development. Documentation is described in further detail in Chapter 2.

## Teacher Research on the Writing Process

In the early 1980s in the United States, teachers working with writing practice began to do and publish research based on their work teaching children to become authors (Atwell, 1987; Calkins, 1986; Graves, 1983). One of the earliest cited works by these writing teachers is a study by Emig (1971) on the composing processes of 12th graders. The curricular approach was called writing process, because teachers gave the *process* of writing—brainstorming, drafting, revising, and editing—just as much focus as the final product. Writing process also makes extensive use of a routine called the writers' workshop, where the classroom becomes a community of authors who collaborate as audience and critics of one another's emerging work. The teachers take part in this community of authors as well, serving as audience, mentors, and sometimes fellow authors. Teacher researchers such as Lucy Calkins saw inspiration for doing teacher research in the same personal vein as the "voice" they supported in the writing of their students. Thus, teachers did research on children's writing because as they modeled writing within an inquiry stance, they wrote about what surrounded them daily—the writing of their students. These writing process teachers came to see that they had important things to say to other teachers of writing about the ways they understood their students' thinking and learning as writers and as inquirers. In the same way that they conceived of the writing workshop providing their students the physical, psychological, and social spaces to find their voices as authors, so they saw their own voices emerging as they wrote about their teaching practice. These teachers did not have a long-term view on the role of practitioner or action researcher, but they were writing specifically and consciously about the idea of the "teacher-as-researcher."

In the field of educational research, these writing process studies generally were categorized as case studies, or simply as "how to" books for writing teachers. That the teachers did the work was often not highlighted, and that this work was a form of qualitative research typically was not noted. Even currently, it is difficult to use the term "teacher research" as a keyword search for information databases. Teacher research studies are still buried within educational case studies, with the fact that a particular study was done by a practicing teacher not highlighted.

The influence of writing process on the teacher research movement in the United States is still powerful. Teachers doing research on writing, and literacy more broadly, remain the single largest group of teacher researchers, especially teachers working at the elementary and early childhood levels. For example, the early childhood journal *Young Children* receives a majority of manuscripts with language and literacy themes (personal communication, Derry Koralek, editor), a pattern that includes submissions to the new column on teacher research, "Voices of Practitioners."

## Narrative Inquiry in Education and Teacher Memoir

Narratives are stories, monologues told by an often-invisible narrator, that describe characters facing a situation with a beginning, middle, and end. Research that takes a narrative stance uses stories to frame the problem of interest and to suggest solutions. Narrative research (Clandinin & Connelly, 2000; Lyons & LaBoskey, 2002) values a multiplicity of perspectives and relies on the power of an audience to interpret a meaning. It is valid within a narrative approach that different readers would draw different sets of conclusions because different aspects of the story would be meaningful to individual readers. The stories told within narrative inquiry are true, based on real events, although narratives are crafted to capture the aspect of the situation that the researcher wishes to focus on.

Memoirs as a form of teacher research are narratives that involve focused stories of self. Memoirs make inquiry by relying on the artistic and creative act of capturing moments in one's life history with accuracy and focus. Teachers may choose to write memoirs that center primarily on professional experiences, or they may write personal memoirs to consider a theme, like learning differences, by describing their own lives as children in school, as juxtaposed with adult experiences as teachers (Hankins, 1998).

## Japanese Lesson Study Approaches

Lesson Study is an approach widespread in Japanese education as a form of self-improvement and teacher evaluation. Teachers meet in groups to observe one another teach a model lesson. Often these lessons also are videotaped so that a wider group of teachers may view the teaching approach. Teachers then meet to discuss the qualities of the lesson and to critique the event. Another teacher may then repeat the same lesson, and the cycle of critique furthers the lesson refinement.

Within Lesson Study, teachers' inquiry is focused squarely on the materials and techniques of the lesson; therefore, the approach provides a concrete way to undertake a study. Key to success of the approach is collaboration among teachers, the teachers' willingness to criticize a colleague, and the presenting teacher's willingness to be open to frank critique. Culturally, both the level of collaboration in search of a common and best approach, and the presenting teacher's willingness to be humbled by colleagues, are more common to Japan than to North America. Lesson Study has been championed in the work of Catherine Lewis (Lewis & Tsuchida, 1998) as relevant to work in North America and has been adopted for professional development in funded projects within some school districts in the United States.

## Self-Study of Teaching Practices

Self-study is a form of research that uses an inquiry of self as central to the research (Bullough & Pinnegar, 2001; Hamilton & Pinnegar, 2000; LaBoskey, 2004; Loughran & Northfield, 1998). Questions may involve identity, teaching effectiveness, privilege, or bias. Self-studies must be introspective, personal, and open to outside critique for verification. There are many methods embraced by those who do self-study, and a variety of stances taken about the nature of self that the teacher studies. For example, self-studies may be ethnographic, use memoir, focus on the products of student work, look at the effectiveness of a program, or be an artistic performance. Self-studies are a form of action research because they look at how the self-as-teacher affects students, and seeks ways to improve those interactions. Self-studies directly embrace the subjective experience of teaching but problematize the personal by presenting it publicly for critique.

## Descriptive Review

The Prospect School in Vermont, with the leadership of Pat Carini (Himley, 2000), originated the Descriptive Review method, which is primarily conversational in form and approach. The Descriptive Process has been adopted by other groups of teachers as a means for grassroots inquiry about school reform undertaken through a collaborative, oral format (Abu El-Haj, 2003). Descriptive Reviews may be focused on a child, an example of a child's work, a portfolio of a child's work, or educational issues. Many Descriptive Reviews are focused on a single case study child, so I will use that form to explain.

There are three roles for collaborators within the Descriptive Review: (1) the presenting teacher who poses the inquiry for others' responses; (2) the chairperson who may be a teaching colleague, administrator, or professor and who takes a guiding and facilitating role throughout; and (3) the collaborating teachers. The presenting teacher must begin the process with an inkling of a question and willingness to prepare and present. The presenting teacher, with a child of interest and general question in mind, then meets with a chairperson. The presenting teacher typically comes to this meeting with a verbal sketch of the child and some work samples, but uses this initial conversation to determine the shape and scope of the inquiry. Following this meeting, the presenting teacher often gathers additional classroom data and writes up a more formal description of the child. To give shape to these reviews, the description follows a prescribed five-part format that includes a range of ways to capture the child (e.g., gestures, learning strengths, relationships). With the support of the chairperson, the presenting teacher then takes about 30 minutes to describe the child to a group of collaborating teachers. These teachers ask questions to clarify, then in a nonjudgmental way conversationally join the teacher in extending the inquiry (seeing other angles to the question, describing related children or situations in their own practice, noting points of contradiction or resonance), posing solutions, and uncovering broader policy implications. All participants take notes, which become part of the final record of the Descriptive Review, but the product of the review is the oral inquiry itself, and the strengthened collaboration among the participating teachers.

TEACHER RESEARCH COMES from teachers and addresses aspects of their daily work with children. Teacher researchers can ask all kinds of questions and focus at any level—from themselves, to the children, the curriculum, the institution, or society. Teacher research is an approach with a long history. It has been reinvented multiple times by different groups of teachers who have found themselves in situations that call for taking action or supporting the development of a professional voice. Philosopher John Dewey and the progressive movement, which followed in the wake of his work, are key in the history of the teacher research approach. The progressive movement's orientation to education fits within an inquiry stance that is central to undertaking research as part of daily professional practice.

Piaget's influence on constructivist teaching and Vygotsky's on a social-constructivist stance also relate strongly to progressive education. In the constructivist and social-constructivist traditions, the role of the teacher as researcher is not always as strong, but it is still present, most particularly in the work of Duckworth (1996). From different beginnings, similar trends can be found in the Montessori approach. Action research is a relative of teacher research, but the two traditions are distinct. Most people taking a field-based participatory stance to research in education choose either the teacher research or action research label. Teacher research is the label that we feel best describes the stance taken in this text.

Several recent influential movements, including project-based curricula, the Reggio Emilia approach, the writing process, Japanese Lesson Study, and Prospect School's Descriptive Review, have given teachers new ways into the arena of teacher research. I hope that teacher researchers will be able to use this history as a backdrop as Daniel and I discuss particular strategies for doing teacher research. As teacher researchers understand more about this kind of inquiry from doing it themselves, I hope they will return to this review of the literature to see how the structure and spirit of their own projects are mirrored by a tradition that is at least a century old.

### Suggested Teacher Research Activities

1. Write down your own definition of teacher research. How does it compare with the definition and explanation given in this opening chapter?
2. Make two columns on a piece of paper. On the left side, make a short list of those elements of teacher research described in this chapter that you find interesting. Then on the right side, make a new list of those

elements that you believe are "doable" for you at your early child-hood site.

3. Again make two columns on a piece of paper. On the left side, list the curricular models (like the project approach) and educational philosophies (constructivist education) that you believe in. Underneath each model, jot down a few key elements (such as, for constructivist learning, active discovery, children as researchers). Then, on the right side of the paper, transfer over those ideas and elements that you want to become the cornerstone or foundation of your current or future teacher research work.

4. Think of your current work situation—whether caregiving, teaching, administration, or policy—and consider possible obstacles to carrying out teacher research (not enough time, for instance). Then consider how you might go about making a structural or scheduling change or two (or approaching your administrator with this idea) in order to pursue a teacher research project at your site.

5. When talking informally with colleagues, raise the idea of undertaking a collaborative teacher research project together. On a blank piece of paper, make a web of what you might focus on as research partners, starting with the focus (such as conflict in the playhouse) and then web out what kinds of data you'd like to find (Are there too few props and toys in the playhouse? Should we get more boys into the playhouse?)

# CHAPTER 2

# The Process of Inquiry— The Art of Doing Teacher Research

Outer Space Meals

*Do you know what space meals are?*
*I will tell you now,*
*I love ratatua,*
*I love wormatua,*
*I love squidatua*
*I love spideratua,*
*I love Beetletua.*

—Darius Roffe, age 7

Guiding Questions

1. What are effective places and ways to start a teacher research project?
2. How and why can a research question help frame inquiry? What are helpful questions to ask?
3. What are effective ways to begin a teacher research project?
4. What is the role of graphic displays of data in a teacher research project?
5. What is the value of documentation panels? What are effective guidelines for creating and evaluating such panels?

## FINDING A PATH OF INQUIRY

As Darius's poem asked, "Do you know what space meals are?" we may ask, "What is teacher research? (and why would I want to do it?)." The best way to answer this critical question is, as with many things, just to try it out. So in embarking on a teacher research project—whether alone or with colleagues, your children, your families—find a path to begin a line (or lines) of inquiry. Beginnings are so important, as the Reggio educators often say. With the start of research, teachers frame questions they wish to answer, or even just formulate a set of ideas they have been wondering about. These questions may be little or big, but the important thing is to start. By just looking at our classrooms with the lens of inquiry, we allow ourselves to see our practice in new ways. We wake up to our ordinary world and open ourselves to change.

Here is an example of how by framing a question, or by just looking, some children began to see the world outside their car windows differently. One summer, as we drove to and from swimming lessons, my children and their friends, then 4 and 6 years old, began playing a game called *Punchbuggy*. The game requires the players to count VW Beetles. We competed each afternoon, the children against the adults. As the summer progressed, the game evolved, both as the children played and depending on which children were in the car. The relationship between this game and setting up a question for inquiry is that by just looking for Punchbuggies, the children began to notice cars and their neighborhood in different and new ways. For example, they learned to see the curve of a car roof to spot a Beetle at a distance, they identified the location of a driveway or side street where a Beetle was likely to be parked, and they learned how to distinguish between an old VW (worth 2 points, by the evolving rules) and a new one (worth only 1 point). So, too, they learned more about numbers and competition. Four-year-old Amanda once asked me with excitement, "We're still winning, we're winning. The kids are still winning, right?" She had noticed another trend. The adult in the car needed to play to make it fun, yet I always seemed to lose.

In this case, the game became a tool where the rules and the competition allowed the children to notice things they had not seen or thought about before. They began to think about car models and makes, which had not been a prior interest; they began to ask specific questions about which way home we would take, making a more complex mental map of our city; and to see how much they were winning by, they asked and answered many questions about numbers, such as, "How many more is 28 than 16?"

The children's game serves as a metaphor for action-based inquiry because it shows how when we take the time and effort to look, we find something, even if we didn't know what we'd find when we began. But there are differences as well. Although the game does create a kind of discipline, the children's inquiry of looking for Punchbuggies is entirely a game. The work of a teacher researcher looking for a type of behavior, language, or creation is disciplined, with the benefit that this heightened purpose also gives us pleasure and satisfaction, like skillfully playing a strategy game. Also unlike the children, the teacher is aware of the intention of the research, notices what is changing, and sets goals to seek why these changes take place. As the 4-year-olds played *Punchbuggy*, they were not conscious of the changes that took place, either in the game or in themselves. In contrast, the older children knew the importance of the rules and were interested in manipulating them to make the game more interesting (and more to their benefit). For example, the older children created and kept track of a number of variations in point values. First they developed the rule, "2 points for convertibles." Then they instituted the rule, "1 point for new cars and 2 points for old cars." Soon they added, "2 points for metallic paint." Then to further the complexity, they doubled the score for driven cars because they reasoned that moving cars are harder to spot than parked cars. So by the end of the summer, if anyone spotted an old, convertible Beetle with metallic paint that was being driven down the street, it would be worth 12 points. Quite a coup!

But even as the older children kept careful track of their rule changes, they were unaware of the changes that took place in themselves as they played this game, because awareness of such a shift requires self-reflection. Self-reflective inquiry is, in fact, more sophisticated than awareness of changing practices (the game's rules, in this case), because selfhood is so fluid and in the moment. Self-reflection requires a consciousness of self, which is frozen in time for inquiry through some means of representation. For example, we can look at ourselves more clearly in writing, in graphic documentation, or through ongoing conversation with others. In this way, earlier perceptions of self are made available for later reconsideration. Such self-reflection is central to teacher research.

Teacher researchers look intensively at themselves engaged in a practice, often over an extended period. The question a teacher researcher asks is important because it will soon take up a lot of time. This question will shine a particular lens on teaching practice, will stand behind research efforts of data collection and analysis, and will guide professional development spent with collaborating colleagues. Therefore, the question a teacher researcher asks should be one of genuine interest. Teacher researchers come to know their question much better than my children and their friends came to know Punchbuggies that summer, so it's valuable to choose carefully.

## RESEARCH QUESTIONS

### Finding a Question

So how do teacher researchers find good questions? (Seven-year-old Darius, in the poem at the beginning of this chapter, asked, "Do you know what space meals are?"—a good question that makes us pause and wonder.) Good questions in teacher research do something similar—they arise from ECE teachers' direct experiences with children, families, and teaching colleagues. They don't come from other people's experiences, from books, or from research articles. For example, one teacher asks, "How can I help my 3s and 4s be less aggressive?" Another asks, "How useful are those computers the school installed in our rooms?" And a third asks, "What makes for a secure and positive attachment between our young toddlers and me, as their caregiver?" These questions come from the teachers' classroom lives and gradually shape themselves into researchable or "doable" questions to address through a study of their practices.

The teachers' questions cited above all identified beginning points that seem simple enough, yet in a real sense this staring out is a significant first challenge for teacher researchers. Teachers are surrounded by so much activity every day, and since they work with young children, most of the work is physical, immediate, and full of emotion. How do teachers discover their inquiry when conscious planning, analysis, and implementation pull at such a different part of the brain than the flow of daily care? Most teachers will find that even here, at the start, there are at least two phases to this search for a question: The first is to find an area that provokes curiosity, passion, or concern; the second is to set out on a focused plan to collect and analyze evidence—but that's next. I start by showing how I, and many teachers I've worked with, have found our questions.

We begin, as often as not, with the child who puzzles us. Sometimes a child's learning, social, or emotional interactions are the spark. Most often, such naturally arising case studies focus on children who are struggling in one way or another in the ECE setting. Teachers wonder how to reach students who learn in ways not well supported by the classroom curricula, materials, or social climate. In one case, a teacher wonders about her role in providing better facilitation for a child who is not learning at a pace similar to his or her peers. In another, a teacher finds she needs to work in close proximity to a child who lashes out physically. Teachers also spend more time and effort helping shy and sensitive children adjust to the busy climate of a school or group-care setting. Any of these case study–driven questions can be framed with the general question: How can I help [. . .] become more successful in learning and developing in my classroom?

At other times, teachers find their questions in the teaching environment. Perhaps a teacher's attention is drawn to how the children use a space, like the block area, the science area, or the outdoor play yard. A space may be underutilized, constantly in a state of disarray, or the scene of too many conflicts. Alternatively, a teacher's attention may be drawn to the complexity of children's play within a space, the way relationships form through a certain kind of play, or the unexpected nature of a child's invention or language usage.

Practitioners new to teacher research, and new to teaching as well, often begin by focusing on a negative aspect of their experience, and therefore use teacher research as a tool for immediate problem solving. How do I organize this classroom? How do I support the children's socialization skills? How do I communicate with families? In contrast, teachers and administrators with more experience often find questions that spring from a deviation from their expectations, or reawaken them from the inertia of a job that no longer feels fresh. Experienced ECE professionals also find teacher research useful as a way to evaluate the success of a new curriculum or management approach. Projects exploring the effects of those changes are similar to projects of new teachers.

Yet in my work with teacher researchers, I have seen that experienced teachers and new teachers face opposite challenges in developing their questions. New teachers tend to work reactively because they know so little about what may happen next. Reactive responses make for unruly research, and the new teacher, who is also a new teacher researcher, must repeat the mantra, "There is no bad data; it is all evidence, I must just make sense of what I have found." In a positive sense, unruly research can be groundbreaking, because the new teacher can be open to how things turn out. In contrast, the experienced teacher often is guided by an educational vision, which lends structure to the question and the unfolding project. Yet the experienced educator must resist asking a question he or she doesn't honestly mean to test, for example, "Is play important to young children's learning and development?"—a question that the teacher who posed it had no intention of disproving. I describe this contrast not to judge the path taken by either new or experienced practitioners, but to provide evidence that teacher research is a flexible tool that can serve teachers' needs throughout their career spiral.

Not surprisingly, most people find the experience of selecting a question for research anxiety provoking. Choosing a starting point is hard, because it rules out the infinite universe of other possible starting points. Teacher researchers have described this stage of the research project like feeling a door closing just as you rush through. A choice made means infinite choices not made, yet because teacher research is focused around a qualitative research methodology, the spiraling process of data collection and analysis allows the researcher to discover the full nature of the question within the process. Therefore, the initial decision, while significant, does not so much represent the action of a door shutting as of a traveler setting out on a path.

Indeed, this "setting out" represents the second major step in the process in undertaking a teacher research project. A case study child, a curricular innovation, an environmental focus—each provides a start, yet every project needs greater specificity and detail, all building to analysis that is coherent and deep. Setting out begins this journey, and the research question matures as the teacher researcher collects, organizes, and begins to analyze data.

There are parallels between the focusing of a teacher research project and the focusing of a project-based curricular unit. Teachers new to project-based work face the need to make their curriculum child-centered and wonder how to select project topics that will work, or "have legs." As a project choice begins to gel, the children become collaborative researchers, exploring their topic through observation, data collection, asking questions, and making representations of their findings. Of course, the children can take only a part of the responsibility. Much more responsibility lies with the capacities of the educational environment to support child-centered inquiry, and the skills of the teachers in supporting the children's memory of events and awareness of their own ideas, and in providing questions, materials, and activities that push children to extend. A project, then, takes shape not simply because of an initial interest, but due to sustained interest that the teacher provides in conscious, creative, and caring ways.

So, teacher research has many parallels to project-based work, and teachers engaged in teacher research find this synergy gives them the impulse to do their research on emerging projects. Yet teacher research goes beyond a description of a project-based curriculum. Teacher research, like a strong project, is conscious and intentional, and involves planned methods of data collection and analysis. Teacher research goes beyond the chronological description of a project. Instead, teacher research strives to answer a question or paradox that stimulated the research or that arose in the course of the teacher research process. While a teacher research project is rich with description of events, these descriptions must narrow to tell a particular story that answers a question. The simple chronology of a project can seldom accomplish real inquiry.

## What Kinds of Questions Work Well?

Teachers and ECE administrators ask all kinds of questions about their work with children. Teacher research should be engaged, focused, and systematic, but at least at first, unlike in traditional experimental research, the question need not be narrow, form the basis for a controlled experiment, or have a testable hypothesis (if . . . , then . . . ). Teacher researchers also do not need to be experts on the academic theory and research of the chosen topic. As teacher researchers work on their inquiry, they will need to develop some, but not all, of these elements. For example, most teacher research studies are not designed as controlled experiments. The classroom rarely affords us those conditions, and even if it might, it is rarely ethical for a teacher to run an experiment on his or her students. If there is a teaching approach that we believe will benefit our students, we cannot withhold it from some so that they can serve as the traditional "control group."

The question itself also will change. Indeed, many teacher research questions have a habit of undulating, growing from narrow to broad and back again. This shifting happens because as research unfolds in the complex world of a childcare center or school that is filled with young children (each with his or her own agenda), a single question has the nasty (or exciting) habit of splitting into multiple questions. Then a teacher researcher must begin to focus on a subset of those. Yet as inquiry unfolds, even new questions come into focus. Although this multiplicity may feel unsettling, the shifting of focus and gradual zooming in on the "what" of the research are the norm for all kinds of naturalistic research. The teacher's goal in undertaking inquiry is not to better control the environment and the children, but to understand them better to gain flexibility and insight.

Some teacher researchers working from the tradition of action research (e.g., McNiff, Lomax, & Whitehead, 1996) ask questions that begin with the phrase, "How can I . . . ?" This questioning strategy puts the self squarely in the center of the inquiry and allows the teacher researcher the greatest chance for effecting an immediate change in the situation. Shelly Swanegan (Stackwood, 2001) put herself in the center of a study in which she described and evaluated a culturally relevant curriculum for character development that she had developed for her kindergartners. In another study where the instructor's teaching was at the center, Christine Olsen (2001) worked to describe and assess the effectiveness of applying an active constructivist teaching practice to students studying to become early childhood teachers.

Other teacher researchers prefer to put a child or children in the learning environment in the center of the question, asking a question such as, "How useful are computers in this preschool (ages 3–5) classroom?" as posed by Lori McGaughey (2001); or, "How do my African American kindergartners develop literacy in ways that reveal a foundation in home language (Ebonics) and a shift to standard forms?" posed by Jennifer Day (2003). Others foreground the adults within their programs, for example, doing studies that assess the quality of attachment between young toddlers and their caregivers in early childhood settings, a question researched in different ways by three teacher researchers. Cathy Richardson (2001) combined observation and interview to compare teacher responsiveness (Arnett, 1989) with the security of the child's attachment to the caregiver (Waters & Deane, 1985). Jessica Fickle (2003) used memoir and photography to understand how her identity and artistic sense allowed her to form strong attachments that allowed her toddlers to stretch away from her and grow. Roxanne Latif (2006) used narrative inquiry to frame key moments in her semester as she formed new attachments with the toddlers in her care.

Within teacher research, the content and the passion behind a teacher's question matter a great deal. However, the form, the focus, and the nature of a research question will evolve over the length of the study. The first round of evolution begins as teachers ask, "What kinds of data can I collect to document and test my question?" The next section moves on to look at kinds of data one might collect, and how teachers can deal with these in two contrasting ways, first by counting and then by creating documentation panels.

## How Do Questions Develop?

After teacher researchers pose a question, they then see the complexity of what they are asking and how to work with that complexity in generative ways. Here are some ways that teacher researchers have taken their overarching questions and fleshed them out in more focused and practical ways.

Cathy Richardson's study (2001) began with her assessing toddler–caregiver attachment in her classroom, yet also asked:

- How can I measure a child's level of attachment to a caregiver? How can I measure the overall effectiveness of the teacher? What are the comparisons between these two measures?

Lori McGaughey's study (2001) began with finding a way to measure the usefulness of computers in her ECE setting, yet also asked:

- How do children respond to the computers? Is more socially driven play replaced by individual play on the machines? What do the parents think about having computers in the classroom? How do the teachers respond to and make use of the computers?

Shelly Swanegan's study (Stackwood, 2001) began with her developing a culturally relevant curriculum for character development in her public school kindergarten, yet also asked:

- What values are important to this parent group and how can I assess that? What kinds of lessons and homework can I develop to help the children build an awareness of their own characters? How do I respond to eruptions of negative behavior even within the course of this extended unit? How do I measure overall effectiveness of the unit, especially from the perspective of the parents?

Christine Olsen's study (2001) began as an application of active constructivist teaching practices to her preservice ECE teachers, yet also asked:

- How do my teacher training methods during our intensive training sessions match my intentions for my students' repertoire of practice? How do different students respond to the training sessions? How do the teachers show they have understood and can apply social-constructivist methods during their work in the semester in the lab school? What assurances do I have that their training will affect their practice once they graduate?

## DATA COLLECTION—FINDING THE LITTLE GEMS

### Finding Data to Count

What makes for data and how do early childhood teachers and administrators begin to collect types of data? Data are whatever you choose. Think of the objects, conversations, and scenes that surround us every day. What makes these into data is a self-conscious eye looking for them, and some way to keep track. Going back to the children and their *Punchbuggy* game, we see the VW Beetles become "data" that are counted through a series of three steps.

1. A car is observed by a player.
2. Each car is called out to be verified by other players.
3. Cars are added onto the running total for the kids (or rarely, the adults).

Taking the *Punchbuggy* game as a metaphor, in a school setting, what might be the corollaries? Preschool teacher Leanne Foley (2003) wanted to understand how she could interest her preschool boys in art. She realized that first she had to notice what the boys were doing in the art area. She created a table with the names of the boys down one side and the different art activities that took place over a number of weeks down the other. By creating this simple means for keeping track of what was happening, Leanne began noticing in new ways what the boys in the class were doing with art. A final tally revealed that among the six boys she was observing, there was a range of participation from one boy who participated in nearly all (15 of 16) of the art activities offered, to another who participated in only half. This range of participation alerted her to the developmental and individual differences among the boys. Yet long before she had calculated these final totals, Leanne realized that when the activities were open-ended, such as painting on the easel, drawing, or using the play dough, the boys were interested in art far more than she had thought.

On the other hand, her intuitive hunch that the boys were not interested in art also had some truth to it, as she documented that on average the boys were less interested than were the girls in her prepared art project of the day. Therefore, like the children playing *Punchbuggy*, Leanne noticed a trend, found a way to verify and document it, and then made some comparative counts. Overall, these counts were only part of her study, but they were a key turning point in her understanding of how the boys were receiving her art instruction.

Finding something discrete to count is a great way for many teacher researchers to get started because it provides a way to focus. In addition, keeping track through tally marks is so doable; it feels like a good place to start. If you have an analytic kind of mind (for example, if the "pro–con" list for selecting a research question suggested at the end of this chapter seemed the best approach to you), there is a great deal you can do with numerical data. Even though teacher research tends to be primarily qualitative, many studies use a combination of quantitative and qualitative methods. The following chapters will give examples of how teacher researchers have analyzed more deeply textured kinds of data, like conversations, collections of children's work, and photographs.

## Audiotape Recordings of Children's Speech, Transcribed

As discussed later in the book (Chapters 4 and 5), audio recording is a key element of data collection. There are several reasons for this. First, it is easy to get an audio recorder and set it up to record normal classroom speech. Second, hearing oneself teach and hearing the children in one's classroom talk to one another, in or out of the teacher's presence, gives the teacher researcher a new way to understand one's teaching and one's classroom. From personal experience hearing myself teach, especially when I've transcribed excerpts and analyzed what I've heard, almost always has given me "ah-ha" moments. Audiotaped data let teacher researchers add to the fieldnotes one has been able to scribble while also teaching, because audio allows teachers to slow down time and re-experience events that one could see from only a single perspective while teaching. Audiotape is so easy to collect, it also will be easy to collect far too much of it. There is only so much slowed-down time a researcher who is also teaching children can stand. I know from experience in my own teacher research projects that hours and hours of unheard audiotape will not help the analysis. Instead, establish a routine that is systematic, but limits audiotaping. For example, select one half hour to record, and then record another half-hour segment later the same day. If using traditional analogue tape, be systematic about labeling the tape with date, event, and participants. On the cardboard facing, also note participants and some detail that will allow recognition of the lesson or interaction. Set a discipline that requires listening to a tape before taping anything else.

Typical problems with audiotaping (once you figure out how to turn the thing on) are that initially the children take interest in the taping and act differently, that voices in a busy classroom are hard to hear or sort out from one another, and that it is hard to decide what should be transcribed from the half hour. The best way to deal with all of these problems is with consistency, realizing there is nothing perfect in this process.

First, taping several days in a row during a particular routine will eliminate the children's distracting and detracting interest, especially if the teacher makes a tape recorder available for them to use in play or for their own research. Next, listening the day of or, at latest, the day after the taping will allow the teacher researcher to understand what is being said because the event is still in short-term memory. Brain research shows that our memory of ordinary events is quite sharp in the first 6 to 8 hours, and remains good over the next 24 hours. After that, the memory trace fades and we have less access to details, even when prompted by a record like a photo or audiotape. If a teacher researcher can get back to the tape in a day, he or she will mostly recognize the children speaking and will have a good idea what they were saying because the teacher will remember the context. This is less true when recording children playing or working collaboratively without the teacher's immediate presence. In these cases, when a teacher researcher hits what sounds like an interesting patch, but isn't sure what the children are saying, timeliness still works in one's favor because the teacher can replay the segment for the children and ask them what they think they were saying. Children won't always remember (or know how to respond to a teacher's question), but the interaction around this segment of tape often creates some other useful data on the question. Another point to keep in mind is that ethnographers, anthropologists, and linguists always struggle with unintelligible speech. In fact, unintelligible speech doesn't ruin a transcript and often holds some meaning, as the speaker may have been less than clear to others during the conversation, prompting different kinds of responses from others than if his or her speech had been enunciated clearly. Because unintelligible speech is unavoidable in making transcripts from tape, there are typographical conventions that account for these muddled patches. Fully unintelligible speech is often depicted as empty parentheses, while speech made out the best one can is spelled out, but put in parentheses to indicate it is a "best guess."

Finally, don't overwhelm oneself in transcription. Limit and structure the approach by choosing, for example, a single 1- to 3-minute segment to transcribe from an hour of tape. Then, present this transcript to someone else, ideally a consistent group of responders such as one's critical colleagues, prefacing the transcript with one point or question it raised that explains why it was chosen as a highlight. I've found there are a number of useful twists in the process of transcribing data to share. The reasons one has picked the segment at first may shift while transcribing, because the close listening practice required by transcription often reveals a new insight. In talking to critical colleagues, a teacher researcher might present these contrasting reasons, or just one's recent revelation. As the next section explains, audiotape also can enhance graphic documents that teachers create as part of the inquiry process.

## UNDERSTANDING YOUR DATA
## THROUGH DOCUMENTATION

### Graphic Documentation of Inquiry

Graphic documentation is probably one of the most important means I've found for helping teachers see their question and simultaneously extend and better represent their project-based work with children. Documentation creates graphic displays, but really it is a form of teacher research that is displayed visually and typically undertaken collaboratively by several adults working in one room. Therefore, there is more importance in the process of undertaking the documentation than in the product. Many early childhood teachers have been inspired to try documentation because they have seen the work of the Reggio Emilia teachers while visiting the site in Italy or through the traveling exhibit, "The Hundred Languages of Children." Focusing on such products, unbalanced by the perspective of a group of collaborators or a school struggling to implement the process, can make teachers think they need to set as their goal the creation of museum-quality displays (a virtually impossible task, of course). In contrast, what's most important to learn, and to develop strategies to support long term, is the process itself, which includes many components. Working in spiraling ways, the teacher researcher creating documentation must frame a question, identify data sources, collect and analyze data, collaborate with others to verify findings, recast the net of the research question in better ways, and then present the findings publicly. These elements parallel the journey of teacher research described throughout this book. The documentation panel stands here as an encapsulated example of how teachers can begin and complete a form of action research that collects and makes use of multiple data sources to address a question that will allow them greater insight and flexibility in their work with children. Since doing documentation is a challenge, I provide specific examples of how to create a product, mixed with a measure of why this kind of work matters to teachers and the children and families their work touches.

In my work in teacher education, I've been influenced by the Reggio Emilia municipal early childhood centers, whose teachers embrace documentation of many forms. The documentation panels, portfolios, books, and diaries are key to the *progettazione*, or projects, that they implement (Gandini & Goldhaber, 2001; Vecchi, 1998). These graphic documents most commonly are seen as display panels, or documentation panels, where the children's words, photos of the children engaged in work, the children's work (often artwork at Reggio), and the teacher's voice are all represented in a manner that reveals the chronology of the project. Katya Alvarado's documentation panel appears in Figure 2.1.

**Figure 2.1.** Katya Alvarado's documentation panel.

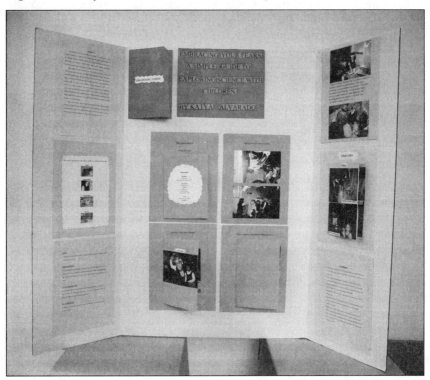

The panel used fold-out books that gave more information about the preschool children's exploration with the science materials. Making the panel three-dimensional provided more space for content and made the panel more visually appealing.

Robust documentation will evolve over time and will be an integral part of the project. That is, without the documentation, the project would not develop at all, as deeply, or in ways as well tuned to the children's emerging ideas and interests. For example, as teacher Michael Escamilla (2004) began his project on shadows, he put up a few of the portraits the children had completed that day, and then asked them the next day at circle what they noticed about the pictures he had displayed. He then took the drawings down to photocopy, and children added to or redrew them to represent new ideas. The panel grew to show these changes. In this way, the documentation provides a means for the children to give input to the evolution of the project and to see a visual reminder that their ideas, words, and work matter. In its final form, good documentation shows the complexity of a project by using a paired focus on the children's work and the teacher's intentions. Through organization and graphic simplicity, a strong panel allows the viewer to understand the story of the project—beginning, middle, and end—and also allows viewers to raise their own questions.

In these ways, documentation is a form of teacher research. The structure and discipline of creating a panel as a project-based curriculum unfolds, provides a way for teachers to simultaneously undertake many aspects of the work, including:

1. engaging children in the inquiry,
2. clarifying a teacher research question for themselves,
3. collecting and organizing a variety of data sources,
4. engaging in ongoing analysis of data, hand-in-hand with teaching,
5. representing findings through multiple forms of data,
6. sharing findings of a project with a broader audience, and
7. collaborating with others.

I'll use a more extended example to illustrate the process of creating such a panel. Jeanne Soulé (2003), a transitional kindergarten teacher, used a documentation panel to make inquiry about the marble raceways her 4- and 5-year-olds were building in the block area during the free-choice period. At the start of the project, she saw the children used a few formulaic ways of building the ramps and connecting lanes. A child working alone, or with one friend, would have built each of these early compact structures. She took digital photographs of the children at work, writing some quick notes as she did so. Then, either later the same day or within a day or two of taking the photos, she used her laptop to show the photos to those pictured and ask what they had been doing. She added these comments to her notes.

Jeanne also used some time during circle to show the photos, read out the captions, and discuss highlights of the raceway constructions with the whole class. At the same time, she started laying out the photos (a sort of proto-panel)—beginning with the earliest, or "baseline" photos, and gradually adding photos that showed innovation or challenge. The display Jeanne created at this point was intentionally in progress. Captions were handwritten, photos came and went, and other than following a simple chronology, there was no real design or polish to her layout. Yet the children enjoyed looking at the photos and reading or asking about accompanying words. These verbal and graphic conversations made two changes to the children's construction. First, in proud response to their teacher's interest, the block builders focused almost exclusively on marble raceways. Second, and more significant, this focus allowed them to interact in more complex ways. Cooperation became common, so instead of three or four little ramps, they worked together, using all the blocks so that they could create one big raceway. As they built together, they also found creative new ways to combine elements and solve raceway problems. The cooperative work and their growing mastery of the materials made for some remarkable raceways and strengthened the social climate of the classroom.

The success of the project was due, not in small part, to the role of the in-process panel. Far more than a static record of their successes, the display served as a tool for the children. That is, in the midst of building, a child often would get up and go look at the photos to remind himself how to create some of the trickier elements built successfully on an earlier day. Children also looked together at the photos during times other than their free-choice period, making plans for raceways they'd build the next day.

Marble raceway fever never cooled that academic year in Jeanne's class, but as the semester ended and graduate school projects came due, Jeanne formalized the panel for presentation. This way, her work could serve the different purpose of communicating the progress of her students' learning to adults who didn't work directly with the children, including the parents and her teacher research colleagues. In formalizing the panel, she clarified her own goals in pursuing the project, deepened her analysis of the children's learning, and made links to the literature in cognition, specifically to the social cognitive framework that guides her teaching practice. This second layer of work on the display placed her findings in a broader context and helped to verify her claims about why and how the project had been a remarkable learning experience. If Jeanne had not begun the panel and used it as a springboard to talk with the children about their work, it is unlikely they would have done as much with the materials. The panel also had served as an entry point for other children to join the builders, because they could pick up on the ideas and the developing norms of the raceway-building project from the photos and the circle time talk.

At the same time that the project supported and revealed the strengths of the learning in Jeanne's classroom, it also raised questions from those in her teacher research group. For example, since almost exclusively boys had participated, we wondered if she should have done something to offset the gender imbalance among the builders? And was it a problem that building choices in the block area had been limited by marble raceway mania? The emerging "raceway pros" had gained exceptional access to materials, teacher attention, and opportunities for negotiation with peers. Therefore, while the project had created powerful learning opportunities, many children had not taken part, and those who had, needed to limit their individual choices for how to work with the blocks. As a teacher researcher, Jeanne Soulé is open to critique of her inquiry. Yet as a teacher, she responds to these final questions with comments that highlight how a project-based approach requires complex teaching, and that necessarily, many events unfolded in her classroom that fall semester that went beyond the scope of her data collection, and of this particular documentation panel. Jeanne says,

> I think it is important to note that as early childhood educators in project-based classrooms—if we know what we are doing and are doing our work intentionally—then we can have projects like the marble project with a majority of boys *and* we can still be running a fair, supported, high-functioning class with all the remaining students. There can be more than one project happening in a class at one time, on different intensity levels, by different teachers. . . . I want to ensure that the goals of project-based classrooms don't [appear to] work [in a way that some are ignored]. All young children are not interested in working on long-term projects. Many children prefer other ways to be invested in the classroom on a daily basis.

As this example shows, a strong documentation panel tells a story of a project and allows the teacher to present a detailed portrait that highlights some of the children and some angle of their classroom. At the same time, the story it tells leaves open space for new stories to be told or new questions to be explored.

## How to Create Effective Documentation Displays

Effective documentation mixes a variety of media and uses the same media to different effect. The most common media that teachers use include photographs, drawings, text, and small constructions. It is sometimes useful to have a DVD or videotape available if you'd like people to borrow the recording, or a computer nearby where they might view the disc. Describing how to craft an effective video presentation is beyond the scope of this book, but the availability of digital video cameras, digital still photography, and digital editing makes this choice possible and appealing for some. Creating the work in a digital form also makes the documentation portable and easy to share online or by disc. Nonetheless, the impact of physical panels displayed in a classroom should not be underestimated. The simplicity and permanence of paper and ink provide teacher researchers with tools that allow them to assess learning and development and inquire about the effectiveness of teaching practices. In using documentation panels in my teacher education and graduate classes, I have created, with input from my students, a rubric for panels that provides further detail on effective final products.

I turn now to each of the major forms of media that teacher researchers use in documentation panels.

*Photos.* What should teacher researchers think about as they take photos? Most photos should highlight the work itself and the activity of the children at work, although I have seen four kinds of photos used. Most common are photos of the children at work, at play, in social negotiation, or in contemplation. As with the process of using audiotape described earlier, the teacher needs to use a camera frequently and casually enough that the children learn not to "cheese" for the picture. Second, teachers photograph the children's constructions, especially those that are temporary like block or sand structures, or those too large to present with the panel. Photographing only the constructions is helpful when the panel needs to be shared with a larger external group, and the teacher faces a school policy that limits the use of photographs that reveal a child's identity. Third, photos of the classroom or outdoor space, empty of children or not focused on the children, provide viewers not directly familiar with the space or its uses a way into the classroom context. Finally, teachers sometimes use photographs taken by the children. This allows them to draw on the perspective a child photographer has chosen as another way into the children's understanding of a situation.

*Drawings.* Related to photography, and providing key evidence on many panels, are drawings. Four kinds of drawings are most common: children's drawings, teachers' sketches, floor plans or maps, and graphics. In deciding which children's drawings to use, the teacher researcher should consider these kinds of questions: Which of the drawings are exemplars of a pattern common among the children? Which drawings raise a new insight a child has had? How can a set of drawings be grouped to show contrast across time or across children? Teachers who use documentation panels come to see drawn representations of ideas as an important way for children and adults to learn and to communicate. Therefore, documenting teachers encourage their students to draw frequently, so the children use drawings to observe closely or express ideas. With teacher research, teachers also learn to systematically collect this work, and they soon have available hundreds of drawings. Digital scanning followed by resizing the image, or taking digital photographs of the artwork, provides a way to effectively display more artwork on a manageably sized panel. Yet, this cornucopia of images leads to a problem similar to the hours of unheard audiotape. In doing qualitative research such as teacher research, the inquiry process requires the systematic choice of data, coupled with an analytic eye that asks, "So what?" Through this process, data can transform and become evidence for a claim to knowledge. Again, the message here is "hold back." The panel should feature children's drawings, but viewers must be able to understand how these images relate to the research question.

A different kind of drawings used in panels is sketches of events made by teachers. Teachers sometimes sketch from or trace over photos if they cannot use photos for sharing the panel outside of the school or clinical setting. Teachers also sketch events they were unable to capture through photographs, or use their artistic interpretation of a sketched event to understand the unspoken perspective. Teachers who are artistic by training or temperament feel most comfortable with this approach, but all of us can find ways to sketch that help uncover our assumptions and reveal insights initially hidden beyond language (Tidwell, 2006; Waddell, McDaniel, & Einstein, 1988).

Documentation sometimes benefits as well from the use of floor plans or maps. Simple floor plans marked to highlight an element relevant to the inquiry (e.g., classroom use patterns, zones of conflict, or changes made to a physical space) are most useful to the viewer. Commercially produced maps can be included (e.g., a section of the community under study, a map gathered while visiting a field trip site) but should be used sparingly and for a good reason. The impact of professionally produced graphics easily can overpower a panel, which should always strive to highlight the local perspective of the children and the teacher researcher.

Finally, teachers sometimes include simple graphics to capture the abstract. Two simple examples are a brainstorm map created with the children as a project begins, or a Venn diagram to illustrate contrasts and similarities. Some teacher researchers have created novel graphics to communicate a concept their inquiry helped them discover, (e.g., a kind of cycling waterfall by Simon Lee, 2003) while others have drawn on the literature of visual organizers, using hierarchical, chained, or nested figures to show relationships that emerged through their study.

*Text.* Although documentation displays draw on the visual to represent ideas, they always use text in one way or another. Because panels are viewed in short spurts, often while standing or even moving, the text should not overwhelm the viewer. In most cases, even when the documentation is created as a book or portfolio, text should be secondary to the visuals. Hand-lettered captions are great for the early stages of making a panel, but because it is so difficult and time consuming to create hand lettering that doesn't distract from the content, the final display text should be done with a computer and printer. Consider design principles in using text for titles and longer sections. Use fancy display fonts sparingly, if at all, and only for large titles. Clean, easy-to-read sans serif fonts (e.g., Arial, Optima, Helvetica) are best for titles or brief captions, while contrasting serif fonts (e.g., Times, Palatino) can be used for longer descriptions. Font size should be a minimum of 16 point, with fonts up to 48 useful for titles. Pay attention to the size of text blocks on the panel. Keeping them to 4" x 6" is one rule of thumb to avoid fatiguing your viewers. If you have much more that you'd like to describe, consider including a pocket on the panel for enclosing a pamphlet that interested viewers can take away.

As with photographs or drawings, teacher researchers should use a variety of forms and source materials for the text included in their documentation. One form that always should be present is representation of the children's voices. These can be captured through audiotape, or in field notes taken during the event, and added as captions under drawings or photographs. If the research is with preverbal infants or young toddlers, capture their babbles in the captions. Although it may be tempting, don't fake these goo-goo-ga-gas. Children's noises and early word approximations are powerful when they are captured accurately. Families will recognize their children in the sounds represented, and the sounds and their melodies communicate meaning that a teacher researcher's analysis can reveal. Just as in work with older children, use at least some audiotape to really listen to the babies' sounds. Just as important, capture the babies' communicative attempts by describing their gestures and explaining the meaning in the event's context, as needed.

A second source for children's speech is what they say in response to seeing or hearing their work or thoughts reflected back to them. As Jeanne Soulé did in her marble raceway panel, show the children photos of themselves at work, or read back statements or questions they made as they worked. As children become literate, their voices are also present in their written texts. Include these writings with a caption providing translation or explanation as needed.

Next, the panel should include the teacher researcher's voice as teacher, which balances the voices of the children and moves the board from description to inquiry. Creating a panel is about describing and reflecting on teaching practice. Therefore, text should describe the teaching intentions behind a lesson, interaction, setup of an area, or interactional strategy. Teacher reactions written during the teaching event are valuable to practice-based inquiry as they capture in self-reflection what unfolded in the moment, that is, *reflection-in-action* (Schön, 1983). These little moments of "Ah-ha!" or "What's happening?" as we teach reveal how in our teaching we draw on stores of deep or tacit knowledge, but we also must be alive to improvise, as children's thinking and behavior never go exactly as planned. Teacherly analysis after the events also should be included as a contrast. These are what Schön calls reflections-*on-action*, and they capture a stiller, more objective way of understanding events, allowing the *in-action* shifts to permeate our consciousness and change us more deeply. Finally, many panels benefit from inclusion of relevant quotes from poetry, song, fiction, or memoir. Including brief quotes from the theoretical or research literature in education, child development, linguistics, or neuropsychology helps the teacher researcher to connect from the new insights of the current project to the broader literature in related fields.

*Constructions.* Samples of constructions made by children add lively energy to an otherwise two-dimensional documentation display. For example, I have seen teachers include glued wood constructions, collages made from mixed materials, clay figures, wire sculpture, folded paper, and beadwork. The materials can be laid out on a table in front of the panel, hung from above, or set up on ledges that the teacher has built into the panel, typically by using cardboard blocked underneath with wood. The constructions should be integrated into the story of inquiry that the panel tells, by using photos of the children at work on this or similar products, and with text capturing children's and the teacher's voices on the process and products displayed.

In contrast to the children's art, teacher researchers I have worked with also have used a range of materials to make their own artistic representations. This art fits with the documentation because it represents a teaching insight that resulted from the inquiry. Oil paintings, quilted fabric, picture collages, mobiles, and paper maché constructions are some examples. The art serves the same conceptual purpose in the displays as do graphics, such as brainstorm maps or Venn diagrams, mentioned earlier. Teacher researchers sometimes find these alternative modes for expressing their insights more motivating and satisfying than abstract and formulaic modes. Additionally, the discipline and engagement of creating the representation allow teacher researchers to gain better and different insight into their findings.

My earlier *Punchbuggy* story shows how when people look for something, they begin to see everything with different eyes. From a brain-based standpoint, we can say we're experiencing the preconscious work of our reticular formation (an evolutionarily early part of the brain) that helps us process the patterns of our world. Yet these blips of noticing begin to matter, and to be maintained as something to look for, only because of the social systems and the collaborative supports such looking can create. The *Punchbuggy* game worked that summer only because we all enjoyed playing it.

In terms of beginning a teacher research study, finding a good question for your focus feels stressful to many would-be teacher researchers because as teachers we feel that we either know too little (What could I ask?) or know too much (Then, what won't I be able to ask?). We just need to start on our inquiry. Having a critical colleague to work with or other more complex supports—through the ECE site, higher education, or a cross-institutional fellowship—helps keep us accountable to starting and maintaining inquiry. There is no perfect question, and even if we were to find it, any question needs to shift and grow within the open-ended analysis cycle of qualitative research. Nascent teacher researchers can try the exercises I've suggested below to find a focus for a question, but any routines, rituals, or tricks for getting yourself rolling with a new task (much like increasing your exercise, lowering your stress, or taking up knitting) would work here. Becoming a teacher researcher is a life-changing event (maybe big, maybe small), and our call here is that you find a way to represent to yourself that you have something you'd like to say with authority about your professional life. The examples of starting and branching questions give some idea of the range and specificity of questions early childhood professionals we've worked with have researched. (These questions are described here in the framework of beginning your own study, not as general suggestions of what can work, as in the first chapter.)

The next step is for teacher researchers to identify data sources and ways to collect and organize them. For simplicity's sake, I push us off the couch by suggesting that finding something, anything, to count is one good way to start the job. Taking an opposite tack, I ask all teacher researchers to consider audiotaped conversation as a basic and necessary element of their data set. I use the creation of Reggio-inspired documentation to raise the how and why of a number of other sources of data work. Framing these through the documentation discussion helps to move back to the whole, so that data are collected in exchange with curriculum and, in a cyclic manner, are organized, analyzed, and presented until they are a final product for presentation to a broader audience—that is, a completed piece of teacher research.

## Suggested Teacher Research Activities

How, then, do teachers find the kind of question that can begin an inquiry? Maybe you already have some ideas for your research. But if you don't, or if you think there may be a better question lurking out there, here are four ideas for a way to start. Each of these exploratory exercises takes about 20 minutes. Choose the one suggestion that feels most comfortable for your strengths as a thinker, or try a few to see what common thread emerges.

1. *Create a list of issues within your center or school.* Make two columns so that one side shows what works well at your site, or what you love about your work with children, while the other shows problems or aspects of your teaching position that you dislike or find problematic. Simply brainstorm this list for 5–10 minutes. Now review the list, marking with asterisks patterns you see such as these:

   - Topics that arise multiple times in different guises
   - Any topic that shows up on both the positive and the negative side, suggesting a paradox that will make looking at it revealing.
   - Any single item or pair of items that jumps out for you as something that really matters about your teaching or your school.

   Using these items, generate a short set of questions that these key issues raise for you.

2. *Take a set of photographs at your site.* Sort through them, looking for one or two pictures that best represent what teaching at your site means for you. Look for the aesthetic, but also for the content. You may select a picture that includes children, families, or teaching colleagues. Alternatively, it may be a picture highlighting materials, equipment, the classroom, or the outdoor space. Find a colleague who understands that you are trying to frame a teacher research question. This person might become your "critical colleague" who will help you think about your research throughout your inquiry process. Explain to your colleague what it is about this picture that is important to you. You might want to audiotape this conversation as early data, or have the tape simply to listen to later to clarify your question. After you finish explaining, take 5 minutes to write down a set of questions or hunches that capture what is going on in the picture that makes it interesting to you. Ask your colleague to do the same. Now read your key questions to each other and discuss a bit further.

3. *Take 5–10 minutes to draw a picture about your work.* You can make a representational picture, maybe about a child, a lesson, or an object, or you can draw a more abstract or symbolic picture. Use the picture as a springboard for discussion with a critical colleague, as above. Then each of you should write a set of three to five questions that the picture and the conversation sparked. Exchange lists, and then discuss these questions. Rewrite any questions that are interesting, but not yet on target. Now, as the teacher researcher, highlight the question that best reflects your interests, then explain why to your critical colleague.

4. *Tell a critical colleague a story.* Talk about what most affected you in your work with children last week. For example, it could have been a warm and nurturing moment, a troubling one, a confusing one, or one where you had an insight. Ask your colleague to listen without engaging in conversation until you are completely done. After you finish the story, ask your critical colleague to restate what she or he saw as the most striking part of the story, in her or his own words. Clarify or extend on the story as needed, so that you both understand why the incident matters to you. Now, through conversation, uncover the potential questions that lie beneath this anecdote and write these down.

# CHAPTER 3

# Using Teacher Research to Understand and Promote Children's Play and Interaction

*The spider's web is soft like*
*my mother's hand*
*which is noiseless when she moves it.*
    Michele, Oahu, Hawaii. In *Small Kid Time Hawaii* (Chock, 1981).

Guiding Questions

1. How can teacher research help us understand how and why children play? How can it improve our guidance and support of children's play?
2. How have selected teacher researchers designed and carried out teacher research projects on children's play?
3. What are successful elements and features of these projects, and what can be strengthened?
4. How have teacher researchers used the research literature to support their projects on children's play?
5. How have these teacher research projects inspired the teachers to make practical changes in their classrooms to promote children's play?

As in Michele's poem, when we look more closely at how and why children play and interact with one another, we essentially are looking to find what is "soft" and "noiseless." These qualities help us learn more about the inner workings of children's play and interactions, and what makes them run smoothly and with synchrony. I discuss examples of teacher research that get at this element of children's play and socializing. As in the previous chapters, which portrayed the work of teacher researchers focused on language and literacy, I present the work of teacher researchers carrying out projects in their own classrooms and educational settings. In particular, I focus on projects pertaining to the play development of toddlers, pretend play in preschool, children's invented play and games in preschool, and the play interests of preschoolers.

## TODDLERS—BUILDING COMMUNITY THROUGH PLAY

Jacqueline Paras-Frei (2004), a Montessori teacher of toddlers, conducted a teacher research project in her toddler classroom. Jacqueline shares the classroom with another caregiver, and each teacher is responsible for five toddlers. The toddlers range in age from 13 to 24 months. Jacqueline had three questions to frame her project.

1. Do toddlers like to be in a community, and do they "naturally" desire to join a community?
2. If building a sense of community is important in early childhood, what do we mean by a community of toddlers? How do toddlers "view" community?
3. What is my role as a teacher in promoting classroom community through the classroom environment, curriculum, and my relationships with toddlers and parents?

Over the course of 4 months, Jacqueline looked for signs of togetherness in her toddlers that would answer these three basic questions. Over the course of her project, she stayed with these questions, finding them useful guides for data collection and analysis. Using written fieldnotes, a personal reflective journal, and a digital camera, she documented instances where her toddlers interacted, played, and communicated with one another. Jacqueline, who previously had taught preschool and was somewhat new to the world of toddlers, was especially interested in using the project to learn about how and why toddlers interacted, and how she could build on this to create a sense of community.

Jacqueline discovered many signs and indications of toddler "togetherness," and with her digital camera, took hundreds of photographs capturing her children's interest in one another. Since toddlers have few oral language skills, Jacqueline knew beforehand (and this was reinforced during the project) that photographs would be critical to documenting the children's interactions and play.

During the project and after the project ended, Jacqueline reviewed and reflected on the large volume of data she had collected through her written notes, reflective teaching journal, and photographs. She started to sort the material into piles that indicated signs of togetherness according to behaviors that indicated children's awareness of one another, where they were when they were playing and interacting, and their favorite activities and routines. After putting the data into these three large groups, Jacqueline made smaller piles of the data to tease out smaller factors and characteristics for each. For instance, in terms of the children's awareness of one another, Jacqueline discovered that the children:

- gazed at another child who was involved in an activity
- gazed at another child even when they themselves were engaged in an activity
- watched and then imitated a peer's actions
- gathered and played near peers in certain classroom areas

For example, in terms of the last characteristic of peer awareness, Figure 3.1 shows three children in the sensorial area.

**Figure 3.1.** An example of peer awareness.

Dan watched Chris play with the nesting cups while Gina stood close by and tried to figure out what to do with the nesting cups. In the next sequence of interaction, Chris, Gina, and Carlos were in the dramatic play area. While he "ate" his own food, Chris watched Gina and Carlos exchanging food. Jacqueline used photographs to show the children's physical proximity to one another, and their gazing and interest in the play of their peers.

Jacqueline also found that her toddlers engaged in other behaviors in which they directly focused on a peer. These included:

- giving or taking an object to or from a peer
- using the same object or a similar object
- gross motor activities (ball throwing, crawling, running, pushing, sliding)
- banging games
- peek-a-boo games
- displays of affection and helping one another
- smiling, laughing, and vocalizing

For example, in terms of the gross motor activity of ball throwing, Jacqueline learned that her toddlers loved this activity for both the joy of throwing the ball and also the social interaction. Jacqueline documented one ball-throwing episode in which Jon "initiated the ball throwing with a small blue ball that he had been carrying around in the classroom all morning." When he first threw it, Samantha and Nicole did not notice. When she did see the ball, "Samantha picked it up and threw it, while Jon went to get another ball. Nicole then joined in and got another ball. They were all gathered in front of one of the playhouses (outside), while at other times they would run and fetch the balls. This time, as they often liked to do, they laughed and watched each other. I had observed Samantha throwing the ball before, while Nicole would ride her tummy on top of the ball. For Nicole to join in with Jon and play with the balls, she was exploring a new way of playing with the ball with Jon's help." Based on this and other similar scenes from her data, Jacqueline concluded that "the children's imitative behavior and need for fun seemed to bring a common experience that the three of them shared."

Jacqueline learned a great deal about her toddlers and the ways that toddlers promote a sense of community all by themselves. Jacqueline reflected that her toddlers "revealed that they are truly social beings. They were very aware of each other, and often gave special attention to each other, and wanted to be physically close. My toddlers like to look at what each other was doing, sometimes imitate each other, and often gravitated and gathered around an object or activity that was interesting and intriguing." Jacqueline's project, in an overall way, provided data and evidence for reaffirming her personal and professional belief in the value of community and togetherness.

Jacqueline reflected that "a community of toddlers really is one of watching each other, learning from each other, being together, gathering physically close together, doing things together, of laughing, having fun together and sometimes not always getting along with each other." This project helped her "see how much being together and in a community is important for toddlers and also how much my direct involvement is crucial in helping promote a sense of togetherness and community." Jacqueline realized that her project would have been strengthened if she had collected more data on her own role in the classroom. Since she wanted her "observations to be as naturalistic as possible," and given the "nonintervention role" from her Montessori training, Jacqueline originally decided not to play a direct role in facilitating the children's interactions. She might extend and strengthen the project in the following ways:

1. Take a more active role with the children and therefore collect more data on how she herself promotes community
2. Experiment with taking fewer photographs, which might enable her to become more involved with the children
3. Collaborate with her co-teacher and become co-researchers, both collecting and analyzing the data, which could be used as the basis for discussion and reflection about their shared group of children
4. Extend the length of the project over a year or more; this most likely would result in the collection of less data and more infrequent data collection

## PROMOTING MORE SOPHISTICATED PLAY AND INTERACTION IN PRESCHOOL

In the following section, I highlight the projects of 3 experienced preschool teachers who focus on, respectively, pretend play in a Montessori environment, children's spontaneous outdoor games, and children's strong interests during independent play. All three projects reveal the value of teacher research for veteran educators seeking new ways of understanding children's play development.

### Understanding and Creating Opportunities for Pretend Play

Julie Vazquez-Torres (2004), a teacher who has taught in Montessori preschool environments for 7 years, carried out a teacher research project on her children's fantasy play. Julie wanted to understand and improve a source of frustration for her in her classroom—the lack of opportunities to encourage pretend play. Before starting her project, Julie reflected on her previous teaching year: "I spent a good amount of time discouraging children from engaging in pretend play. I either stopped it altogether or redirected their attention to a more academic use of the materials in my room. I discovered, though, that when I stopped their fantasy play, the children often returned to it later. I became frustrated because I wasn't honoring the child."

Julie wanted information on how to promote her children's pretend play, and she wanted to see whether there were ways to incorporate this play within a Montessori reality-based curriculum. Over the course of 4 months, Julie used written observational notes, a data collection sheet, an audiocassette recorder, and a reflective teaching journal to collect data on instances of pretend play in her classroom. Julie's data collection sheet included the following items:

- Date
- Time
- Children observed
- Materials used
- How the materials were used
- My interventions
- "Play" as peaceful or aggressive
- Duration of the play
- Language used
- Notes to self

Data collection sheets are designed as efficient and handy ways to record data when observing and/or participating in a teacher research setting. It is best if the sheets are simply done, so that they can be photocopied and clipped onto a clipboard or kept in a folder for easy access and use. The sheets can be revised over time as data collection gets underway, as either its direction changes, or the teacher researcher has new ideas for making the sheet more efficient and useful—such as using the graphics and information to capture the essence of what the teacher researcher is interested in, that is, the most important elements, strategies, or behaviors. The sheets also can be organized and designed with preset categories and elements borrowed and/or adapted from the research literature or curriculum materials.

Julie also wanted to find out what other Montessori teachers thought about the role of play in their classrooms, and so she designed a short survey of 12 questions. The questions ranged from, "Do you find that children in your classroom use the Montessori materials for ways other than they are intended?" to, "Regardless of redirecting students away from pretend play, on average, do they continue their pretend play?" to, "If pretend play is not practiced at your site, why not?" Julie sent the survey to 12 local Montessori educators. She wanted these data to supplement the data she obtained from her classroom observations by adding the perspectives and experiences of other teachers on the issue of fantasy play in a Montessori environment.

Over 2 months, September and October, Julie watched for and observed instances of fantasy or pretend play among her 23 three- to five-year-olds while they were engaged in the Montessori activities and work areas with the Montessori materials (called "works"). Once she had watched and observed on several occasions, Julie was able to focus on particular children whom she felt exemplified certain aspects of the fantasy play she was seeing. Like Jacqueline in her project, Julie did not start out looking at a few children, but looked more globally at all the children. Later in her data collection, Julie sat down with her collected data and "divided the material into the three themes of house play, solitary fantasy play, and mixing works together." She observed several children enacting house play, and selected Hanna and Amelia to provide examples of the children's fantasy play, and chose Benjamin as a focus child to show how the children mixed Montessori "works" together.

Just as the digital camera allowed Jacqueline to quickly record the children's actions, Julie's data collection sheet helped her quickly and efficiently record the children's play behaviors and language. Julie reflected, "I created the data collection sheet as a guide to make sure that I captured the specifics of each child's play." Julie also relied on an audiocassette recorder to capture the children's conversations during the fantasy play. Like many other teacher researchers who investigate their own teaching practices, Julie had to teach *as* she observed. The audiocassette recorder freed Julie both to observe and also to assist and guide the children as needed. With the tape recorder running, Julie knew that she would listen to the tape later when she was not busy with the children. She found it valuable to audiotape "the children's stories and language in their pretend/fantasy play," and that it turned out to be most beneficial to "audiotape the children engaged in house play since that afforded the most dialogue." Julie transcribed the tapes at the end of her data collection period.

In her teaching journal, Julie complemented her audiotaping and data collection sheets by writing down "thoughts and reflections on the day regarding the children's play." She also recorded notes on conversations she had with her co-teacher on fantasy play. Julie noted, "The journal reflected the times I felt frustrated as well as contented." The teaching journal strengthened her other data collection by providing Julie with a personal, reflective space for jotting down her inner thoughts and feelings in a quick, immediate way regarding the progression of her project. It thus enabled her to capture a different kind of data (more internal than the external data from her classroom observations and surveys) that would enrich both her ongoing data collection and her future data analysis once the project was completed.

As Julie started to collect her data, she quickly encountered a dilemma—she wanted to see and document the children's play, but her initial teacher training and the philosophy of her current teaching position discouraged children's pretend play. This issue stayed with Julie throughout the course of her project and in the end became one of the key aspects of her findings.

Julie was also "surprised" by the survey results. All of the teachers surveyed "experienced fantasy play within their environment, but no teacher had in any way thought of truly incorporating it into their teaching. Every teacher admitted that pretend play was valuable to children's development, but most were reluctant to change their traditional Montessori model of education." The teachers, then, were in a similar developmental place to Julie's—aware of the value of fantasy play but not incorporating it into their teaching and classroom environment.

As noted earlier, Julie found three main instances of the children's fantasy play: house play, solitary fantasy play, and mixing Montessori works together. In an example of the first instance, Julie discovered several children who liked to transform the classroom library into a playhouse (the classroom had no established playhouse or area).

> Ruby and Sara wanted to play house. Then went into the library and brought out their work rugs. Ruby used her pillow to make a pillow and blanket for Sara. Ruby made the couch into a bed and they pretended to sleep. After a few minutes, Ruby made a rooster sound indicating it was time to get up. Sara then became a kitty. Ruby said, "It is breakfast time. It's your party today Kitty, Kitty." Ruby then saw me watching her taking another rug. She asked me if she could get a rug and use it as a blanket. I said, "Yes." Ruby then asked me if she could use the math manipulative objects for Kitty's breakfast. I said, "Yes."

Julie continued to observe that "Ruby then instructed Sara on how to pretend to eat the "food."

> Sara replied, "Yucky, I don't like it." Ruby said, "It's your favorite soup, eat for pretend. Do you want to play with it?" "Yes," said Sara. Ruby then dumped out the shapes and they started building things with them, which is what the activity is supposed to be for.

Julie reflected on this incident of spontaneous pretend play: "Normally, this type of play would not be OK and I would say no. Ruby knows this and this is why she asked me before she took things. However, I wanted to get a feel for what the girls' strong urge to play house was all about. I also wanted to practice what Montessori preached, which was to follow the child. To me this was a perfect example of that."

Julie's reflective teaching journal allowed her to deepen her data collection and ongoing data analysis as her project progressed. For example, in one entry Julie continues to reflect on the dilemma of teacher intervention.

> This morning the girls played house again in the library. My co-teacher saw that I was watching this and started talking to me about this. She is concerned because if two girls are playing house in the library and someone else would like to use the library to look at a book, they cannot. My co-teacher said she agreed that children need the space to act out dramatic play and she wouldn't stop it, but what about the children who want to read a book? I told her that is why we should have a dress-up area. This way the children wouldn't need to use the library. She disagreed and said that then we impose adult rules on the children; it is as if we say, go and play and don't bother us now. In this way, we would be limiting their imagination, and they would engage in pretend play in all areas of the classroom, so what would we do about that?

The teaching journal allowed Julie to begin wrestling with the possible meaning of her data—in terms of what they meant for her teaching philosophy and teaching practices with her co-teacher—even before she had collected all her data and sat down to analyze it.

Later on, when she finished her data collection and began her data analysis, Julie looked back over her data and tried to see how it all might influence her teaching and the philosophy of the school toward play. Her project provided numerous instances of the children's spontaneous fantasy play and showed Julie that her children wanted and needed regular outlets and avenues for this kind of play in her classroom. Julie reflected on the value of her project: "I have grown as a teacher as a result of this project. I am much more comfortable with allowing the children to engage in pretend play. Although I must admit it happens more often when I am teaching alone in the afternoon than in the morning session when other teachers are around. Although this is also becoming difficult because my director is considering changing the afternoons to a pre-K time."

In considering the implications of her project for potential changes in her own classroom and her school in general, Julie commented, "I feel that we are not in full agreement with my feelings about fantasy play. However, I do feel that I opened the door for discussion and am hopeful that this topic will be discussed in the future. As for me, I will always respect the philosophy of the director at this particular site. I will have to find a balance for myself between following what I learned from this project and the educational vision of my director."

To strengthen and extend her project, Julie might consider one or more of the following ideas:

1. Enlist her co-teacher as co-researcher so that both teachers who share the classroom can share in the collecting and analysis of the data, and then make decisions with the director about possible changes to the philosophy and policy regarding fantasy play
2. Visit the sites where the survey respondents work to observe the children and talk with the teachers (Julie did start this: "I decided that I wanted to visit and compare play-based sites and Montessori schools in terms of what each kind of program does with pretend/dress-up areas. For example, I just visited a Montessori environment, and when I entered the classroom I was very surprised to see a dress-up area there. Unfortunately, I was not able to engage in a conversation with the teacher about her thoughts on pretend play. The school and teacher follow Montessori practice. I did observe that the area did not distract in any way from the other areas in the room. Children would spend some time in there and then move on to something else.")
3. Talk with the children themselves regarding their interest in play and what they would like to see in their classroom
4. Talk with the children's parents to begin a dialogue on the expectations regarding play [Julie noted, "When I am speaking with parents (especially visiting parents) I explain that there are lots of materials in the room to engage the children academically; however, our main desire is to help develop the character of the child. This is a time for relationship building and self-discovery. The academic materials are there when the child is ready, not when we think he/she should be ready. If they are forced upon him/her, the child will reject them altogether and we will have lost him/her forever."]
5. Present her project to her colleagues and director and begin a dialogue on the potential role of play in their Montessori environment. (Julie commented later, "My director said that because parents are paying so much to send their children to school, we are obligated to make sure they are engaged in academic learning [versus free play]. I know this stems from pressure.")

## Child-Directed Play and Strengthening the Peer Culture

Aaron Neimark (2005) had taught preschool for 6 years and kindergarten for 3. He carried out a teacher research project focusing on how children's self-directed play strengthened the peer group. His site was a play-based preschool serving 30 children grouped in three clusters: two pre-K (4–5-year-olds) and one of mostly 3-year-olds. Since Aaron taught in the mornings, he decided to conduct his research in the afternoons, which freed him to conduct observations and watch and listen to the children closely. This gave Aaron more time and energy for data collection than if he were teaching at the same time, and also allowed him to see the reactions and comments of his teaching colleagues as they interacted with the children during their play. His afternoon data collection, though, also became a bit problematic, for a few reasons. Occasionally, a child would want to hang out with Aaron, rather than play with the other children, and Aaron would have to help the child disengage. Aaron was also not sure what to do with some things he saw in the children's play—should he let his colleagues know what was going on, or just let it go? Last, although it was interesting to see his colleagues in action, there were occasions when a teacher would say or do something in reaction to children's play that Aaron disagreed with or would have handled differently.

As Jacqueline and Julie did, Aaron wanted his project to improve his teaching and support of young children's play. Aaron wanted to change his "perspective and approach" to working with his children as they played together. He wanted to improve the ways that he could guide and help children gain entry to play groups, and to help the children maintain child-initiated games and play. As a result of his initial and ongoing data collection and analysis, Aaron reflected, "I changed my perspective and my approach to my children's play both throughout the study and afterwards." Since Aaron kept an open mind, and maintained an awareness of the *immediate practical value* of his emerging research, he was able to integrate new insights and ideas from his project directly into his teaching.

Further, as often happens in teacher research projects, Aaron's initial focus for his research changed and evolved as his project progressed. Initially, Aaron "focused on observing how my children attempted to gain access to group play," and how certain children could or could not gain access to child-controlled play groups. Then, as he collected some initial data, and also read more of the research literature on young children's play groupings, Aaron became more interested "in learning about a locally constructed peer culture, created by specific children and how this related to the children excluding and/or including others."

Aaron's ongoing data collection and analysis were influenced by specific studies and ideas from the research literature on children's play groups. For instance, Aaron particularly liked the work of William Corsaro (1985) on children's play groups and used some of Corsaro's ideas as the "orienting theory" for his project. Aaron especially liked Corsaro's ideas on how young children construct a peer community or culture that is both related to and distinct from the overall adult-directed culture of a preschool. As Aaron notes, "When I first read Corsaro's work, I found myself thinking more about my students' creative worlds of pretend and about their collaborative play. And if I truly understood more about their worlds and their peer cultures, then couldn't I (and other teachers) help to foster more meaningful collaborative play among children? I also thought I could better understand those children who are often on the periphery, not established in a particular peer group."

Over the course of 3 months, Aaron collected data on the children's play choices and patterns on the school's outside play yard. He looked most closely at whom the children played with, their choice of games, and the materials and props they used and how. He recorded what he saw and heard through extensive written field notes, took photographs sparingly, and also kept a reflective teaching journal. In addition, Aaron informally interviewed his colleagues in terms of what he saw in his observations, and audiotaped some of these conversations. Aaron found it helpful to speak with his colleagues and "find out about the difficulties of working in the yard and grappling with intervening and trying to extend the children's play at the same time."

Aaron had a total of 31 play observations for his project, with an average of three observations per week. The length of his project allowed Aaron to see the children's play over an ample period of time, and the frequency of observations gave a rhythm to his data collection and allowed him to follow games and patterns as they quickly evolved and changed. He also made written notes of his ongoing insights and reflections as he taught in the mornings, which ended up helping him make sense of his more formal afternoon observational data.

Aaron also got into the habit of reading over his observations later that same day, or soon thereafter, which helped him reflect on the value of his data. In order to organize his data as he kept observing, Aaron first "indexed" his data by looking for the different strategies that children used to gain access to a play group. A short while later, Aaron did another indexing of his data by looking for when the children "understood the way that a particular play group interacted and played." In doing this, he also indexed the objects that the children used and the roles that they took or were assigned. Thus, Aaron did a great deal of data analysis *as* his project progressed, collapsing the data into children's access strategies for play, the objects used in play, and the children's play roles. Aaron could then overlay these windows of analysis onto his detailed descriptions of the children's games that he captured in his written field notes.

Aaron found a total of 14 games and creative play activities that related to the children's peer culture, access and affiliation in play, and spontaneous play. Based on his data, and his ongoing analysis, Aaron realized that the essence of the children's play was a kind of "goofy culture," which was at once "resistant" to the official teachers' view of playing in school and also humorous to the children themselves. This dual desire—to rebel a bit against the established order of how you are supposed to play in preschool while also having a goofy fun time—motivated the children's play together and their cooperative, collaborative creative games and play activities.

Aaron found that the children created five games that specifically enhanced their sense of a shared peer culture. Aaron called the games No Entry (boys limited the number of other children allowed to play), Jewels (girls limiting play entry), Instant Monster (chase games), Power Girl (boys and girls chasing and taunting), and Hang a Broom (hanging brooms upside down from outdoor play structures). In No Entry games, for instance, children exclude others as a way to reinforce their own friendships. In one observation, Aaron jotted down notes on the play of Miguel and Ray, and then in his write-up of his project, turned these notes into a more fully formed No Entry play scene.

> Miguel and Ray are in the dress-up room, standing in the loft overlooking the lower area which is furnished with a table and chairs, kitchen appliances, plastic ware, food, numerous stuffed animals and puppets, babies, baby bottles, clothing, shoes, jewelry, and more. The boys are high enough to get a close look at the hand-painted ceiling, depicting tropical vegetation, animals, and a partly cloudy day. They have been up there for about 10 minutes pretending that they are Lego Knights, each holding stuffed animals. Max arrives, looks in the dress-up room, and then begins to climb the ladder leading to the loft. Miguel blocks the ladder, hindering Max's access to the loft. Almost immediately, Max calls out to a teacher, "They won't let me come up," expecting swift justice.

Reflecting on the significance of this game, as exemplified by this scene, Aaron admits that this "type of game is quite common in early childhood settings, and that it raises concern or even alarm for many teachers." Yet, based on numerous observations of this kind of play, as well as the other data that he collected on the children's other kinds of play, Aaron learned to see this and other examples from a peer-culture perspective. He realized that rather than a simple example of peer exclusion that requires adult intervention, "Miguel and Ray do not exclude Max for the sake of being selfish or mean, but because they want to exert control over this aspect of their lives and to preserve their friendship. They thus view the entering child, Max, as a potential threat. Many children like Max who get excluded learn to develop complex access strategies, just as Corsaro found in his study. They adapt to the reality that access to play must be negotiated in some way."

Aaron also discovered five other games involving the inclusion/exclusion issue through the use of specific play props and objects. He called these games *Goofy Brooms*, *Get My Hat*, *Cone Head*, *Rings*, and *Throw a Chair*. Aaron identified 12 objects commonly used in these games: brooms, soccer balls, plastic cones, hats, rings, chairs, strollers, basketballs, tennis balls, babies, toilet paper rolls, and bristle blocks. He collected data on how the children used the objects in each game and on how each game worked in terms of inclusion/exclusion, and then thought about how teachers might view each game and how each reinforced the children's peer culture.

In *Goofy Brooms*, children hung brooms upside down on the basketball hoop, as shown in Figure 3.2. Aaron observed Greg and Jack playing this game one day, and again Aaron converted his detailed notes from this observation into a well-formed written anecdote that he used for analysis purposes.

> Greg and Jack take turns hanging the child-sized brooms on the basketball hoop, and then remove them. They climb the geodome (jungle gym) and Jack says, "Ow, my butt!" and they both laugh. Allen, who is usually not a member of this group, watches this from a nearby bench.
>
> Jack makes a joke about Allen's sunglasses, but Allen's facial expression communicates that he doesn't think it's very funny. Immediately following this, Jack asks Allen, "Do you want to see something goofy?" Anticipating Allen's answer, Jack knocks a small chair over and sits on the back of it. Allen, Jack, and Greg laugh. Allen then prances over to the basketball hoop and hangs a broom. Allen then gets a soccer ball and a broom and uses them as a hockey stick and puck.

This type of goofy play often is seen by teachers as needing adult intervention, but Aaron learned a good deal of "play value" in this kind of game for certain children. Aaron reflects, "In play-based programs with a lot of time for free play, some children adjust better than others. For children like Allen, who have some difficulty socializing and joining in with others, it was actually good that he was in close proximity to the *Goofy Brooms* game. He was able to observe Jack and Greg playing, and then to have Jack directly invite him to participate by saying, 'Do you want to see something goofy?'" Aaron, having collected several previous examples of the boys' goofy play behaviors,

**Figure 3.2.** One of Aaron's games, *Goofy Brooms*.

knew that Allen had already seen some of the boys' goofy games. He thus had background knowledge about "something goofy," and was more easily enticed into getting involved with Jack and Greg by getting another broom and a soccer ball and joining in the goofiness.

 Aaron also became interested in the children's spontaneous games, and how they gained or restricted access on their own, as well as the effects of these strategies on the peer culture. Aaron discovered four games that the children primarily used in their spontaneous game playing: *Basketball Babies* (putting basketballs in small strollers), *Chase Me* (chasing and hiding), *Bubbles* (blowing bubbles), and *Water Table* (water table and float/sink objects). For example, in *Basketball Babies* the children used the basketballs, strollers, and babies in "silly ways."

> After finishing snack, Miguel ran outside as usual but I was unable to supervise yet, as we were still eating a snack. Jack and Ray instantly got up and ran toward Miguel. I told them that because I could not supervise the whole yard, they could use only half of it (including only the geodome and the basketball hoop). They quickly climbed the geodome and then ran over to the basketball hoop. Next to it was a double baby stroller with a baby in it. Miguel and Ray took the baby out and put basketballs in the stroller and started pushing it around, laughing hysterically. Jack tossed the baby around, sometimes high enough to go over the fence, and then Ray put it on the water table and threw a basketball at it. I asked them not to throw the baby, appealing to the "no throwing hard things" rule. I suggested that they could blow bubbles on the baby's face, to which they agreed.

Aaron observes that "this scene shows how Miguel and Ray associate goofiness with Jack, and that the circumstance and the timing of being restricted to only part of the yard sparked this kind of spontaneous play activity. The situation also led to resistant behaviors like throwing the baby. Miguel and Ray, however, are not known for this kind of behavior, and their goofy collaborative play related to their spontaneous flexibility at the moment."

Aaron found that *Basketball Babies* and the other three games were all instances of spontaneous collaborative play that was both goofy and resistant. In these ways, these games, like the others he discovered, served to reinforce the children's peer culture both as something in opposition to the official teachers' world and as something fun and motivating to join in on.

In an overall way, his teacher research project helped Aaron see new ways to support and guide the children's own invented play strategies, and also to see ways that he could broaden and deepen his understanding of the intricate and detailed ways children play on their own. Aaron's project also began to have an impact on his colleagues and the role of play at the preschool in general. For instance, one of his directors said in a staff meeting (in reference to Aaron's data on the children's *Goofy Brooms* game), "I just think we have to keep in mind how hard it is for some children to play with others, and then when they do, we stop it by focusing on rules that they might be breaking." Aaron notes that his school's "supportive environment is essential for creating an atmosphere for discussions between teachers and for making change." This helped move Aaron's teacher research project beyond just his work to the larger work and mission of the entire school, teachers, and administrators.

To extend and strengthen his project, Aaron might consider the following changes and modifications:

1. Collect more data in the mornings during his official work time. Aaron could then have more-balanced data for the morning and afternoon sessions, and a nice comparison of the children's play in relation to his own interventions/noninterventions. Morning data collection also would give Aaron experience collecting data as he taught, always a challenging juggling act.

2. Talk with the children. Ask them what games they like to play, how they invented them, why they play them as they do, what they would like to play that they do not, what girls think of playing with boys, and vice versa, what the difference is between inside play and outside play, and so on. This would add the direct voices of the children. Aaron could even use his data on the children's games in classroom discussions—talking about the pros and cons of their games and even turning his data into Project Approach work. This in turn would provide an extra layer of data and of analysis and reflection from the children themselves.

3. Involve colleagues in data collection. Aaron could create a data collection sheet, photocopy a pile, and attach them to a clipboard for a colleague or leave a few clipboards in different areas of the school for colleagues to write down play observations as they spontaneously occur.

4. Talk with parents and families. Ask them whether the children create or replicate these games at home. Ask whether the children learned some of their inclusion/exclusion strategies from older siblings or other children. Ask parents what they think of the children's play at home in general, and their views on the amount of time and freedom afforded the children to play at the preschool.

## Children's Strong Interests in Fantasy Play

Whereas Aaron was interested in studying children's play in groups, veteran preschool teacher Margaret Thrupp (2005) wanted to understand the "strong interests" of individual children as they often played on their own. For several years Margaret had been fascinated with children who had strong interests in certain toys, objects, and games, and with the relationship between their play and other activities, like reading. Her parent cooperative preschool emphasized a play-based program, with a combination of mixed-age and same-age play groupings throughout the school day. Margaret focused her project on her group of 3½- to 5-year-olds, and within this group she selected five focal children (3 boys and 2 girls) who displayed strong play interests. The children and their interests were Michael (airports), James (animals with horns), Kieran (lions), Sofia (horses), and Megan (horses).

Margaret collected data over the course of 2 months, collecting data on random days each week, and sometimes carrying out as many as six short observations in a day. While she focused on the five focal children, she did collect additional data on others with whom they played. Margaret captured the children's play actions and other play-related behaviors in several ways.

- written field notes
- conventional still camera
- audiocassette recorder
- children's artwork
- interviews of selected parents of the focal children
- interviews of three of her former students

While Aaron found inspiration and a direct "orienting theory" from some of the research literature on his topic, Margaret was frustrated to find little direct literature on her focus of children with strong interests. She settled instead for literature in such related areas and fields as social competence, imaginary friends, gifted children, and gender. Similar to Aaron's experience, reading selected literature in each of these areas helped Margaret piece together a helpful theoretical background for looking at children with strong interests and how and why they play alone and with others.

Julie, Jacqueline, and Aaron all became interested in their teacher research projects on play due to years of feeling puzzled and confused about certain issues regarding their children's play. The genesis of Margaret's project, on the other hand, was one particular child.

A few years ago I taught Milo, whom I came to call the "Shark Boy." He just loved sharks. Hammerhead sharks, cookie cutter sharks, great white sharks, and most of all, Carcharodon megalodon, a prehistoric shark. The Shark Boy played with toy sharks, read about sharks, drew sharks, pretended to be a shark, and he consequently accumulated much arcane information about sharks. And the Shark Boy was not alone. I realized that there was also a Train Boy, too. As time went on, I met Dog Girls and Horse Girls and others. These children reflected their strong interests in multiple ways: drawing their topics, reading about their topics, talking about their topics, and pretending to be their topics.

While Aaron came upon the idea of "goofy culture" in the children's play only later as his project progressed, Margaret started her project focusing on "strong interests," with a set definition based on her teaching experiences with these children. She defined strong interests as "when a child is observed over a period of 2 months doing the following: repeatedly using a toy relating to a particular topic of interest or repeatedly pretending to be the topic of interest in their fantasy play." Margaret also stipulated that these children also will "choose books relating to the topic of interest, represent the topic in art, and/or talk about the topic."

After observing and collecting data on the five focal children's strong interests in play, Margaret synthesized a list of several factors in the children's play that she wanted to concentrate on:

- special interest topic
- involvement in pretend or fantasy play
- use of toys in their play
- use of books to supplement the special interest
- representation of the special interest in art
- talking about the special interest with others
- frequency of the involvement with the special interest

This list became the basic toolbox for both her data collection and her data analysis, efficiently linking what she collected with its significance to her overall project focus.

I highlight here a few of Margaret's major findings based on this list. From talking with the parents and observing the children, Margaret discovered that the length of time of the children's involvement with their special interest varied greatly. Michael's interest in airports had been going on for 5 months, James's interest in animals with horns for 2 months, Kieran's interest in lions for a year, Sofia's interest in horses from age 2, and Megan's interest in horses from age 2 also.

Margaret collected a good deal of data on the children's use of toys and other objects in their strong-interest play.

> The use of toys in the children's fantasy play depends on the topic of interest. Many of the children have animals as the topic of their strong interests, and they often play with plastic or stuffed animals, and with such accessories as stables, veterinary sets, houses, blocks, vehicles, trains, and tracks.

Margaret also found that the children used toy animals to create "imaginary scenarios" that varied in their degree of connection to the children's original stories, books and movies (such as *The Lion King*), or their on-the-spot creative imaginations. As in much of children's fantasy, the children had the toy animals talk with one another, carrying on a dialogue. Margaret found only one example of the children directly talking to the toys; the animals talking to one another captured the children's interest and imagination.

The physical markers (toys, objects, places) of the children's interests varied. Some of the focal children had special toys (like horses) that they used at home and at school to support and extend their special interests. They frequently carried around the toys both at home and at preschool, and this was a constant obvious indicator of their special interest. For instance, Sofia loved one particular horse that was so special that her baby brother at home was not allowed to touch it. At the same, Margaret also found that certain children weren't attached to one particular toy or object, and any horse or any lion would do just fine. For example, Megan used any available horse or giraffe in her pretend animal play. Margaret discovered that although the children frequently carried around a favorite toy or kind of animal, they used these favorite toys and objects for fantasy play as opposed to simply as a source of comfort. For instance, Margaret observed Megan's giraffe fantasy play with Sofia.

> SOFIA: (the giraffes scream) (looking at Margaret) I'm playing kind of a scary game.
> MARGARET: What kind?
> SOFIA: The guys want to kill the giraffes.
> (the giraffes talk)
> GIRAFFE 1: Guys, get away from here.
> GIRAFFE 2: Why?
> GIRAFFE 1: Guys are trying to kill us.
> SOFIA: (to Margaret) This giraffe's dead.
> MARGARET: Oh no!
> SOFIA: It got shot. This one's tied to a post.
> MARGARET: Why is it tied to a post?
> SOFIA: Because they'll try to eat them. The one came alive again. The mommy was tied to the post. She was sad and lonely. The baby teared through and she was free. The baby fell and it kinda got hurt but she's OK. The mommy came and and she ended up too. But she came back alive.
> BABY GIRAFFE: Mommy, when did you get out?
> MOMMY GIRAFFE: You have to get tied to the post.
> BABY GIRAFFE: Why?
> MOMMY GIRAFFE: Because this has to be dried. On their noses (wipes all the baby giraffe's noses)

Margaret found this to be a typical scenario, with the key "relationships between the toys, as the giraffes talk to the other giraffes and not to the child.

There is some narration of the story only if an adult is present. Although Sofia cares for the baby giraffes by wiping their noses, she does it on behalf of the mommy giraffe."

Margaret learned that some children were just as interested in a place or "generic" props and objects as in a particular horse or lion. For example, Michael's special interest in airplanes prompted him to create an "airport" scene on the outside yard. In this outdoor scene, Michael's airplane and airport consisted of a gate, a bench (where he liked Margaret to sit), and the hill that served as the site for the customary airline safety movie. Michael also adapted to changes in the scene—when one child dug a hole in the hill, Michael determined that this would become his bath, and he also added a particular place to prepare the airplane's food. Other additions to his airline play included playing with a safety card from a plane brought by a teacher, and carrying around a "pilot's license" that his mother had made for him.

Michael extended his special interest fantasy play in other ways. He built airplanes out of varied materials in the classroom and liked to tell stories involving airplanes, as he did one day with Celeste.

> *MICHAEL:* It's about the little boy who couldn't sleep. OK, this is the story of the airway subway that couldn't fly in the morning. Once upon a time there's a little engine on the airway subway and it didn't go very easily.
> *CELESTE:* And then it would never fly in the morning, then the daylight.
> *MARGARET:* It didn't want to go in the morning because it was too sleepy.
> *MICHAEL:* Then if it was still doing its engine, and one stormy night and one time there was no police at . . .
> *CELESTE:* Happily ever after.

Margaret also found that there were some gender-related aspects of the children's special interest play.

At the outset of her project, Margaret asked, "Why are most of the children I've seen with strong interests boys? Do boys exhibit strong interests more than girls?" Margaret found that "gender certainly changes the nature of play and the nature of the interest." For instance, the boys she observed were involved with such traditional "boy" interests as sharks, baseball, dinosaurs, and trains, while the girls pursued such interests as dogs, horses, giraffes, and pet animals. Margaret found that the toys they used were also related to gender. For instance, the girls liked to use their toy animals to tell and act out stories. Sofia used plastic horses to tell a story as she provided her own narration.

Once upon a time in a little village there lived four horses (she counts the horses). Five horses in a place. A place where horses can live. All day long. And one day a baby horse came out of a mommy's tummy. And this was the horse. And it was yellow and white and cream. She loved her mommy. And she always drank milk out of their mommy's tummy.

Margaret found that much of the boys' special interest play involved more gross motor activity and also contained more violent themes. For instance, Kieran's interest in lions often turned into play sequences where he would "pounce" in pretend play. He even asked Margaret once to make a sign to hang above him that read, "Beware! Lion may eat you up!"

Margaret's project not only helped her understand her children's strong interests, but helped her see new ways to support her children's play.

I have tried to support the interests of the children with strong interests by providing appropriate toys in a way that facilitates open-ended activities. Animals, planes, and trains are available in a variety of settings, including water or sensory tables, in the sandbox, in the doll house, near the blocks, on the train table, and on a table in the art room. The toys are often displayed with props such as blocks, tracks, plastic trays, or clay. Certain children with strong interests gravitated toward certain areas each day.

For example, Margaret observed that James, who loved to play in the sensory area, checked to see which animals were there every day that he might play with. His friends often joined him there, and Megan would too if there were horses or giraffes on the table. Margaret also found it helpful to bring in selected books to complement the children's particular interests, to add certain clothing and props to the dress-up corner to support the children's strong interests, and to turn the whole classroom into a set for dramatic play (airport, post office, birds' nests).

In an overall way, Margaret's teacher research project helped her see the value and effectiveness of her current approaches to children with strong interests in their play. Especially for a veteran teacher with a lot of experience, a research project like Margaret's is likely to yield project findings that, in part, can reaffirm and strengthen the teacher's current instincts and ideas. Margaret's project also helped her see how she might further extend the children's special interests by linking them to her curriculum.

As a teacher researcher, I will continue to observe my children to try and determine how they learn best and how they function in their play. I will try and continue to provide an emergent curriculum which is based on the children's interests and needs. Using the children's special interests helps me in several ways: Children can be encouraged to try new activities if they are connected to their interests (a child who never paints may try to paint with a dinosaur); loners can find playmates when their favorite game is made a theme for the whole class (as when we turned the classroom into an airport based on Michael's special interest); and in general the children can build on their understanding of the world and remain highly motivated by following topics of their own choosing.

To extend and strengthen her project, Margaret might consider the following changes and modifications:

1.  Speak directly with the children, asking them about their strong interests. What are their favorite toys or objects or interests? Why do they like them? How did the interest start? Do they play the same at home and at school? Why do they mostly like to play alone? These are some questions that can be asked at the beginning of the project, and then later on as Margaret has a better understanding of the children's special interests from her other data collection.
2.  Fold the children's strong interests into her emergent curriculum, and then create an expanded teacher research project that documents the interconnections between the children's interests and Margaret's guidance of her classroom's emergent curriculum. This also could complement any conversations between Margaret and the children about their interests, as Margaret could devote time in small- and whole-group discussions on these interconnections. This would facilitate not only the children's talking to Margaret, but their talking to one another about their interests, fostering a new level of exchange and learning among the children themselves. It would be interesting to see whether some of the children's strong interests rubbed off on other children.
3.  Take a more developmental view on her focus by collecting data on the strong interests and play of toddlers and preschoolers within the 2–5-year-old age span. She could stick with her effective idea of focal children and choose three to four children across this span. This would provide her with cross-age data on how, for instance, a 2-year-old's play with giraffes and horses compares with a 5-year-old's. Or Margaret could enlist the help of her teaching colleagues, asking the teachers of the younger children to help collect some data on the strong interests of these children in play. Alternatively, Margaret could look at this age span in mixed-age settings, collecting data on 2- to 5-year-

olds as they played out their strong interests within the same play area or with the same play toys and objects.

4. Compare her data with the experiences of ECE colleagues at other preschools that have play-based and other curriculum models. Julie did this in her project, asking teachers at other Montessori preschools about their views on child-initiated play. Margaret could speak informally with teachers at play-based, academic, Montessori, Waldorf, and Reggio Emilio–inspired preschools to compare and contrast their experiences of children with strong interests. This might yield some interesting additional cross-program data. For instance, in Reggio-inspired programs, is there a greater positive connection between children's strong interests and the "official" curriculum of the classroom and school? In a Waldorf setting, what is the effect and influence of the absence of certain kinds of toys on the play of children with strong needs? Do these children use and/or create other kinds of objects for their fantasy play?

TEACHER RESEARCH, as seen in the projects in this chapter, helps teachers both better understand the theoretical underpinnings of children's play and also find new ways to support play and socialization in early childhood settings. If play is to continue to be a hallmark of high-quality early childhood classrooms and programs, teacher research has an important role in furthering our understanding and support of children's play.

## Suggested Teacher Research Activities

1. *Use a Digital Camera*: Purchase or borrow a digital camera to use, as Jacqueline did in her project. Experiment with taking photographs of your classroom environment, your home, and other areas. Then take pictures of children at work and play in your work environment. Don't worry about a focus; just take the shots so you can practice using the camera. Then practice sifting through these photographs, taking out those that do not seem interesting or are not focused, and keeping those that are intriguing and clear. Finally, consider integrating the use of a digital camera in a teacher research project. Think about an easy way to use the camera in your project, capturing those elements of children's play that you are most interested in. For example, Jacqueline wanted to find those instances where her toddlers were engaged in playful situations that promoted a sense of an emerging toddler community.

2. *Focus on the Play Environment*: Julie's project focused on children's pretend play in a Montessori environment. Examine your classroom

or teaching/caregiving environment, which includes materials, expectations, and routines for children's pretend play. Consider some aspect of the environment that you can change in order to promote children's pretend play. Begin observing and documenting (simple written fieldnotes like Julie's will do) what the children actually are doing (and not doing) in their pretend play. Then document the interaction (or lack thereof) between the children's play or desire to play and the concrete, physical opportunities for this pretend play in the environment. Now begin putting the two together—sifting through the data for instances of a successful match between the children's pretend play and the environment, as well as instances where the children try to engage in pretend play but this is not supported by the current environment.

3. *Look at Children's Play Strategies*: In his project, Aaron wanted to learn more about how preschoolers include and exclude one another in their self-directed play. Consider starting a similar teacher research project. Think about how you would like to improve your children's ability and skill to enter and exit play with one another. Choose a few children to serve as focal children, as Margaret did in her project on children's strong interests in play. Select carefully and see if you can find children with varying levels of play participation with peers: a child who would like to join in other children's play but hangs on the sidelines, a child who readily and easily enters ongoing play situations just by joining in, a child who when involved in play sometimes or often will not allow others to join in, and a child who can successfully join but then has difficulty maintaining participation in the ongoing play. Begin observing and documenting as Aaron did through written fieldnotes, photographs, and informal conversations with colleagues.

4. *Maximize Your Data Collection*: Aaron decided to collect the bulk of his data on the children's play choices and games during afternoons, when he was not teaching. (Julie, Jacqueline, and others presented in this chapter all collected their data as they taught, which was both an advantage—they could look at their own actions—and also a disadvantage—they had less time to observe and record.) If you can, as you embark on a teacher research project on children's play (which requires a great deal of sensitive and time-consuming observation and data collection), consider how you might collect at least some data during your "off" time: break, before or after your work day, during nap when some children might be playing, and other instances where you don't have to be 100% hands-on with the children.

5. *Use a Variety of Data Collection Tools*: In her project, Margaret captured her data via written fieldnotes (for the children's talk and

play behaviors), a conventional still camera (for the children's play objects and scenes), and an audiocassette recorder (for the children's stories and conversation as they played). Try observing a scene of children playing and talking, and then write fieldnotes as you run an audiocassette recorder. Use your fieldnotes to write down the gist of what the children are doing and saying. A premade data collection sheet can help speed the writing down of what you are seeing and hearing. Then after the observation, in the quiet of your classroom or home or car, listen to the audiotape without looking at your notes. Listen for possibly meaningful content (what the children are saying) and style (how they say it). This will attune your ears to the sounds and rhythms of the language of the children's play. Then, on another occasion, listen to the audiotape as you look at your notes. Mark in your written notes—by circling, starring, checking, noting with words—certain elements of content and style that you are finding particularly (and potentially) interesting and significant for your project focus. Then, in the last stage of this process, if you really need the children's exact words and phrasing, carefully transcribe selected parts or all of the audiotape.

CHAPTER 4

---

# Teacher Research and Understanding Children's Language Development

*One day my daughter said to me,*
*she said so softly so quietly*
*Mommy I have a petunia in my ear,*
*That's why I can't hear you so clear.*

—Marilyn, Oahu, Hawaii.
In *Small Kid Time Hawaii* (Chock, 1981).

Guiding Questions

1. What is the value of long-term research on children's language learning?
2. How can we use teacher research to understand the language of infant–caregiver interaction?
3. How can we use teacher research to understand how and why young children use language to make and keep friends?
4. What are effective data collection and data analysis tools to use for teacher research on children's language learning?

## CHILDREN'S LANGUAGE AND THE LANGUAGE OF TEACHER RESEARCH

Children learn by listening to, seeing, touching, and tasting their worlds of experience. They learn with their bodies, hearts, and minds, and often in this particular order. We learn as adults in the same ways, but we have largely forgotten the learning of our childhood. As early childhood practitioners, we spend countless hours and untold moments listening for, reaching toward, and trying to hold onto children's words, sounds, phrases, thoughts, feelings, and ideas. On a daily basis, we engage with the sights and sounds of children's earliest language and literacy experiences. In doing so, we learn to intuit and predict effective ways to observe, understand, and support their learning. All this is a precursor to teacher research in this area of children's development.

For instance, in caregiving with infants, we learn to anticipate their needs through countless experiences of recognizing and understanding their crying and body movements. Working with toddlers, we learn to recognize and understand their interest in social interaction with peers as they orchestrate physical movement, oral language, nonverbal language, and objects. With preschoolers, we sense the more sophisticated ways that children coordinate their expanding first and second language and literacy powers to understand themselves, one another, and their worlds. Working with kindergartners and early primary grade children, we learn to gauge how and where to promote children's burgeoning capacity for using languages and literacies to understand ever-widening concepts, content, information, theories, and ideas.

Within this often-unpredictable and slightly mysterious journey of experiencing the social and intellectual lives of young children, our own use of language as practitioners enables us to stop and hold an event or incident or thought or idea. Language—encapsulating what we think and feel internally, what we say to ourselves and talk about with others, what we record and preserve in our mind and on paper—all this enables us to pause and slow the fast blur of life with young children. As Sylvia Ashton-Warner (1963) notes, "I don't know that ideas develop. They just appear" (p. 20). Children move and think and feel according to their individual interests and experiences, and their thoughts and ideas and actions come at us in unexpected ways from unexpected directions. Again as Sylvia Ashton-Warner notes, the "moving currents of children's interests" (p. 79) fill up our time with children. This is what we react to, think about, ponder, and consider as children talk, interact, draw, write, and read. This is where teacher research—involving *our* own oral and written language—helps us capture, reflect upon, understand, and change the languages of children's work and play.

## COLLECTING AND ANALYZING DATA ON THE LANGUAGE EXPERIENCES OF INFANTS

Caregivers and parents (and other family caretakers) of newborns, infants, and toddlers practice effective and valuable aspects of teacher research on a daily basis. We can expand on this practitioner knowledge through the structured forms of teacher research and engage in organized inquiry and reflection to understand the very beginnings of children's language learning.

## Infants—The Beginning of Long-Term Data Collection

When Kaili, my daughter, was born I started to collect data on her earliest attempts at communication and expression. I continued to collect data on her growth over the next several years. I didn't realize it when I started—I just saw myself as an overeager parent ready to chronicle his child's every move!—but I had embarked on a long-term data collection and analysis project that has considerably sharpened my teacher research knowledge and skill.

When Kaili was a newborn, I used an audiocassette recorder to audiotape her crying, sighs, cooing, shrieks, and breathing. I also used a video camcorder to capture her earliest movements, gestures, facial expressions, body movements, and interactions with objects, her environment, and people. I also wrote down in my research notebook Kaili's nonverbal and oral language as it emerged in chronological order. As she progressed through toddlerhood, preschool, and kindergarten, I continued to collect data via audiotape, camcorder, and written observational notes. In analyzing and understanding Kaili's language growth (now 8 years worth of data), I have relied on these three tools to provide different windows onto her learning and development. The three tools each bring different kinds of data to my interest in understanding the origins of children's language development and seeing how one child's language experiences play out on a daily basis—moment by moment, minute by minute, and hour by hour—over the course of several years.

Every research tool has its particular strengths for capturing and understanding children's language growth. The audiocassette helped me concentrate solely on the sounds of Kaili's language growth. As I engaged with or watched her as an infant, and had the audiocassette going at the same time, this amplified my listening for Kaili's earliest attempts at communication and expression. This tool helped me become a better listener, observer, *and* participant as Kaili cried, cooed, babbled, screeched. Most important, it improved the quality of my engagement with Kaili and her blossoming linguistic powers, attuning my ears to her particular language talents and repertoire of sounds.

In addition, the video camcorder captured both Kaili's oral and nonverbal language at the same time. This tool allowed me to see and resee, and to hear and rehear, Kaili's oral and nonverbal language in concert. While the audiotape isolated sound, like a musical piece without any visuals, the camcorder put sound and sight together, like a play with the actors both acting and talking. I also used my camcorder to document her earliest physical explorations and language inventions and interactions with others. Most of the time, as an infant, Kaili was not distracted by the camcorder and went about her busy infant life unfazed. I have continued to use the camcorder through her current 2nd-grade year. The video recordings of her language and literacy play and work are interspersed with video footage of her birthday parties, playdates with friends, gardening, playing with her grandparents, and other daily routines and activities of her home, family, and community life. The camcorder has recorded her language and literacy growth over 8 years, starting in infancy, and has embedded and contextualized this learning and development within the familiar, warm, and comfortable surroundings of home and daily family life.

In my research notebook, I also wrote down what I thought her crying and various other noises sounded like, and also wrote down a brief description of where and how (and sometimes why) her language evolved and occurred. I also noted any instances of nonverbal, physical movements that I felt were essentially linguistic and communicative and expressive in intent and in effect. For the past 8 years, I have recorded her language in my research notebook, using the simple split-page format of the date in the left column, Kaili's language in the middle, and explanation and context of her language in the right column. If my notebook was not handy, I wrote down Kaili's language on scraps of paper, the back of my hand, grocery lists. Over the years, there have been numerous occasions where we were driving in the car and Kaili would say something, and I had to hold it in my head until we came to a stoplight or stop sign and I could write it down. When she was a preschooler, my impromptu note taking and recording even got to the point where Kaili would say, "Aren't you going to write that down?" if I didn't write something she said right away.

Caregivers, teachers, and parents who care for the same children over the course of a few years or more have valuable access to children's language growth over a long developmental span. This length of experience is critical for seeing and understanding the breadth and depth of children's linguistic development, and for searching over time for children's particular language talents, needs, and developmental milestones. For example, from recording in my research notebook, I have seen over the years how Kaili's earliest efforts at sound making and nonverbal communication turned into later attempts at mastering English phonology (sounds), syntax (word order), semantics (word meanings), and pragmatics (social use of language) during her toddler, preschool, and kindergarten years.

## Infancy

1/1/99 (2 days old)
DATA: crying, loud and long; varied length of time; varied pitch; pace
    of breathing varied
INTERPRETATION: her earliest physical exploration of her own voice;
    coordination of crying and breathing

3/10/99 (3 months)
DATA: opens hands, curls fingers; moves head from side to side; gazes
    and smiles at adults
INTERPRETATION: increasing sophistication of nonverbal and physi-
    cal expression and exploration with self and others

9/12/99 (9 months)
DATA: crawling; looks and follows when adults point at object; bab-
    bling and cooing; smiling and laughing; early attempts at "mama"
INTERPRETATION: continuing coordination of vocal powers and
    physical exploration; early articulation of sounds, words, names

## Toddlerhood

5/5/00 (15 months)
DATA: said /buhbuh/ for "bubble" when kinder gym teacher blew bubbles
INTERPRETATION: expanding efforts at articulation and pronuncia-
    tion of new vocabulary in new contexts

1/3/01 (2 years)
DATA: "That's too big for me" (said sing-songy) when picking pieces
    of papaya in a bowl
INTERPRETATION: single- and multiple-sentence oral language; play-
    ing with the rhythms of syllables, words, and phrases

## Preschool

12/5/01 (3 years)
DATA: "I haven't seen Cody (her cousin) in a few while."
INTERPRETATION: continuing efforts to get English syntax just right

7/16/02 (3.7 years)
DATA: "It looks like a butterfly of lights" (lights at night on a hillside)
INTERPRETATION: increasing awareness of and experimentation with
    using language to compare experiences

Kindergarten

6/28/03 (4.6 years)
DATA: "They were babies and then they growned."
INTERPRETATION: still incomplete mastery of English syntactical
    structures and inflections

6/26/04 (5.6 years)
DATA: "Where does color come from?" "Who made the earth?"
INTERPRETATION: using language to inquire and understand physi-
    cal phenomena

This kind of long-term documentation of children's language growth is made
all the richer when our data collection and analysis start in infancy. It is in
infancy that we can see the roots and the beginnings of children's earliest
attempts at oral language and nonverbal communication and expression—
all this is the foundation of a lifelong engagement with language. It also can
reveal key patterns, factors, and influences in our own caretaking, teaching,
and parenting that affect (positively and negatively) young children's language learning. It challenges us to look over years of changes in critical areas
of children's language growth, and therefore sharpens our teacher research
knowledge of combing through a lot of data and looking for key examples,
vignettes, stories, and moments that illustrate important teaching and learning. Further, documentation of language growth from infancy gives us years
of data to look at, try to understand, and apply to our continually evolving
understanding of the role of language within children's general development.

## The Language of Infant/Toddler–Caregiver Interaction

Kelly Lopez is an experienced trainer of infant/toddler caregivers. Kelly is
interested in using teacher research to improve her work with caregivers and
also strengthen her knowledge of important connections between language,
play, and infant/toddler and caregiver interactions. She carried out two projects,
looking at the role of language and interaction between infants and their
caregivers in infant/toddler settings. Kelly looked specifically at how caregivers
notice, respond to, and understand nonverbal cues from infants and toddlers.
From experience, Kelly knew that these cues come from the small moments of
human interaction, and she wanted to use this knowledge to improve her own
practice as a trainer of caregivers.

As I work with programs and learn what types of assistance they
need, whether it be with the types of materials the program needs, a

training/workshop on interactions or using language with children, or educating and helping programs implement a relationship-based curriculum into their infant and toddler programs, I rely on those moments that I engaged with children on a one-on-one basis.

In one project that lasted 7 weeks, Kelly observed selected caregivers and infants at a daycare center where she worked as a trainer with the faculty. Kelly looked in particular at "caregivers reading and understanding nonverbal cues, including visual attending (looking at objects and people in the environment), facial expressions (smiling and frowning) and body movements (pointing at and reaching for objects and people)." She used a one-page data collection sheet with columns to record the children's actions, behaviors, and language.

The heart of Kelly's project involved close, detailed observations of caregiver–infant interactions between Theresa and 12-month-old Ashley. The following data snippet shows how Theresa engages and extends play with Ashley through developmentally appropriate oral and nonverbal language.

> (Theresa sits down in front of Ashley and rolls the ball to her but does not let go.)
> (Ashley raises her arms and, slightly flailing, looks wide-eyed at the ball. She leans forward toward the ball, slightly arching her back.)
> ASHLEY: Ah!
> THERESA: You're so excited . . . you want this ball! (Puts the ball in her lap.)
> ASHLEY: Hmmmm . . . hmmmm. (squeals) Ah! (Arms flail back and slightly arches. Her eyes get bigger. She slaps and pounds on the ball. Squeals again.) Ah! (Lets go of the ball.)
> THERESA: (rolling ball back to Ashley) Rolling ball to Ashley.
> ASHLEY: (With eyes on the ball, lifts arms again, squeals.) Ah!
> (Pounds ball with hand and lets go of the ball and it rolls back to Theresa.)
> THERESA: You made the ball roll, Ashley.
> (As Theresa rolls the ball back, Ashley's eyes follow the ball, her upper body slightly flails and arches back slightly, and she opens her arms wide.)
> Here's the ball. (Puts ball in Ashley's lap.)
> ASHLEY: (Slaps at the ball and squeals again.) Ah! (Lets go of the ball and arms flail.)
> (Theresa rolls ball back to Ashley's lap.)
> ASHLEY: (squeals) Ah!

Kelly notices (as she watches Theresa and Ashley) and simultaneously records (on her data collection sheet and in her memory) the intricate interplay of sounds ("Ah!"), words ("ball"), sentences ("You made the ball roll, Ashley"), physical actions (Ashley's arms moving, back arching slightly), movement of objects (rolling ball, patting ball), and the entire tenor and feel of the exchange (the ease and pleasure of their interactions). Kelly's extensive experience as a caregiver and as a trainer of caregivers has sharpened her on-the-spot data collection techniques and skill in sensing language to look for and to record. For example, Kelly noticed that "Theresa is able to observe Ashley's body movements and focus with her eyes as a signal to continue with the activity of getting the ball back to Ashley after Theresa releases it."

As her project continued, Kelly noted that "audiotaping became a major data collection tool" but that she "felt so overwhelmed by so much data collected" with this tool. Kelly liked what Hubbard and Power (2003) say about the value of translating "raw" data into "cooked," or more synthesized, notes. She began to look for patterns and key elements in her collected data and realized that "language held the key for Theresa to extend her interactions with Ashley, and to link language with feelings, emotions, and objects." Two weeks after the above observation, Kelly again observed Theresa and Ashley.

> THERESA: (walking around the classroom to look at a fish mobile) Ashley, let's say good morning to the fish.
> (Ashley looks at the fish, then back to Theresa, and then back to the fish.)
> THERESA: Hanging fish. (Touches a fish and the mobile moves.)
> (Ashley smiles, looks back at her, and reaches out for the fish.)
> You want to touch the fish? (Holds her up close to the fish to touch it.)
> You can touch it. See the blue fish?
> (Ashley looks at Theresa, looks back at the fish, and reaches for the fish.)
> You did it! You touched the fish, the blue fish. It's hanging on the string.
> (Ashley holds out her hand again.)
> You want to touch it again? Let's find the yellow fish. (Points to the yellow fish and touches it.)
> ASHLEY: Ah! (Ashley reaches for the fish, slaps it, and squeals.)
> THERESA: You made the fish move. You like the fish. Mobile hanging.

Again, Kelly captures the wonderful small moments of gesture, movement, sounds, words, and objects between caregiver and infant. Kelly subsequently observed that this snippet reveals "Theresa's ability to really being tuned into Ashley's interests, and to read Ashley's cues for wanting to explore the fish mobile. She continues the interactions through questions and allows Ashley to engage with the fish to help her understand what it is she is exploring." Kelly noticed that Theresa uses "short, quick phrases (*hanging fish, mobile hanging*) that provide Ashley with the key words for linking object names/ referents, physical movements, and verbal descriptions." And, "Theresa's quick verbal response (*You made the fish move*) to Ashley's verbal sounds of interest (*Ah*) link the entire interaction."

Kelly also interviewed and spoke with Theresa to gather information on Theresa's thoughts and feelings underlying her interactions with Ashley and other infants.

> I know that one of the things that attracted me to the work here is that the program believes that infants and toddlers learn best when they have a strong and supportive and safe place to learn. The caregiver must develop a solid and trusting relationship . . . and needs to be responsive to the needs and wants of the children. . . . I really want the children to understand what is going on around them as well as what is happening to them. That is why I work hard at slowing down when I am with the children.

Theresa's wonderful insight into her own caregiving—slowing down what she is doing in order to see and hear and feel the infants in the moment of interaction—is essentially what Kelly has done in her teacher research project. By creating (and subsequently revising) a data collection sheet, observing caregiver–infant interactions, and recording and documenting infants' in-the-moment nonverbal cues, Kelly uncovers critical elements and factors influencing positive, rewarding interactions and caregiving.

Reflecting on the value of this teacher research project, Kelly thought that "to see another caregiver in action has allowed me to see the importance of using those one-on-one opportunities for exploration, language, observation, and eventually reflection on my own practice. This project re-emphasized my feelings about how quality responsive caregiving is reflected in the infant–caregiver reciprocal interaction." In turn, Kelly can take new data (the snippets from Theresa and Ashley) and new insights to strengthen the understanding and knowledge of nonverbal cues and engagement of other caregivers with whom she works.

If Kelly were to carry out her project again, she might strengthen and extend the project in these ways:

1. Extend the duration of the project to see possible developmental changes both within the infants (as they grow and develop in general) and in the caregivers (as their understanding grows of powerful ways to interact and support the infants under their care).
2. Bring her own work and training of the caregivers into her teacher research project, gathering data on important connections between what she sees "on the floor" between the caregivers and infants and her training with caregivers on selected aspects of infant language and communication and caregiver support and guidance.
3. Enlist the help of the caregivers as co-researchers, asking them to keep an observational log and observe one another's interactions with the infants, and also keep an individual caregiver journal or log of their own internal thoughts and reflections on their work.
4. Use a video camcorder to record and document the nuances of the nonverbal infant and caregiver interaction and body language.

In a second project lasting 3 months, Kelly continued her research and teaching interest in the language of infant–caregiver interaction (Lopez, 2005). This time Kelly did use a video camcorder as her main data collection tool.

> Videotaping provided me with an amazing option to look closely, over and over, at infant–caregiver interactions. The ability to rewind, observe the adult separate from the child, and vice versa, provided me with the ability to look at them individually, and then together, in order to see what each brought to the language of the interaction and relationship. My hours of videotape also gave me the audio to listen to, decipher, analyze, and reflect on. If I used only fieldnotes to gather language, I would have lost the little nuances from both the caregivers and the infants.

The camcorder allowed Kelly to collect detailed audio and video data. For example, Figure 4.1 shows a set of six detailed interactions between Julie (the caregiver) and Sara (the infant), and the transcript shows their accompanying detailed oral and nonverbal language interactions. The letters (a–f) in the transcript correspond to the photos (a–f) in the figure.

> (Sara is casually eating Cheerios, but also dropping them on the floor. She sees Rachel, another child, being given crackers.)
> [Photo a]
> JULIE: (to Sara) Let's make you a bottle.
> SARA: (Turns and looks up at the counter, points and says urgently) Ahhhh. Ahhhhh. [Photo b]

**Figure 4.1.** A series of interactions between Julie (caregiver) and Sara (infant).

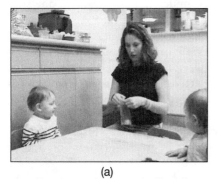

(a)

(b)

(c)

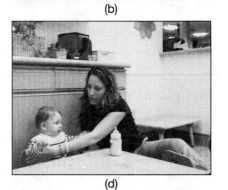

(d)

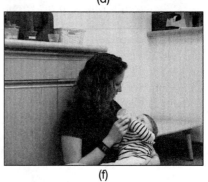

(e)

(f)

*JULIE:* (Observes and hears her and gives her a couple of Cheerios.) Here are a few Cheerios. (Quickly makes a bottle as Sara eats Cheerios. Sits down next to Sara and shows her bottle and then puts it on the table.) Are you ready for your bottle?

*SARA:* (Sees bottle and quickly stands up.) Ahhhh. Ehhhh. (Sits back down.) [Photo c]

*JULIE:* (Puts out arm in front of Sara to pick her up.) [Photo d]

*SARA:* (Puts arms up and out.)

*JULIE:* (Picks Sara up and puts her in her lap. Puts bottle close to Sara's mouth.) [Photo e]

*SARA:* (Leans back and grabs onto bottle.) Ahhhhh.

*JULIE:* (Looking at Sara as she drinks eagerly.) That's what you were waiting for. Cheerios are nice, but this is better. [Photo f]

This detailed audio and video data allow Kelly to make informed and sophisticated interpretations of the language of the interactions. Kelly reflects, "In this interaction, Julie was tuned into the needs of the children she cares for. At this time, she knew that it was time for Sara to have her bottle. She knew because she knew Sara's eating schedule, but also because she observed that Sara was not really eating the Cheerios in a manner that showed Julie that she was eating them because she was hungry for them, but rather she was hungry for something. So Julie verbalized to Sara about what she needed, sending the message appropriately, and let Sara know that her needs were important and that when she expresses her needs, Julie will be there to support her."

This kind of rich audio and video data enriched Kelly's reflections and analysis.

> When I wrote down what happened in the video segments, this provided me with a narrative of what I observed, with video allowing me to link different segments together. Transcripts of the audio from the videotapes allowed me to be specific in the kinds of language being used and the impact of this language on the quality of the infant–caregiver relationship. These transcripts held most of the information that I needed, as my focus was the role of language. They held so much information in a small amount of time.

## TODDLERS—ENTERING WORLDS OF DISCOVERY AND LEARNING

Early childhood educators working with toddlers are faced with the complex task of both understanding and promoting language development in children who are just beginning to speak and interact with peers. Teacher research plays an important role in helping us pay closer attention to the nonverbal and budding verbal talents of toddlers, and to uncover critical factors in caregiving and the environment that influence toddlers' language learning. This section highlights teacher projects focusing on the role of language in peer interaction, friendship, and a sense of community.

## Learning to Interact with Peers

Cary Crawford, a director of a daycare center, conducted a short-term (2-week) project on one child's peer interactions at her center. As the director, Cary wanted to support her teachers and understand the value of conducting periodic observation and research to understand the daily challenges that the teachers and children experience. In particular, Cary wanted to support the teachers' efforts to help Lexi, a child in need of new strategies for successfully getting along and playing with her peers. Cary reflected on the initial reasons for her project.

> The teachers began to focus on how to help Lexi effectively use her words during interactional conflicts with other children. I began the teacher research project to better understand the behaviors used by Lexi during interactions with other children and the conflict resolution strategies used by the teachers. We also looked at how Lexi transitioned from the toddler room, where she was the oldest child and one of the only ones talking, into the 2- and 3-year-olds' room where she was the youngest child and the majority of the children have already gone through the vocabulary spurt and talk in sentences. I wanted to see which of the teachers' intervention methods helped Lexi and whether or not the older children helped her use her words in peer interactions.

Cary's project is an example of a short-term teacher research project designed to address a practical classroom issue in need of a solution—intervention strategies to help Lexi not bite other children and to play and interact more effectively with peers. The project is also an example of teacher research in two settings—the toddler room and another classroom for 2- and 3-year-olds. As such, it shows the possibilities for teacher research to help us understand an important issue associated with the social and interactional challenges that this age group faces in their varied developmental oral language.

As the site director, Cary wanted to define her role in the project clearly.

My role in the project was strictly as observer for the periods of time that I observed and collected data. Because I spend a lot of time in the classroom, the children (including Lexi) all know me very well and that sometimes made it hard to only play the role of observer, as they were sometimes coming to me for assistance and, especially the younger ones, for nurturing.

Cary conducted two observational sessions, for 4 hours each, over the span of 2 weeks. Cary carried out this data collection plan once in the young children's room and then again when Lexi transitioned to the 2- and 3-year-olds' room. Cary designed these two different observation sessions "to see if the conflict intervention methods used by the teachers had an effect on Lexi's behavior, and to look for a decrease in aggressive behavior and an increase in Lexi's use of words." In half-hour increments, Cary looked for the following behaviors: biting (B), biting attempts (BA), hitting (H), and pushing (P). She used a data collection sheet that marked out the time periods on the left side and recording areas to the right to write down the behaviors and the corresponding codes for aggressive behavior (B, BA, H, P). The codes helped Cary start her data analysis *as* she collected her data.

Once she had collected all her data, Cary then looked for specific evidence of changes in Lexi's language and social interactions.

Was Lexi's behavior decreasing in the toddler room, and if so, was it because the teachers were effectively encouraging her to use her words? Or did Lexi's behavior decrease once she made the transition to the new, older children's room, and if so, was this the result of being around children who used verbal skills to effectively communicate their needs?

In analyzing her data, Cary looked over her observational notes and the codes or categories for aggressive behavior (biting, biting attempts, hitting, pushing), and looked for the most prominent patterns and key factors influencing Lexi's conflicts with peers. Cary discovered that most of Lexi's interactional difficulties occurred as a "result of space issues or conflicts over toys, and sometimes attention from the teacher."

For example, on one occasion, Cary observed an interaction regarding space issues and attention from a teacher.

A child sat on a teacher's lap and Lexi walked up and attempted to push the child out of the teacher's lap. The teacher gave Lexi the option of sitting next to them or waiting until the child got up. At this point, Lexi attempted to bite the child, which the teacher was able to stop.

Cary reflected on the teacher's action and noted that the teacher "could see the incident coming and so was able to stop the bite from occurring."

Cary also looked at issues of space, toys, and closeness with teachers in light of one teacher's effort to "shadow" or stay close to Lexi in order to help her. In another incident that Cary observed, the children were getting their lunch boxes when a child picked up Lexi's lunch box and ran off with it. Lexi then bit that child. This incident showed Cary that the shadow teacher (who was helping distribute lunch boxes) could not always be right near Lexi, and so this was not an entirely effective strategy to help Lexi interact with peers.

Cary's observations also revealed that the teachers presented a "clear alternative" to biting for Lexi by using such phrases as, "Remember to use your words," "Say mine," or "Tell him no." Cary found that this worked well only when the teacher was quick enough to intervene and directly help Lexi. Overall, in the toddler room, Cary did not observe a decrease in Lexi's biting and pushing, although the teachers encouraged Lexi to use her words.

When Lexi transitioned to the 2- and 3-year-olds' room, the teachers "decided against shadowing Lexi in the hopes that being around other children who use language to communicate would have an effect on Lexi." Although some of the children in the new room still pushed and hit, most used words "to express all of their needs from being hungry or needing a diaper change, to telling someone 'no' over a toy." In looking over her written observations and the number of times that Lexi used aggressive behavior, Cary noticed that Lexi "only attempted to bite once and she didn't actually bite at all." For example, when Lexi and two other children played at a table, and the teacher was at the other side of the room changing a child's diaper, a child tried to take one of Lexi's beads. "Surprisingly, Lexi pulled on the bead and said, "No, it's mine."

Based on her short-term teacher research project, which involved close observations of a child in need of social and linguistic support to interact with peers, Cary concluded that teachers, the environment, and children's peers all play critical roles in this process of positive peer interaction and play. The project also helped reaffirm for Cary, as the director of a daycare and preschool center, that a director's role also includes conducting occasional teacher research and that this kind of professional work opens windows onto ways to support both children and teachers.

Here are a few ways that Cary might extend her teacher research project:

1. Extend the time period of the project, observing for a longer overall period of time, and observing more frequently within this time
   span (keeping in mind her very busy schedule and responsibilities
   as director).
2. Invite the teachers working with Lexi to serve as co-researchers, gathering data on Lexi's peer interactions in a more formal and organized
   way. For instance, the teachers (especially the teacher taking the role
   of the shadow teacher) could take turns writing observational notes.
   Further, Cary and/or one of the teachers could videotape small incidents that could be played back in staff meetings for discussion and
   professional development.
3. Find and bring in articles and information on facilitating successful
   toddler interactions, and the issue of biting and other nonverbal actions that impede peer play, and discuss them with the teachers in
   light of what they were seeing (and not seeing) with Lexi and the
   other children in the two classrooms. This would provide extra food
   for thought for extending the data gathered in the classrooms and
   lead to a larger discussion of toddlers' general social and linguistic
   development.
4. Involve children's parents in discussions and data collection focusing on the challenges for toddlers of social interaction without strong
   oral language skills. First, parents could be given a data collection
   sheet to record instances of interactional difficulty at home and also
   to note their own examples of helpful linguistic phrases used with
   their children. Second, Cary could organize parent discussion sessions,
   of which Cary could record selected segments, where parents would
   discuss issues and examples of successful (and not successful) ways
   of helping their toddlers use nonverbal and oral language in social
   interactions.

## The Language of Friendship and Togetherness

Jessica Fickle, a Montessori teacher of toddlers (24 to 40 months of age),
conducted a short-term project (three months) on the connections between
the budding language abilities and friendships of three girls in her classroom.
Initially, Jessica was drawn to this project because she wanted to find out
more about the connections between language and friendship for toddlers,
and for three of her children, Emma, Ilana, and Jeanette, in particular. Jessica chose Emma and Jeanette because of "the complexity of their friendship, the strength of Jeanette's bond with Emma, and the magic these two
girls had when they played." Jessica knew from one incident that the two

girls had something special in terms of their friendship that would be interesting and valuable to explore further in a teacher research project. One day, Jessica observed, Emma and Jeanette were playing and another child, Ilana, tried to make friends with them. Ilana wanted to play and be friends with Emma in particular.

Jessica designed a small project that examined the girls' friendship and language both inside and outside the physical space of their classroom. Inside the classroom, there were Montessori materials and freedom of movement for children to work alone and with others. Jessica also included the outside because there were places on the yard, such as the tire swing (fits three children at a time), that were favorite spots for children to gather and play together. Jessica also knew that when the children swing, and also wait on the bench to swing, they "talk with one another, share stories, and sing songs." The tire swing, the waiting bench, and other places on the yard, like the sandbox, were rich in potential for language, interaction, and friendship.

Over the course of 3 months, from February to April, Jessica observed and recorded evidence of Emma's, Jeanette's, Ilana's friendship patterns and their corresponding use of language. Jessica observed and took written observational notes once a week during morning drop-off, play, and work time. While Jessica could have just looked at the girls' inside play choices and use of language, and thus eliminating looking outside and the use of the other two data sheets, the combination of inside and outside play choices and language use expanded the breadth and depth of Jessica's project. It made it more comprehensive and interesting, and more richly captured the full range of the three girls' interactions, language use, and friendship patterns.

Throughout her project, Jessica "constantly watched the girls' friendships grow and change but only recorded specific data" once a week. This is an example of a "doable" teacher research project, especially one in a classroom of busy and active toddlers in which Jessica needed to teach and observe, and so she devoted only one day a week to actually recording data.

Table 4.1 shows Jessica's data sheet for capturing the girls' inside play choices. Jessica focused on the girls' play with manipulatives, puzzles, babies, art, and books. In tracking these data, Jessica noticed that the three girls participated in an average of "three different language play interactions a day," and that "more of these interactions occurred during art activities and while using manipulatives." Jessica also observed that "Jeanette began to play alone with Ilana in the playroom before she started to play with her alone outside. Jeanette was more accepting of Ilana in the playroom." Further, since Ilana loved puzzles and was better at doing puzzles than Emma and Jeanette, the inside playroom offered a material (the puzzles) and a smaller shared space for Ilana to form a friendship with the other two girls.

**Table 4.1.** Inside Play Interactions

| Date (2001) | Manupulatives | Puzzle | Babies | Art | Books |
|---|---|---|---|---|---|
| 2/15 | J and E | J and E | | J and E | |
| 2/22 | | I and E | | I and E | I and E |
| 3/1 | I and J | I and J | | | I and J |
| 3/8 | | I and E | I and E | I and E | I and E |
| 3/15 | | | | J and E | |
| 3/22 | | E and J | | | E and I |
| 4/4 | E and I | | E and I | E and I | E and I |
| 4/11 | I and J | I and J | | I and J | |
| 4/16 | I and J | | I and J | | |
| 4/23 | I and E | I and J | | I and E | I and E |
| 4/30 | J, E, and I | | | J, E, and I | |

E = Emma; J = Jeanette; I = Ilana

Table 4.2 shows Jessica's sheet for recording the three girls' outside play choices. Jessica focused on the bushes, hill, bikes, swing, sandbox, climbing, and complex games (defined as the girls devising their own rules for running and playing in different parts of the yard at the same time). She observed that the hill, bushes, and bikes were the most popular places and activities for the three girls. Jessica found that "the hill was the most common area for the three girls; here on the hill, they had interactions every day and usually more than once a day. They liked to look for rocks, sticks, and leaves. The hill also provided the girls with a great view of the yard and a great place to hide, play, and climb." The second most popular area, the bushes, consisted of three separate sets of bushes. The girls used the bushes for hiding, playing house, and singing and dancing. Jessica also noticed that Jeanette was more hesitant to play with Ilana on the hill and bushes than in other places on the yard; "it seemed as if Jeanette felt as if she had more claims to Emma on the hill and bushes than elsewhere on the yard." She seemed to be protecting her play space. At first, "Jeanette would tell Ilana 'no' that she couldn't play, and only let Emma play with her near the hill and bushes. In the end, Jeanette accepted Ilana and asked her to play with them."

Jessica looked for and recorded five different kinds of language use.

1. two words ("Emma come")
2. simple sentences ("Pretty hair . . . Jessica I like")

**Table 4.2.** Outside Play Interactions

| Date (2001) | Bushes | Hill | Bikes | Swing | Sandbox | Climbing | Complex game |
|---|---|---|---|---|---|---|---|
| 2/15 | J, E | J, E | | J, E | E, I | J, E | |
| 2/22 | J, E | J, E | E, I | E, I | J, E | | |
| 3/1 | J, E E, I | J, E E, I | J, E, E, I | J, E | E, I | J, E | |
| 3/8 | J, E | J, E | | J, E J, I J, E, I | E, I | E, I | |
| 3/15 | J, E, I | J, E | J, E | J, I, E | J, E I, E | J, E I, E | |
| 3/22 | J, E E, I | J, E, I | | J, E J, I J, E, I | | J, E | |
| 4/4 | J, E J, E, I | J, E J, E, I | J, E | J, E, I | J, E J, E, I | J, E | |
| 4/11 | J, E J, E, I | J, E J, E, I | J, E | J, E J, I J, E, I | J, E, I | J, E J, E, I | J, E J, E, I |
| 4/16 | J, E, I | J, I | J, E, I | J, E J, I J, E, I | J, E | J, E, I | J, E, I |
| 4/23 | J, I | J, I | J, I | J, E J, I | J, E, I | J, E, I | J, E, I |

E = Emma; J = Jeanette; I = Ilana

3. complex sentences ("No Emma . . . Gabby push tire swing. No Emma three kids no room Emma")
4. short stories ("I go Alex's house. Emma go. My mommy take me good cake. I like.")
5. longer more complex stories

Jessica found evidence of most of these language forms for all three children.

Jessica found that Emma's language skills for communicating (as seen through the above five categories) developed and became stronger over the course of the 3-month research project. As Emma's language skills for communication improved, she acted as a "scaffold for both Ilana and Jeanette's language development." With her expanded language skills, Emma also could extend her friendship connections with Jeanette and Ilana, as seen in more sophisticated greetings and play interactions.

Table 4.3 shows Jessica's sheet for documenting these greetings over the course of the 3 months. From her experience as a toddler teacher, Jessica knew that the early morning drop-off time was a critical time for her toddlers to make social connections with peers, and that their greetings to one another were an important linguistic element of this social process. The three girls usually arrived in the classroom in this order: Emma, Jeanette, and then Ilana. Jessica documented how Jeanette approached Emma, and also how Ilana approached both Emma and Jeanette. Jessica also looked at whether the greetings changed over the course of the 3 months.

In looking at the data from Table 4.3 *as she collected* and wrote down the data, and then *later* when all data had been collected, Jessica noted particular ways that the three girls changed and grew in the use of nonverbal and verbal language (and assistance from adults like a parent or Jessica) in making social contact with one another. For instance, Jessica noticed that in the beginning, "Emma came up to Jeanette and invited her to come and play. There was very little language used at this time, and when Ilana first started greeting the other two girls, Jeanette did not give Ilana a warm greeting."

For Jeanette, Jessica noticed that in "February Jeanette needed Emma to approach her (she said, "Hi, come on" to Emma and then they both ran off). In March, Jeanette needed her dad to help her approach Emma (Jeanette approached Emma with her dad and then said "OK bye Daddy" and then said "come on, go bikes, bye daddy" again to her father). By April, Jeanette was running off without her dad and waved goodbye to him from the hill (Jeanette, with her dad, approached Emma and said, "Hi, Emma." Emma said, "Jeanette, I went to the zoo and saw iguana." Jeanette then said, "Oh my daddy zoo," and then both girls ran to the top of the hill, where Jeanette waved goodbye to her dad).

In these and other instances of the girls greeting one another during morning drop-off, Jessica discovered that over time the girls' efforts became a ritual. As such, something to be counted on to start the day on a positive social footing, "it became the most important part of their friendship. This ritual of greeting became so important that if there was a change, such as Emma not being at school, then Jeanette had a hard time leaving her dad. When Emma greeted Jeanette, it made the drop-off much easier."

In an overall way in her project, Jessica learned a great deal about important connections between language and friendship for toddlers.

As an educator of toddlers, I need to try and understand these connections. The different observations in my project helped me

**Table 4.3.** Greetings

| Date (2001) | Emma | Jeanette | Ilana |
|---|---|---|---|
| 2/15 | Emma went up to Jeanette and said "hi . . . come on" | Emma approached her and after greeting Jeanette ran off | NA |
| 2/22 | Emma went up to Jeanette and said "hi . . . come on" | Emma approached her and after greeting Jeanette ran off and said "bye daddy" | Emma approached her. "Hi Lala come play" after greeting Ilana hugs mommy one more time and goes over to Emma and Jeanette . . . Jeanette says no . . . Ilana come back to me |
| 3/1 | Emma went up to Jeanette and said "hi . . . come on . . . go hill?" | Emma approached her and after greeting Jeanette said "ok" and ran off then said "bye daddy" | Emma approached her. "Hi Lala come play" after greeting Ilana hugs mommy one more time and goes over to Emma and Jeanette . . . Jeanette says no . . . Ilana come back to me |
| 3/8 | Jeanette, with her dad, approached Emma. Emma turned and smiled and said "hi . . . come on . . . go hill . . . bye daddy" (to Jeanette's dad) | Jeanette approached Emma with her dad. Jeanette dad said "Hi Emma" Jeanette said after greeted by Emma "Ok bye daddy" | Emma approached her. "Hi Lala come play" after greeting Ilana hugs mommy one more time and goes over to Emma and Jeanette and plays with both of them |
| 3/15 | Jeanette, with her dad, approached Emma. Emma turned and smiled and said "hi . . . come on . . . go hill . . . bye daddy" (to Jeanette's dad) | Jeanette approached Emma with her dad. Jeanette dad said "Hi Emma" Jeanette said after greeted by Emma "Ok bye daddy" | Ilana approached Emma and Jeanette with me. Ilana says "Hi Emma" and they begin to play |
| 3/22 | Jeanette, with her dad, approached Emma. Emma turned and smiled and said "hi . . . come on . . . go bikes . . . bye daddy" (to Jeanette's dad) | Jeanette approached Emma with her dad. Jeanette said "Hi Emma" Jeanette said after greeted by Emma "Ok bye daddy" | Ilana approached Emma and Jeanette with me. Ilana says "Hi Emma" and they begin to play |

**Table 4.3.** (continued)

| Date (2001) | Emma | Jeanette | Ilana |
|---|---|---|---|
| 4/4 | Jeanette, with her dad, approached Emma. Emma turned and smiled and said "hi . . . come on . . . go get sticks . . . oh no stick at school go hill . . . bye daddy" (to Jeanette's dad) | Jeanette approached Emma with her dad. Jeanette said "Hi Emma" Jeanette said after greeted by Emma "Ok bye daddy" | Ilana approached Emma and Jeanette with me. Ilana says "Hi Emma Jeanette . . . Ilana play?" yes says both the girls and they begin to play |
| 4/11 | Jeanette, with her dad, approached Emma. Emma turned and smiled and said "come on . . . Jeanette let go find Ilana . . . bye daddy" (to Jeanette's dad) | Jeanette approached Emma with her dad. Jeanette said "Hi Emma" Jeanette said after greeted by Emma "Ok bye daddy" | Ilana approached Emma and Jeanette with me. Ilana says "Hi Emma Jeanette . . . Ilana play?" yes says both the girls and they begin to play |
| 4/16 | Jeanette, without her dad, approached Emma. Emma turned and smiled and said "come on . . . Jeanette let go find Ilana" | Jeanette approached Emma without her dad. Jeanette speaks first . . . "hi Emma . . ." Jeanette said after greeted by Emma | Ilana approached Emma and Jeanette with me. Ilana says "Hi Emma Jeanette . . . Ilana play?" yes says both the girls and they begin to play |
| 4/23 | Jeanette, without her dad, approached Emma. Emma turned and smiled and said "Jeanette . . . Jeanette . . . come let go . . . bikes or hill" | Jeanette approached Emma without her dad. Jeanette speaks first . . . "hi Emma . . ." Jeanette said after greeted by Emma "go hill" | Ilana approached Emma and Jeanette with me. Ilana says "Hi Emma Jeanette . . . Ilana play?" yes says both the girls and they begin to play |
| 4/30 | Jeanette, without her dad, approached Emma. Emma turned and smiled and said "Jeanette I went to the zoo and saw iguana" | Jeanette approached Emma without her dad. Jeanette speaks first . . . "hi Emma . . ." Jeanette said after greeted by Emma "Oh . . . my daddy zoo" | Ilana approached Emma and Jeanette with me. Ilana says "Hi Emma Jeanette . . . Ilana play?" yes says both the girls and they begin to play |

come to an understanding of toddler friendship and its influence on language development. The observations also became important information for planning the classroom environment and my toddler program. I realize more strongly now the importance of building and guiding friendships for toddlers. As someone who works with toddlers, I need to learn the different cues that toddlers use, and to see how I can model these different cues to promote friendships. The project also helped me see more clearly the value of promoting activities that the children are interested in and that can build language between them. For instance, as I observed the three girls in this project, I noticed how much all three liked rolly pollies. So I decided to add a rolly polly tank to our classroom environment. This tank activity then created several formal and informal language interactions among the children.

Jessica's project captured interesting complexities of language and friendship between her three toddlers. The use of the three data collection sheets enabled Jessica to collect a rich array of data on her focus. Since she looked at only three children, and three children who often played together (so she could observe them all at once in an efficient manner), Jessica uncovered many little gems about how their language skills and friendship connections became stronger over the course of the project.

If Jessica were to extend the project, she could make the following modifications:

1. Extend the time span of the project and start the project at the beginning of the school year to see more growth from September through August.
2. Enlist the help of her teaching assistant, who also could record observational data, and then she and Jessica could compare and contrast their data. This might well help Jessica focus her ongoing data collection and ongoing analysis in new directions that she had not thought of.
3. Speak with the girls' parents and ask about their hopes and expectations for the girls' social development and friendships in and out of school. This would add an important layer of family and home life, and also out-of-school play patterns and language use, that would give more "depth of data" to Jessica's project. It also would provide her with more information for supporting and guiding the girls' interactions and play at school.
4. Have brief informal discussions with the children themselves about where they play and with whom. This might lead to changes in the

way that Jessica guides and observes their "spontaneous" greetings, play, friendships, and language growth in these areas.

The teacher research projects in this chapter, both short- and long-term, show how data collection and analysis on particular areas of interest and need help us better understand children's nonverbal and oral language development. The examples also show how teacher research focuses on the small moments of children's language use—words, babbling, shouts, grimaces, smiles, sentences, ideas, and gestures—that are all part of young children's expanding toolbox of linguistic talents and skills.

## Suggested Teacher Research Activities

1. *Create a Data Collection Sheet*: In considering the focus for your teacher research project on language, play, or interactions, try out a few different data collection sheets. For example, look again at the data collection sheets that Jessica used in this chapter to capture aspects of her toddlers' emerging language use and friendship connections. If you are collecting a lot of data or specific different kinds of data (as Jessica did, for example, in looking at the children's greetings versus where they played), then try devising more than one data collection sheet. Once you have one designed, the best way to see its benefits is to try it out. After you try it a few times as part of your data collection, you can revise it one or more times to make it more efficient and useful.

2. *Use an Audiocassette Recorder*: If your project involves children's oral language, and/or your own language, then experiment with using an audiocassette recorder. If you audiotape, simply listen to the tapes without transcribing for the first few times. Then after you have collected more data, and are at a point where you feel that some analysis of those data is helpful, listen to one of the audiotapes again. Do not transcribe the whole tape, but select one or more short passages (5–10 minutes of audiotape) to transcribe. Remember that just 5 minutes of a tape can take over an hour to transcribe, especially if there are a few children's voices (and yours) on the tape. If possible, borrow a transcription machine, which allows you to use a foot pedal to rewind the tape several times in order to hear and rehear a certain segment of the tape. It also frees your hands to write or type, and you don't have to continually move your hand to start and stop and restart your tape recorder.

3. *Use a Digital Camcorder*: If you work with infants either as a direct caregiver or as a trainer, try using a digital camcorder, as Kelly did, in your teacher research project on infant language growth. Use the

digital camcorder to record the intricate, back-and-forth verbal and nonverbal exchanges between caregiver and infant. Replay parts of the video as you collect data, looking for ways both to improve your technical recording techniques and also to look at aspects of the caregiver–infant exchanges that are of most interest to you. Use the digital camcorder to freeze-frame, as you would take a photograph with a conventional camera, certain scenes that exemplify aspects of the exchanges. Catalogue and index these stand-alone photos for ongoing and later analysis.

# CHAPTER 5

# Teacher Research and Children's Projects and Literacy Learning

Sweet December

*When I was born*
*I swam with whales*
*and ran with elephants*
*like wild shadows*
*climbing over mountains*
*and into the oceans.*

*Then it was like the vast seas*
*blended in watercolors*
*while hungry elephants*
*touched*
*the water's edge.*

*And when the wild ones danced*
*in the forest and the whales swam*
*in the seas, that was when*
*I was born.*

—Keenan Dung, age 10

Guiding Questions

1. What is the value of teacher research for understanding how children discover, theorize, and converse in project-based work?
2. What are effective data collection strategies for a project on young children's storytelling development?

3. How can teacher research help us understand how and why young children participate in and learn from story dramatization?
4. What are effective data collection tools and data analysis strategies for understanding children's early reading and writing development?
5. What are good reasons and ways to form collaborative teacher research partnerships to research children's early literacy learning?

When young children discover and learn about the wonders and the joys (and some frustrations) of the world of literacy, they can, as in Keenan's poem, feel like they are swimming and dancing and have a new kind of voice. This is what we as educators want for the young children in our care and in our classrooms—a stronger voice, a stronger passion for sounds and words, and a stronger desire to become lifelong readers and writers and talkers about books and stories. Teacher research can help us as practitioners to strengthen the ways that we bring literacy to children, and improve the possibilities for young children to come to literacy on their own terms and in their own ways. Teacher research, then, strengthens our conceptual view and understanding of how young children can learn to become lifelong readers and writers, and it also can promote the practical strategies and methods that we use in our daily lives with children as we talk, read, dictate, tell stories, write, and dramatize our literary lives. The ECE teacher researchers in this chapter show us, through their teacher research projects, how we can integrate this attention to conceptual understanding and practical application in their teacher research projects.

## UNDERSTANDING CHILDREN'S PROJECT-BASED LEARNING

Working on long-term projects with children is an effective way to promote children's interests in their worlds and to integrate conversation and dialogue, art, literacy, and other curricular areas. Project work and play have important parallels to teacher research—children discover interesting phenomena and experiences and ask questions in dialogue with one another, a process that mirrors what we do as teacher researchers.

### A Dialogue with the Shadows—A Project from Kindergarten

Michael Escamilla, a veteran Spanish/English bilingual preschool and kindergarten teacher, is interested in the value of long-term projects associated with the project approach and the use of art and conversation from the

Reggio Emilia framework. In a project that Michael called "A Dialogue with the Shadows" (Escamilla, 2004), he and his assistant teacher, Melanie Sanchez, and their kindergarten-aged children used observation, conversation, dictation, writing, and drawing to explore the forms and functions of shadows. The project did not start with a research question but, like all of Michael's project work with young children, it began by his noticing the children's interest in a phenomenon or object or experience. As Michael says, "When children stop and think about an object or something they are experiencing, then we are doing our job. In project work, we observe and we listen. If not, we have no ideas to investigate or explore."

When the children found a snail in the school's garden, they brought it into Michael's classroom.

> We took the small snail inside the classroom and put it on a white sheet of paper on one of the tables next to the windows. The children looked at it very carefully with magnifying glasses and made a few remarks about its slow dragging motion. Trying to seize the opportunity, we supplied them with paper and pencils so that they could draw the likes of our visitor.

As Lilian Katz says about one of the goals of project work, the children quickly became "passionate about discovery." And this, too, was happening to Michael and Melanie, as they watched and listened and began documenting the children's new interest in the snail. In turn, the children's drawings and dictations about the snail were the project's first artistic and linguistic representations of the children's reactions to and understandings of the snail (see Figure 5.1).

Notice how the children are immediately encouraged to become the principal investigators of the snail—What does it look like? How does it move? How does it make me feel? What is it doing? What do I think of it?—and in

**Figure 5.1.** (a) A snail out for a walk. (b) A snail in love (Kevin N.).

(a)

(b)

this way, the children lead the research component of the project. Michael is not leading the research; rather, he is gently facilitating it (bringing the snail in and putting out white paper and letting the children draw) and also observing and listening and recording (actually the children's own drawings and conversations and dictations). So right from the start, the children are doing the data collection and early data analysis.

As the children made their first drawings, "the sunlight came through the window, which created the snail's shadow on the white paper. This incident led the children to try to draw the snail and its shadow." The children then moved from their personal and playful interpretations of the snail (Figure 5.1) to representations of the snail in the immediate environment (see Figure 5.2).

The children's drawings and dictations are early evidence of their research—collecting and analyzing data simultaneously. For example, Michaele's dictation, "A small snail has a small shadow," and Kevin's, "A big snail has a big shadow," indicate their insights into the relationship between the size of an object and its corresponding shadow. Joe's comment, "The shell has a shadow, but not the snail," indicates his discernment of which particular components of an object (or animal) might or might not influence or produce a shadow.

At the time, later the same day, Annie showed the class the fourth version of a self-portrait in which she showed her new very short haircut, as viewed from the back with the help of a mirror held by her friend Camilo (see Figure 5.3).

Later in the day, at circle time, some of the children shared their snail drawings and discussed their meanings. The group of children who had been

**Figure 5.2.** (a) A big snail has a big shadow (Kevin L.). (b) The shell has a shadow, but not the snail (Joe). (c) A small snail has a small shadow (Michaele).

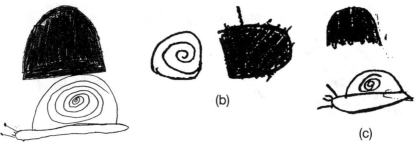

(a)

(b)

(c)

**Figure 5.3.** Annie's self portrait: (a) front (b) back.

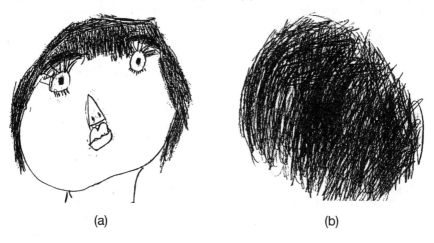

(a) (b)

working on self-portraits showed their latest versions. At the same time, Annie presented and shared her two-sided self-portrait of her new haircut.

> When the children who drew the pictures of the snail and its shadow presented their drawings to the rest of the class, they engaged in a discussion about shadows and their attributes. We tried to agree on a definition, but every child seemed to have his or her own very individual concept of shadows. When Annie presented her self-portrait, most of the children couldn't reach a consensus on whether the dark-colored portion of her drawing was a shadow of her head or the head seen from behind.

So, what happened by chance in the morning—the discovery of the snail, the children's drawings, the sudden appearance of the sun that made a shadow for the snail, and the children's interpretations of the relationship between the snail and its shadow (and any object and its shadow)—extended itself in the afternoon with the sharing of the children's shadow drawings and Annie's self-portrait of her new haircut. It is a good example, too, of the children's own research work as they looked at the drawings, shared their thoughts and observations, and tried as a group and as individuals to interpret what drawings might mean in terms of a definition of a shadow. So the children's research nicely parallels, as often happens in richly arranged and guided project work, Michael and Melanie's own teacher research. They, too, are looking at the same drawings and listening to the children, trying to look for interesting patterns or divergent thinking and the next direction to go in. In teacher research, we are constantly stopping here and there in our projects, assessing where we are (do I have good data? do I need more? different data?) and deciding on the need for new directions for data collection and analysis.

Michael, too, sensed the importance of the brief evolution of the children's actions and thinking—as represented through the children's own observation and drawing and dictation and discussion—for further study and research (both for the children and for himself and Melanie).

> We thought this was a good opportunity to record their ideas in order to present them back to the children on another occasion. From then on, we tried to follow up on the children's interests in shadows. This marked the beginning of the Shadows Project. We planned to ask the children a few more questions that we thought would be relevant to elicit more comments from them. These questions, along with their responses, were typed up and posted on the walls to keep as reference. The dialogue, the drawings, our teacher comments were the beginning of our documentation, which we hope is always a little different and better than the documentation of our previous project.

Michael guides the children bit by bit, taking cues from them and letting the documentation process keep pace with the children's interests and discoveries. It is important to point out that he and Melanie are not leading the children to a predetermined point; rather, they are thinking of "a few more questions" that would "elicit more comments" from the children. In this way, Michael and Melanie are learning along with the children, and the children's own research process (insights, discoveries, questions) become Michael and Melanie's research, too, as captured through documentation (drawings, conversations, dictations, and photographs). Thus, the "beginning of the Shadows Project" for the children is also simultaneously the beginning of the heart of Michael's teacher research of the project.

Further, it is Michael's intent to make documentation in this project "a little different and better" than previously. This effort means that Michael and Melanie are thinking and wondering where and how to support the children next, and how to use documentation to help in this process and also help their own teaching hearts and minds. As Katz and Chard (1996) point out, "Documentation is an important kind of teacher research, sharpening and focusing teachers' attention on children's plans and understandings and on their own role in children's experiences" (p. 3).

Conversation and discussion are sophisticated forms of oral language development for young children, and they played a key role in the Shadows Project.

We had a discussion with a group of 18 children. Ten felt confident enough to express their ideas, comments, and theories in public. We are finding that most of the time the children are better able to contribute to these discussions or conversations in small groups. However, it is very important to hold these large-group discussions to keep the doors open to anyone who wants to throw in an idea, a question, or comment. For example, in the dialogue below, Tommy sat silently throughout the discussion but at the end made a powerful statement. This indicates that he was following the conversation attentively. In these conversations, our role is to facilitate the dialogue with open-ended questions. All the children's answers are accepted and written down on the board so that they feel that all of their ideas are valued and equally important. It is not important that their answers are right or wrong; it is important that they are expressing their thoughts and formulating theories.

In the following dialogue, Michael and Melanie ask "meaningful open-ended questions and try to take the children's answers seriously." In the conversation, note how the children are "becoming aware of the connections between themselves and their shadows, the shadows and light, the sky, the clouds, and the ground." Michael and Melanie used an audiocassette recorder to capture the dialogue.

> *MICHAEL:* I think that we have shadows because the sun is shining.
> *FRANCO:* I think that we have shadows because the sun is shining.
> *PEDRO:* I know. Because the sun is bright and the sun comes out and the shadows come out. And then, when the moon comes out, the shadows go away.
> *LUPE:* When the sun follows you and the . . .
> *FRANCO:* (interrupting Lupe) The sun doesn't follow you! The shadows follow you. When it is very hot the shadows follow you every place you go.
> *HAN:* (still thinking about Pedro's statements about the shadows going away when the moon comes out) At night time, we don't see the shadows.
> *MALKA:* But if you come home and then you turn the lights on, then you have your shadow.
> *LUPE:* When it is night time you can see a little bit of shadows.
> *MALKA:* When you turn off the lights then you don't see the shadows.
> *MICHAEL:* When you don't see your shadow, where do the shadows go?
> *SALMA:* Maybe they go underground.

*FRANCO:* Maybe they go away at their house and their house is underground.

*KELVIN:* I think the shadows go into the clouds.

*JUNE:* (unsure of what to say and repeating what Josephina whispers in her ear) The shadows go . . . to . . . go the water.

*MICHAEL:* Why do you like your shadow?

*FRANCO:* I like my shadow because when I walk down the street it goes with me and goes across the street and it goes on and on and on until I stop and the shadow stops, too.

*BETTY:* I like my shadow because it follows me and it can't go the other way.

*SALMA:* I like it because when I crawl in the grass, then the shadow crawls in the grass, too.

*KELVIN:* I like my shadow because the shadow has legs and it likes to walk.

*MICHAEL:* How many shadows do we have? (Nobody answers. "Maybe this was not a good question," Michael thinks to himself. After a few moments, Tommy speaks. He is the only one with an answer.)

*TOMMY:* We have one shadow because there's only one sun.

This snippet of the children's conversation shows their high level of interest and engagement in one another's comments and ideas, and how their emerging ideas and theories take into account those of their peers. And Michael does not explicitly lead their discussion other than asking a couple of thought-provoking questions that he and Melanie have prepared in advance. So just as the children are extending their project learning in conversation with one another, so too are Michael and his assistant extending their research in response to the children's ideas and explanations.

The children then studied shadows indoors and outdoors, and learned about shadows "at two different levels": shadows projected on the ground because of the sunlight, and shadows projected on the white screen with the help of the light from an overhead projector. The children continued to make important discoveries, some of which made sense to them while others were perplexing. For example, when the children's shadows were projected on the screen, they were not attached to their bodies, while the shadows projected by the sunlight were. But when the children made representations of these phenomena through drawings, "it was a challenge to draw the position of their shadows in relation to the sunlight." In their first attempts at drawings, the backs of the children's bodies were all colored in to represent a full-body shadow on the body itself. Seeing this challenge, Michael and his assistant decided to make chalk drawings of the children's shadows outside. For example, they traced Franco's shadow several times over the course of a single day. "The children were then able to see that although the shadow seemed to move every time we went out to trace it, it always remained attached to Franco's feet." The children then drew more of their outdoor shadows, and linked their bodies with their shadows.

The Shadows Project continued for several weeks and Michael and Melanie continued to gather and analyze data, which were essentially the children's comments, dictations, writings, and drawings from their project work and play. The children also used books as reference material, and Michael asked the children's families to send in books, too. In this project, the children's curricular learning and the teachers' research go hand in hand, each fortifying and nurturing the other—with the children "leading" and inspiring the teachers one moment, and the teachers assisting and leading the children the next. Michael sees the foundation for rich project learning as the same as that for fruitful and rewarding teacher research.

> When you are doing projects, you have to talk and collaborate. You have to coexist and work together. Many times I think in our work we separate out things for the sake of organization. But the more that I do project work, and document and research this kind of learning and teaching, the more I think that we have to co-depend and collaborate. This sense of collaboration refers not only between teachers, but also to the collaboration that must take place between teachers and children in order to be active co-learners in the classroom. Reggio Emilia has given us more than a vision; it has given us an inspiration by illustrating what could happen if we really listen to the voices of our children. And what the project approach has given us is a practical, useful interpretation of the Reggio Emilia system. It's been adapted to the American way of thinking about how to do projects. I used to follow the project approach stages 1, 2, 3 as if I were following a cooking recipe—like following steps—but now my way of teaching has become more holistic. I now document and reflect at a deeper level—and can communicate this to the parents—than when I taught using themes. Reflection, the heart of my teacher research and project work, improves my teaching. Reflection means asking, What are we doing? What can we do better? And what are we learning as teachers from one project to the next?

Throughout the project, Michael and Melanie used a range of tools to collect and analyze the children's project play and work: children's drawings (photocopied and collected), dictations, words and conversations (written down and audiotaped), actions (photographed), books (child-made and published from the library), indoor and outdoor exploration, and artifacts and objects. They also put together the most interesting and illuminating of the children's discoveries into documentation panels. Michael believes that documentation "is a window on the past and also a perspective on the future." For example, when photographs and drawings are labeled by the children and the teachers, "sometimes we use the past tense, the present, and the future—we did this, we are doing this, or we might do this at some point." Again, this is an important parallel with teacher research, as ongoing analysis and reflection on data take into account what we did, what we are doing, and what we will do.

If Michael did the Shadows Project again, he and Melanie could strengthen and extend their research in these ways:

1. Find new ways to encourage quiet children and those learning English to speak up more in group discussions. Give some of these children designated lead roles in the children's investigations that do not necessarily require lots of oral language.
2. Involve the children more in listening to portions of the transcribed group discussions. Encourage the children to reflect on what they said (and didn't say) as a way to think back to their earlier ideas and theories.
3. Keep a reflective, dialogue journal in which Michael and Melanie respond to each other's ideas on the effectiveness of their project questions with the children. Teaching assistants often are underutilized in teacher research, and this is an excellent opportunity to strengthen an already strong collaborative working relationship. Michael and Melanie also could create an audit trail (see Pat's project on critical literacy in Chapter 6) to track the data and their interpretations.
4. Involve the families more—ask families to record any data at home involving the children's interests in shadows and bring the data into the classroom.
5. Present ongoing findings to other colleagues on site to elicit their feedback and suggestions for continuing and improving the project and the accompanying research.

## RESEARCHING CHILDREN'S STORYTELLING AND STORY DRAMATIZATION

Children's storytelling and drama are important ways for children to express themselves and communicate verbally and nonverbally. Teacher research can help us understand how children come to stories, and the value of drama for promoting literary learning.

## Multilingual Storytelling in the Preschool

Mary Lin, who uses both Chinese and English in her preschool class-room, is interested in promoting storytelling and story dictation to help as a foundation for her mostly Chinese-American children's literacy learning. The initial impetus for her interest started with one of her children, Fay, who spoke almost no English and also spoke almost no Chinese with Mary or the other children. Mary thought that stories might be a good way to help Fay open up socially and academically. Mary eventually conducted a short-term project of 7 weeks (Lin, 2004), collecting data only on Fay's Chinese and English language use through the lens of storytelling and story dramatization. Fo-cusing on only one child helped narrow Mary's data collection and discour-aged her from collecting an unwieldy amount of data. Mary also utilized the following data sources, data collection tools, and data analysis strategies:

- reflected on the roots and influences of her own personal and cultural knowledge of stories and storytelling
- elicited and recorded the children's stories as dictations on paper and also as oral stories captured on audiotape
- read books and stories to the children and recorded their reactions and discussion
- shared her own stories and recorded them on audiotape
- told stories and encouraged the children to tell stories in both English and Chinese
- transcribed the most illuminating portions of the children's stories
- to understand her data more fully, consulted selected research litera-ture on storytelling

Mary began her research not with a question, but with the puzzle of her own personal transition from storytelling in China to storytelling in the United States.

The word "story" in Chinese is a very formal term that refers to a folktale, fairy tale, fable, or heroic event that teaches people lessons. The people from my village and I had never thought of ordinary people like myself telling stories and never considered that what happened to us were stories. When I came to the United States and people asked me to tell a story about myself, I panicked. My first reaction was that I couldn't do it—I don't have any stories. And when I learned about story dictation here, at first I thought, what's so special about it? The children's "stories" seemed like they were just talking, and on top of that, children are talking all the time and so how to write their stories down?

Mary's 7-week project helped her more clearly see the forms and functions of preschool children's first stories. Mary started her data collection by reading *Goodnight Moon* (Brown, 1947) to small groups of her children. She started with this book because it was Fay's favorite. Mary read it in English and the children retold what they could from the story in English and Chinese. The first time Mary read it, Fay did not speak. But on the next two occasions, as Mary also introduced props to retell the story, Fay became more involved, speaking one word on the second rereading and then the next time telling Mary in Chinese, "I need the book." As she turned the pages, she told her story in Chinese (which Mary audiotaped and later transcribed into both Chinese and English).

晚安月亮 (Goodnight Moon)

氣球 (balloon)
有只牛跳過個月亮 (has a cow jumping over the moon)
三個熊坐呢張木凳 (three bears sitting in chairs)
二只小貓 (two little cats)
二只小襪 (two mittens)
一只小老鼠 (one little mouse)
有一個屋 (has a little house)
有一個梳子 (has a comb)
有一碗粥 (has a bowl of porridge)
有一個婆婆坐張木凳度 (has a little grandma sitting on a chair)
有一只燈 (has a light)
有一個月亮 (has a moon)
有一只牛跳過月亮 (has a cow jumping over the moon)
晚安有一個氣球 (goodnight balloon)
晚安二只貓 (goodnight two little kittens)
晚安二只手套 (goodnight two mittens)
晚安三只熊坐張木凳 (goodnight three bears sitting in chairs)
晚安屋 (goodnight house)
晚安老鼠 (goodnight mouse)
晚安鐘 (goodnight clock)
晚安沒人 (goodnight nobody)
晚安碗粥 (goodnight a bowl of porridge)
晚安老婆婆 (goodnight old grandma)
晚安星星 (goodnight stars)
晚安空氣 (goodnight air)
晚安電話 (goodnight telephone)
(translation: Annabella Tong)

Balloon. Has a cow jumping over the moon. Three bears sitting in chairs. Two little cats. Two mittens. One little mouse. Has a little house. Has a comb. Has a bowl of rice porridge. Has a little grandma sitting in a chair. Has a light. Has a moon. Has a cow jumping over the moon. Goodnight balloon. Goodnight two little kittens. Goodnight two mittens. Goodnight three bears sitting in chairs. Goodnight house. Goodnight mouse. Goodnight clock. Goodnight nobody. Goodnight bowl of porridge. Goodnight old grandma. Goodnight stars. Goodnight air. Goodnight telephone. The End.

With this breakthrough story, Mary realized that opportunities for storytelling in Chinese would help Fay's confidence, language growth, and storytelling knowledge. As in many teacher research projects, the discovery of one object of fascination (*Goodnight Moon* in this case) and one critical event or small moment of learning (retelling the story in Chinese) enable a project to gain a newfound research *and* curricular strength and direction.

Validating Fay's home language helped me to create a safe nest for her to reach out and open up to me. I remember myself having the same feeling when I came to this country. I thought that my children were better able to adapt and were not as conscious of making mistakes as I was. I was wrong. Fay needed the extra support, too. So Fay really opened up. She told many more stories in Chinese. All her stories were about family, the things she likes to do at school, and the things she does with her family on the weekends or the night before.

So Fay started to speak more in Chinese and English in the preschool classroom and slowly began to make some friends and speak up more with teachers and children. Fay's academic storytelling breakthrough slowly carried over into little breakthroughs in terms of friendships and also initiating interactions. Three weeks after the *Goodnight Moon* story, Fay put two things together—storytelling and taking the initiative socially. Fay came over to Mary and gave her a poke on the back and pointed to the container of writing pads and pencils, which Mary used to take the children's story dictations. "Oh you want to tell a story," Mary replied. Fay smiled, and told her new story.

I know sing song.
Let me think.
I know dance.
I like sing sister kindergarten's song.
I like sing Old Mary Mack.

I like play with little friends.
I like play bicycle.
Mommy see doctor. Baby come out first then see doctor.
I think Joey not coming school today. He need see doctor.
Joey told me.
He didn't tell teacher Mary.
He play with me, tell me.
I finish telling.

Mary also collected language data from Fay in other language activities. For example, when the children were doing an All About Me book, Mary asked an assistant teacher to work with Fay and talk with her in English. At first, the teacher gave fill-in-the-blank phrases for Fay like, "My name is _____." But Fay did not answer. Only when the teacher switched to asking questions, apparently a more familiar English construction, did Fay begin to answer. "What is your name?" (Fay); "What school do you go to?" (Monarch); "What do you like to eat?" (carrot, chicken, soda, chocolate milk, apple juice); "What colors to you like?" (pink, blue, purple, green, and red). Mary used this additional linguistic information to gain a more well-rounded picture of Fay's emerging English talents and the teacher strategies that best supported Fay's English development. Mary then could apply this information to her other work with Fay on storytelling and story dictation.

Several weeks after she first retold *Goodnight Moon* in Chinese, Fay retold it again, and this time in English.

Cow, the moon. Three bears on chair. Goodnight cat. Goodnight moon. Goodnight cow. Goodnight bear. Goodnight house. Goodnight mouse.

By collecting data on the same activity and material—retelling the same story—Mary was able to compare and contrast data over a period of several weeks. This is an excellent strategy in teacher research, to keep the data collection simple and doable (and it fit right into Mary's curriculum and teaching) and to revisit a phenomenon or activity or material again and again over time. This affords a mini-lens or window onto children's incremental gains and growth, and provides those wonderful "little gems" of data for reflection and understanding on the part of the teacher researcher.

From this short new retelling of *Goodnight Moon* in English, I saw that Fay's vocabulary was expanding. She also followed part of the structure of the story. She picked out the things that she could name in English, and said goodnight to each one. These are still not full sentences in English yet; Fay used single words and more phrases. And she said it all in English. Also, by comparing this retelling to the one she did earlier in Chinese, I noticed how much stronger her Chinese vocabulary is.

In a general way, Mary found that teacher research gave her a deeper understanding both of Fay and of her own teaching.

> The project helped me look at Fay more closely. Although I looked mainly at her storytelling, I got to know Fay more as a whole child. I now have a better understanding of her school life and home life through her stories. Storytelling also helped me bring the family closer to the school. One day recently, Fay's father came to school and wanted to know who Joey was. He had heard about Joey from Fay's stories of school in their home. "I want to meet Joey," Fay's father said.

So not only had the research and teaching focus on Fay helped her socially and academically in the classroom, it also strengthened her home–school connections.

If Mary were to carry out this project again, she could strengthen and extend it in these ways:

1. Read books in both English and Chinese, giving Fay a foundation for stories in Chinese that most likely would transfer to stories in English. Mary then could more fully compare and contrast Fay's comprehension and use of story language and structure in Chinese and in English.
2. Read back Fay's dictated stories in Chinese and English, asking Fay if she would like to add or change anything. This would give Fay another opportunity to reflect on her own stories, and give Mary more one-on-one time with Fay discussing her stories.
3. Enlist her teaching assistant more fully, asking her to become an official co-researcher collecting and analyzing story data from and with Fay. Mary and the assistant could keep a dialogue research journal, in which they each would write down their observations of Fay's stories on any given day, and then write a short reflection on these data. Mary and the assistant then could respond to each other's reflections as an ongoing dialogue.
4. Ask Fay's parents to also become co-researchers, enlisting their help in recording or writing down stories in Chinese that Fay might tell and also recording stories that the parents or older siblings might read and tell to Fay.

## Story Dramatization in the Preschool

Sivinee Traiprakong, a novice preschool teacher, is interested in children's dramatic re-enactments of children's literature. Sivinee carried out a teacher research project at her preschool (Traiprakong, 2004), in which she read four children's books (*Caps for Sale, The Mitten, A Mother for Choco, Anansi the Spider*) over the course of 10 weeks. Sivinee devoted approximately 2 weeks to each of the four stories, rereading the story each day and leading story dramatization activities 2 days a week. She worked primarily with small groups of children, aged 2.3–5.1, who wanted to join the story dramatization as their chosen activity. For each of the four books, Sivinee followed the same basic routine.

> I set up the stage made from a long white fabric as a semicircle at the corner of the school's sandpit. After snack, I asked the children who wanted to join in the story dramatization activity. I led the interested children near the stage, and we always sat down on a blue blanket on the sand. I then read the story. Afterward, the children themselves decided if they wanted to dramatize the story. Sometimes I had two children and sometimes I had seven. The total number of children did not matter, as I learned to cut or add roles as needed. Sometimes one child would play two roles at the same time. There were also always children who helped me set the stage. I then asked children to sign up for roles by putting their names down (I helped them write if they needed it) on a big piece of paper. I read out the roles to confirm their choices, and then gave them a short summary of the story before the children chose costumes and props. After each child had on their costume, I asked them to stand at center stage, hold hands, and bow to their audience (whomever happened by to watch). The play then began. The children made up their speaking parts and their movements.

This is another nice example—as it was for Michael's and Mary's projects—of the need for the curriculum to make good developmental sense for the children in order for the accompanying teacher research to make good teaching and research sense for the teacher researcher. Sivinee created a format and routine—with materials and ways to participate—that were doable for her and the children. For example, the first two books that she chose for dramatization required the children to speak little in the way of dialogue. In this and other ways, since the learning and participation demands were not overwhelming for the children, Sivinee could teach and *at the same time* had the energy and time to collect data.

Each time the children acted out a story, Sivinee recorded the following:

- Children (Who are the children participating in the drama?)
- Roles (Which roles from the stories do they choose?)
- Choices (How do the children choose the roles?)
- Entrance (How do the children enter and join the drama?)
- Props (Which props do they choose and what is the effect?)

Sivinee took these elements and put them into a chart, which she photocopied and attached to a clipboard. She used this as a handy data collection sheet, jotting down notes during each story dramatization.

For example, when the children were enacting *Caps for Sale* (their first story) on one particular day, Sivinee recorded data on their participation.

Children

Mira, Juan, Cal, Mika, Sally, Joanna, Isa

Roles

Cal as a monkey
Mira as a monkey
Mika, Sally, Isa as trees
Juan, Cal, Joanna as peddlers

Choices

Cal likes monkeys
Sally says the tree is the easiest role
Cal wants to be a peddler
Joanna and Juan follow Cal (as peddlers)
Isa follows Sally (as trees)

Entering

Cal, Mika, and Isa began the play, and then their friends joined in

Props

Two green skirts and leaves for the trees
Many kinds of caps

This careful documentation allowed Sivinee to keep track of the *same* key elements of the children's dramatization across four different children's books, different children, different props, different teaching and facilitation strategies, and a time span of 10 weeks. It gave her project *descriptive breadth*, which in turn gave it *analytical depth* and helped her more deeply understand *what* her children were doing, *how*, and *why* in their story dramatization.

As in Jacqueline's project on toddler community (featured in Chapter 3), the use of photographs also helped Sivinee's data collection and ongoing data analysis. Using a digital camera, Sivinee took photographs of important phases of several of the plays that the children performed based on the four books. When Sivinee finished her data collection, and started writing up her project, her photographs were helpful in re-enacting the small moments of the children's drama play and work. For example, in recreating the dramatization of *Caps for Sale* by three children (Arthur, Emilia, and Juan), Sivinee used eight separate photographs that depicted key actions, props, and decisions by the children. Sivinee also added a lot of text to explain the photographs, and the text stood on its own as both description and analysis. I provide the text here without the photographs to illustrate the vividness of her "key moment" descriptions.

1. Arthur, Emilia, and Juan and I sat on a nice blue mat inside the stage as I read *Caps for Sale* to them.
2. After finishing the story, Arthur and Juan chose to be a tree, and Emilia chose to be the peddler. The children chose their own costumes and props.
3. Arthur and Juan wore green wraps. Arthur hid behind the stage before the play began, while Juan wanted to stay inside the stage.
4. After everyone got their costumes and props, all the children met at the center stage and bowed to the audience.
5. At first, nobody chose to be the monkey, so Arthur switched roles, from being a tree to being a monkey. The monkey stole caps and hats from the peddler who slept under the tree.
6. The peddler was still sleeping and she didn't know that the monkey had already taken her caps and hats.
7. The peddler woke up and found that she had lost all of her caps and hats. The monkey teased the peddler, saying, "Tzzz . . . Tzzzzz . . . tzz."
8. The peddler was angry and said, "You monkey . . . give me back my caps!" Then the monkey gave all of the caps and hats back to the peddler.

Sivinee took some notes as the play unfolded and also took photographs. She later sifted through the photographs to find the best sequence of eight or so photographs (eight small, 1" × 2" photographs fit well onto one page) that depicted key elements (props, costumes, roles, action, dialogue) in the drama. If Sivinee had only taken photographs, she would not have captured the children's actions (such as Arthur changing roles) and their language (The peddler said, "You monkey . . . give me back my caps!"). Conversely, if Sivinee had only taken written notes, she would have missed out on the visuals of the photographs to recreate the drama.

This project helped Sivinee learn about effective ways to promote story dramatization with young children and also to sharpen her observational and analytic skills as a preschool teacher.

> As I watched the plays and took notes, I realized that I didn't understand a good deal of what was going on. But writing down key elements of their plays (on a data collection sheet) and keeping a journal on my own role helped me reflect on my teaching practices in this project. I discovered problems and also solutions that I had never realized before. As I looked again and again at my data sheets, my journal, and my photographs, I could hear again the children's voices and see their participation. Reseeing and rehearing this material helped me realize that the story dramatization project was the right place and way for the children to act out the four stories and have a good time with their friends. My final reflections on this project didn't necessarily provide answers, but connected me to new teaching practices and new insights into my children. For example, I realized the value of setting up an attractive stage, making it cozier each week, changing and adding new props even with the same story, letting go of my initial role as stage manager (the children eventually took it over), and that I could always count on a regular group of actors to participate in the story reading and the story acting (while some children were content with only listening to the story and then leaving for another activity).

As in Michael's and Mary's projects, Sivinee's final reflections and insights are focused on both the value of teacher research and new insights into her teaching and her students. She realized that the project didn't necessarily provide her with "new answers" on story dramatization for this age group, but "connected" her with "new teaching practices and new insights" into her children. By project's end, after reading and dramatizing only four stories, Sivinee had several new ideas and understandings of what children do in story dramatization, how they participate, and why (or why not).

If Sivinee were to carry out the project again, she might consider these modifications and extensions:

1. Start off the project with a book or two of her choice (*Caps for Sale* and *The Mitten* are perfect for this age), then open up the story choices to the children, seeking their ideas and reasons for a particular story or book to enact. This would give another level of data collection (the children's interests and how they discuss a story to choose) as well as another layer for her drama curriculum.
2. Discuss with the children (as Michael does about the snails) their theories, reactions, and ideas about what they like about the story dramatization, how they chose their roles and props, and their "choice" of dialogue and actions. This would add a "meta" level of participation for the children, encouraging them to reflect on their drama participation as a collaborative group of 2–5-year-old thespians.
3. Expand the audiences for the plays. Consider having the children perform for different groups of children, who would ask questions and make comments after the plays. This would encourage the actors to "reflect" in a different way about their choice of roles, props, dialogue, and actions.
4. Display the photographs on an ongoing basis over the course of the project on documentation panels, adding photographs over time. This would allow other children, teachers, administrators, and parents to see what was going on, and offer suggestions for changes or new ideas as the story dramatization project unfolded.
5. Videotape at least one of the plays, preferably more than one version of the same story, and then play it back for the children. Encourage them to observe "what stays the same" and "what changes" from story enactment to story enactment. Again, this would give Sivinee another layer of data to collect and analyze—the children's nascent skill at describing and analyzing their own involvement as a group or community of actors.

## RECONCEPTUALIZING CHILDREN'S EARLY LITERACY DEVELOPMENT

I now describe three projects that integrate young children's language and literacy development. An individual teacher researcher carried out the first project in her preschool classroom. One teacher researcher and one university-based researcher conducted the second project in a 1st-grade classroom. Four teacher researchers carried out a collaborative project at four different ECE sites in the last project.

## Balancing Child-Centered and Teacher-Initiated Literacy

Ivy Ng (2006), a veteran preschool teacher, wanted to find effective ways to balance teacher-directed literacy instruction with child-centered, play-based literacy learning. Since Ivy was mandated by her public school district's child development program to teach from a particular literacy curriculum, and also to carry out specific assessments over the course of the year, Ivy wanted to find new ways to teach literacy in an interesting and developmentally appropriate way. Ivy carried out her project in her preschool classroom of twenty-two 3–5-year-olds, primarily children of recent immigrants from China who spoke mostly Chinese at home. Ivy is fluent in Chinese and English, and used Chinese with her students on an informal basis since her site is not an official bilingual preschool.

Over the course of 5 months, Ivy collected data on the children's choices of literacy activities, how they participated with one another in these activities, and her own goals and strategies for introducing literacy to the children. Ivy used these strategies for data collection:

- Personal journal (for reflecting on her teaching and recording her memories and thoughts on what the children were doing)
- Whole-class data (collected data on general patterns across a majority of the 22 children)
- Focal children (selected three children—Anna, Kevin, and Delia—to focus on specifically)
- Fieldnote book (for recording children's conversation, action, responses, gestures, general attitudes, and performance)
- Audiotape cassette recorder (for recording children's dialogue, "reading," and group discussion)
- Camera (for capturing children's literacy products and children in action doing literacy)
- Collection of children's literacy work and play samples (collected and dated chronologically)
- Collection of written lesson plans (for recording the themes, topics of interest, and activities introduced)

Ivy chose the three focal children because they were all learning English, were 4-year-olds who would be going to kindergarten the next year, and had different interests and talents for language and literacy learning. Ivy kept a separate folder for each child and arranged all of the child's literacy work and play samples in chronological order. Throughout the project, Ivy looked over her accumulating data and asked herself, "What do I see behind this picture or piece of dialogue?" rather than, "What is this picture about or the content of this conversation?"

Ivy first looked at her classroom environment, observing how children interacted with one another and materials in ways that were playful and also focused on aspects of literacy learning. This allowed Ivy to have a *broad sweep* of the child-driven or child-centered literacy engagement in her classroom, before looking at her own direct role. Ivy observed the different areas of her classroom and quickly found that the children were engaging in spontaneous literacy activities based on what interested them at the moment on their own or with friends.

For example, all of the children loved Cocoa, the classroom guinea pig, who lived in one particular area of the room. One day, Ivy noticed Kevin and Anna (two of her three focal children) observing Cocoa after they had fed her. They remarked how Cocoa ate the orange so cleanly and drank the water in a funny posture. Then Anna started to draw a picture of Cocoa and copied its name on a piece of paper. Kevin followed Anna and drew a picture of Cocoa, too. They then dictated a written message with Ivy's help. Anna dictated, "This is Cocoa. Cocoa happy. This is Cocoa name. Cocoa happy *because it eats an orange*" (the italicized words were said in Chinese). Kevin dictated, "This is Cocoa. I write the name here. And the cage. Cocoa is inside the cage. She has things to eat. Cocoa. Name." From this scene, Ivy realized how the children made their own little "literacy discoveries," and then benefited from Ivy's simple, guiding additions through dictation.

In another example, Michael and Steven built a city with bridges and roads similar to the book *This Is San Francisco*. As they worked together, Ivy recorded their dialogue.

> *STEVEN:* This one is the road, the bridge.
> *MICHAEL:* If you go there and then you may go back and start there again.
> *STEVEN:* You may go to the tunnel.
> *MICHAEL:* This is the Oakland Bridge.
> *STEVEN:* I'm crossing the bridge. (Holds a car and drives through the bridge.)
> *MICHAEL:* The flag is called the "American." (pointing at a block) The city has a beautiful road. This is American Road.
> *STEVEN:* My dad said our home is San Francisco.
> *MICHAEL:* The city is called California San Francisco.
> *STEVEN:* Ivy, we make a bridge and a tunnel. Same. (Shows Ivy the pictures in *This Is San Francisco*.)
> *MICHAEL:* Yeah, this is road and cars. A city. Look at. (Points to pictures in the book.)

*IVY:* You should make some signs for the roads so drivers can read
the signs and know where they are.
*MICHAEL:* Ivy, can you write the city name for me?

Ivy wrote the words on a piece of paper and let Michael copy them. After
writing the words on paper, Michael put the names of the city and road on
top of the blocks.

By looking at particular areas of the classroom, and collecting data on
the children's small interactions with literacy, Ivy was able to find these kinds
of "little gems" of data. These little scenes, like creating the city with blocks
and signs, provided much early food for thought and reflection.

> Michael and Steven brought into play what they knew about San
> Francisco. Their playful interaction helped them create a story about
> San Francisco (complete with an "Oakland Bridge" and an "Ameri-
> can Road"). I noticed how their pretend play became an essential part
> of their literacy learning, rather than the other way around. Their
> pretend play allowed them to plan together, create a mental represen-
> tation of their city, and showed off their linguistic talents and emerg-
> ing interest and knowledge of literacy. As I observed their play, I saw
> their story-like literacy play. At that point, I wanted to extend their
> learning in reading and writing. So when Steven asked me to look at
> their city, I suggested he make signs for the drivers. I realized that I
> could be a facilitator in helping the children achieve literacy skills
> beyond their current developmental level, and child-centered play
> provided the foundation for this extension.

Without knowing it at first, and not necessarily looking for it in her initial
data collection, Ivy found excellent early examples of ways to balance child-
centered play and adult-facilitated literacy teaching.

Ivy could have restricted her data collection to finding more examples
like the ones with Cocoa and the blocks, similar to how Sivinee focused on
only four children's stories in a tightly focused project. This would have made
for a fine project. But since Ivy wanted to find out how to balance her literacy instruction throughout the entire literacy program, she looked at other
areas of the children's literacy learning. Ivy looked at a range of activities
that she initiated and taught. For example, after reading Leo Lionni's
*Swimmy*, Ivy did a story-mapping activity with the whole class. They discussed the main character ("Swimmy"), place ("in the sea"), the problem
("the big fish wants to eat the red fish"), and the solution ("we have to swim
together to scare the big fish"). At first, though, the children weren't sure
about the main character. So Ivy asked, "Who do you see on almost every

page?" and flipped through the book. "Swimmy," said Kevin. The children had good ideas for the other story elements.

Ivy suggested to the class that they create their own story together.

> I showed them a blank paper. I told them that I did not know the title, the characters, the setting, the problem, the solution. I asked them to help me. In this playful setting, I guided the children effortlessly through the process of creating a story. The children felt that they were participants rather than listeners. I then showed them three things: a saw, a cellular phone, and a car. I asked the children who they wanted as the main character. The children chose a child.

Ivy continued by encouraging and guiding the children in composing a story as a group. As Ivy and the children told the story, Ivy's teaching assistant wrote it down. (In the story below, the italicized parts are told by the children, while Ivy contributed the remaining text.)

> Once upon a time *there was a child. The child had a red car with yellow wheels.* One day, *the child decided to have a ride.* The child drove the car down the road to the city. When the child got to the city, *the child saw many house. The child wanted to go from one house to another house. The child put the car in someone's back door.* When the child got off the car, the child smelled something burning. The child looked up at the sky and *saw fire in the house.* The child heard someone shouting, "*Help, help!* We can't open the door." "*I need the firefighters to help,*" the child said.

> The child took out the *cellular phone and called 911. "Please come. There's a fire at the house,"* the child said. "OK, we're coming," the firefighter said. The child was very scared. *The child ran away from the house and waited for the firefighters.* Weewoo, weewoo, weewoo. *The child heard the siren of the fire truck. The firefighters came and used the hammer to break the door. They told the child to get the saw and the child said, "Yes." The firefighters used the saw to cut the door.* Boom. The door was broken. People ran from the house. Then the firefighters put out the fire. The people said, *"Thank you"* to the child. "*You're welcome,*" said the child. The people said "thank you" to the firefighters. "You're welcome," said the firefighters. Then *the child got in the car and drove back home.* The End

The next day Ivy read the story back to the class, and they identified the story elements, which Ivy wrote down on chart paper: Title (The Firefighters'

Rescue), Character(s) (the child), Problem(s) (The house was on fire. Some people needed help), Solution (the child called 911). Several days later, the children retold the story and acted it out. They also performed it for their parents. This teaching sequence differs slightly from Sivinee's project, in that Ivy had the class collaboratively compose their own story, which they then acted out. In turn, in terms of her research, this gave Ivy a different angle on the children's literacy learning—it gave her data on any direct transfer of story language, content, interest, and participation from children's original stories to their discussion of the story elements and then to their dramatic performance of the story. This gave Ivy a "layered cake" array of data over time that remained child-centered. So for Ivy, the uniformity and consistency of her teaching (all elements of the story's evolution were child-centered) in turn gave "research consistency" to her data collection and analysis. This kind of consistency helps in looking for transfer or carryover of knowledge, skills, experiences, and interests. This teaching/learning/research cycle helped Ivy reflect on the value of this kind of curriculum for the children's literacy growth.

> I found that the freestyle group story promoted the children's expressive language development and social interaction. I really like what Hamilton and Weiss (1990) say about stories, that they have the power to make the "here and now disappear" for children. The children "reread" the story and even used the script in their play. For instance, Anna (one of my focal children) may not have completely understood the stories I read aloud earlier, but this creative child-centered storytelling and story dramatization scaffolded and helped her beginning English skills. She felt confident to "read" our child-created story because she only had to memorize the words. It also increased her comprehension and understanding, expanded her vocabulary and sentence structure, and she applied new words and scripts with peers. I also noticed that she used new scripts in her play, too. Like a chant, Anna added, "Help, help! We can't open the door!" in her play language with her friends.

The project gave important new insights into Anna's (and the other children's) literacy learning through this kind of layered teaching and data collection. In turn, Ivy noticed the transfer of Anna's English language skills (from child-created story to discussion to "rereading" to drama to chants in her play). This gave welcome evidence for Ivy concerning the power and value, for the children and for herself, of nurturing a rich literacy curriculum that integrated child-centeredness *and* teacher-directedness within the *same* activity or project.

Does a balanced literacy curriculum mean half of class time is under teacher-directed instruction and the rest is children's free play? From this project, I now call this "half and half" view inappropriate curriculum. For instance, my three focal children were not really interested in participating in my guided activities. But then I learned to follow their interests and insert my instruction to support their learning as much as I could through our interactions at choice time. I also learned that sometimes a teacher-directed activity is also a child-centered activity, as when we collaboratively told the story about the child and the firefighters. I initiated and implemented these lessons but they were created based on the children's interests. I prepared the ingredients but the children were the chefs. I now see a new cycle for my teaching—planning, observing, and guiding/playing—as *the children guide me* in planning the curriculum.

If Ivy were to carry out this project again, she might consider the following ways to strengthen and extend her project:

1. Read through Michael's project on shadows and consider how she might help the children initiate a project based on one of their interests. She could then "insert" (to use her newfound teaching terminology) teacher-initiated and literacy-based materials and activities within the unfolding of this project. Ivy could then collect the children's drawings, dictations, writings, and dialogues, as Michael did.

2. Create, with the children, an ongoing documentation panel that would show the evolution and transfer of this new mix of child-centered and teacher-directed literacy work and play, again as Michael did in his shadows project.

3. Keep the thread, as she started to in the beginning of her project, of the important role that the environment plays in young children's literacy learning. Over the course of her project, then, she could document the interactions of her three focal children (and other children if she had the time as she taught) in certain areas of the classroom. This would help her understand ways to rearrange, change, and maintain the materials, arrangements, and participation parameters to most effectively promote literacy engagement and interactions.

4. With the assistance of her site director, bring her data to staff meetings to generate a larger dialogue with her colleagues about ways to find a balanced literacy curriculum. Hopefully, this would encourage her colleagues to collect their own data on this focus, which would provide more data from other teachers and other children to

share, discuss, and analyze. This would give Ivy a larger audience of peers to review and respond to her quite comprehensive and broad project.

## Understanding 1st-Grade Writers—
## A Collaborative Project

Susan Kraus (a veteran 1st-grade teacher) and Stacia Stribling (a university-based teacher researcher and former teacher at Susan's school) collaborated on a project on children's writing development in Susan's 1st-grade class-room (Stribling & Kraus, in press). Susan and Stacia collaborated on the project for one school year, as Susan taught the class of 23 first graders and Stacia co-taught 1 day a week for the entire year. This project is an excellent example of the kind of support that a university teacher and researcher can provide in a teacher research project. Susan benefited from an additional teacher (again, this makes good developmental sense for the children and good teaching sense for the teacher researcher) and an "outside" colleague who brought a different pair of eyes and ears to Susan's classroom and their shared research. Stacia benefited, too, by enjoying a close teaching and re-search partnership with a former teaching colleague. Their project culminated in the publication of a jointly written article, and co-presentations at national conferences.

Susan and Stacia pursued their project out of a desire for deeper connections with their children.

> As we reflected on our struggles between what current writing standards demand and what we value as teachers of writing, we came to the realization that we had somehow lost sight of what was important to us as teachers. We wanted to build relationships with our students that allowed us to listen to them, share responsibility for learning with them, and use their insights and needs to guide our instruction. We decided to reconnect with these values through our writing instruction; we focused our research on the writing process of our 1st-grade students.

Their project is an interesting example of teacher research that starts with a concern in one area of education (relationships with children) and then uses another area (writing development) as one window onto that initial concern. Susan and Stacia could have focused on collecting data on their broader re-lationships with the children, but this would have been too general a focus and too loose a research design. Further, they adjusted their research focus over the course of their school year together.

We began in September by asking: What happens when 1st-graders set their own writing goals? By January, we had shifted our focus to look more specifically at the ways in which 1st graders reflect on their writing progress. In early spring, after looking at our interventions and data collection, we realized that all the while we were really concerned with how to improve the content of the students' writing. In the end, our project went beyond the pages on which our students wrote and into the community of learners we created.

This is an excellent example of the dance we undergo between our research focus (where we are going) and our data (what we are looking at). Susan and Stacia's research focus shifted three times over 9 months, as they needed time to discover the best kind of data (content of the children's writing) to illuminate the heart of their research interests (fostering and connecting with a community of learners). They eventually crystallized three main research questions.

- How can we effectively emphasize story content in our writing instruction?
- When we do emphasize content, what emerges within our students' writing?
- What does this journey look like for the students and for us as teachers and teacher researchers?

For data collection, Susan and Stacia relied on their teacher research journals to record the children's behaviors, comments, conversations, and thoughts. They also used the journals to write down their own reflections and interpretations of what they observed of the children's writing development. They also collected, reviewed, and photocopied selections of the children's writings over the course of the year.

Collaboration was an integral component of their data collection and analysis. They debriefed together during lunch and recess, sharing snippets from their observations of the morning writing activities. In these conversations they collaboratively interpreted their observations, which helped push their research and their students' writing forward. Stacia spent the afternoons writing extended reflections on their shared data in her own journal. Susan, as the classroom teacher, wrote down students' exact words and actions as they happened in the classroom. She also took notes during whole-class conversations, recreating the script as it unfolded. Susan and Stacia found that their varied reflective strategies strengthened their collaborative data analysis.

We had different approaches to journaling—Stacia's extensive writing explored the big picture of the children's writing and helpful theories to make sense of the students' writing, versus Susan's detailed description of words and actions as she multitasked her responsibilities as teacher and researcher. But when put together, these approaches provided a rich re-creation of what we experienced and observed and how our thinking unfolded along the way. Later, when we sat down to clearly identify our findings from this research project, we decided to reread our journals in order to get a better sense of our process and highlight patterns. We also went back through the students' writing samples, looking at their development over time as well as comparing the development across students to get a better sense of possible general trends.

By the project's end, Stacia and Susan identified four major factors in the children's writing:

1. There was a disconnect between what the school system wanted students to focus on in their writing and what was natural to them as writers.
2. The researchers had difficulty focusing on the content of students' writing, as they found themselves unconsciously commenting on the way the students' writing looked (conventions).
3. The inconsistencies they saw in children's attention to mechanics was linked to attention to content—as stories gained variety and depth of content, the children's attention to mechanics decreased.
4. Students had complex writing ideas but struggled to make their ideas "look right" because they lacked an understanding of complex writing structures.

Throughout the project, Stacia and Susan struggled to integrate the written language conventions (spelling, punctuation, sentence structure) and the children's writing content. This was a teaching concern or "tension" that in turn became a research concern—they began looking in their data collection and analysis for new ways to make this integration happen. (Interestingly, this is similar to the teaching/research struggle that Ivy Ng underwent in her preschool project on integrating child-centered and teacher-initiated literacy activities).

For example, Susan and Stacia looked at Meredith's writing.

Meredith was a diligent worker who took writing very seriously. When we first met her, she also had a solid grasp of sentence structure. She enjoyed writing stories about herself that were filled with a lot of information. Even so, she stuck with simple sentence structures —naming part followed by action part. For instance, in November she wrote a piece called "My Tonsils Are Out." She wrote, "I got my tonsils taken owt. The let me ceep the mask that put me to sleep. My dad went in with me. He look like a chef." Meredith caught on to our content focus rather quickly and began to incorporate more "story language" into her journal writing.

In December she began using descriptive language and dialogue in her stories. The introduction of these elements in her writing coincided with a decrease in her attention to mechanics. For example, in her "A Cold Christmas Eve," she did not retain her knowledge of punctuation while incorporating new content elements. She wrote, "one could [cold] christmas eve santa and his elf.s wr [were] fleen [filling] the sled with presents lots and lots uv presents eevn no [though] santa is fat and chubby thos reindeer uv his thay can cree [carry] him ok santa sid one uv the elf wus comeing out the door elf ast [asked] santa can I go with you so santa sid yes mreey christmos." We realized from this data that *at this moment* Meredith could not juggle too much developmentally (mechanics and content) as she tried out new content and techniques in her writing. It was as if she sensed that this was a big enough risk to take.

Both Susan and Stacia grew personally and professionally from this collaborative project through their respective backgrounds, interests, and different roles. Susan was pleased with how their collaborative project provided a welcome intellectual dialogue.

Collaborating with Stacia made the project more of a learning process for me. When doing collaborative research, many discussions took place. I wrote notes as the activity occurred, and after mid-day discussions, Stacia wrote the reflections of the day while I taught the afternoon lessons. After school we discussed the day and planned for the next activities. Both Stacia and I have conducted classroom research without a collaborative partner in the room. This is more challenging, because there is not someone to share the immediate questions and "aha" moments with, though the rewards are just as interesting. Our project, like all teacher research, takes time and effort; the days are crazy trying to fit in data collection, but the payoff is worth it when the effort is there.

Stacia welcomed the collaborative opportunity to co-research children's writing, and as a teacher educator she benefited from working with a currently practicing teacher.

> Embarking on this project with Susan was so important to me. Not only did it allow me an opportunity to get back "in the trenches," but gave me the chance to explore an issue that has always been a struggle for me: teaching children to write. . . . My partnership with Susan gave me the courage to critically explore the writing process and take risks as a teacher, researcher, and writer. . . . Together, we were able to construct a new understanding of 1st-grade writers.

If Susan and Stacia were to carry out the project again, they might consider the following modifications:

1. Make it a 2-year project. Another year would give the researchers more time to fine-tune their data collection and analysis, and continue to raise the already high level of their collaboration and interpretation.
2. Invite colleagues to sit in on the classroom writing sessions and also to sit in on the research meetings with Susan and Stacia. The colleagues could be from Susan's and/or Stacia's institutions, and they could offer outside response and feedback on the project. This also would extend the wonderful collaborative nature of their work.
3. Invite the children to serve more fully as co-researchers, keeping track of changes to their writing mechanics and content, and getting them to reflect more deeply as a group on the joys and difficulties of integrating mechanics and content changes in their writing.
4. Use selected theories, ideas, and practices from the pedagogical and theoretical literature on young children's writing to inform their emerging research.

## Multilingualism and Literacy—A Collaborative Project at Multiple ECE Sites

Evangeline Espiritu, Manuel Kichi Wong, Norma Villazana-Price, and I collaborated on a 2-year teacher research project on children's language and literacy learning for 2–5-year-old children (Espiritu, Meier, Villazana-Price, & Wong, 2002). We all knew one another prior to the project and were eager to work together on our first collaborative teacher research project. As Evangeline noted, early childhood educators so often "work in isolation," with little time or opportunity for reflection and inquiry with colleagues. The project was generously funded by a research grant-making institution, the Spencer Foundation, which greatly enhanced the quality and success of our project. I encourage teacher researchers to seek funding for their proposed projects. Outside funding can have a positive impact on the success of teacher research projects by providing funds for materials, books, release time, supplies, readings, conference travel, and data collection equipment.

Writing the proposal for the grant greatly helped us find a helpful structure for our collaborative group. We devised built-in structures for ensuring dialogue and cooperation throughout our project. Since we worked at four different sites, located in two different cities, we needed a clear way to communicate and share our project findings. We initially decided on eight structural components.

> *Component 1: Monthly meetings* We met each month to share and discuss our data and collaboration.
>
> *Component 2: Individual research focus* Evangeline chose the verbal and nonverbal language of toddlers; Manuel chose preschool literacy environment; Norma chose English language learners; Daniel chose the dictation strategies of preschoolers.
>
> *Component 3: Focus children* We each selected two children to focus on specifically.
>
> *Component 4: Fieldnotes* We each wrote and collected notes on our observation and/or participation at our respective sites.
>
> *Component 5: Cross-visits* We intended to carry out two cross-visits to one another's sites each year.
>
> *Component 6: Shared readings* We read selected articles on aspects of children's language and literacy learning pertaining to our project.
>
> *Component 7: Conference presentations* We presented our teacher research work at two conferences.
>
> *Component 8: Project write-up and dissemination* We wrote an article for an early childhood journal about our project's structure and findings.

A few of these components were in place when we started—writing the funding proposal helped us think about them—and we added others as we saw fit as our project progressed. The group also made decisions to change and adapt certain components over the course of the 2-year project, and we ended up finding most of them valuable and useful. The most problematic component turned out to be the cross-visits, which were too difficult to plan and coordinate and demanded too much commuting time.

I highlight two components as most beneficial to our project—monthly meetings and the individual research focus.

*Component 1: Monthly Meetings.* The monthly meetings were central for sharing our individually collected data, asking for help in analyzing the data, and generating new ideas and directions for our project. The long-term nature of our project strengthened our monthly meetings, as we did not have to rush our material and we had a long stretch of time to collaborate and help one another grow as teacher researchers. The meetings were also social gatherings for us, as we strengthened our relationships as researchers, ECE professionals, and friends. Over the course of the project, two of us had newly arrived children, and we shared other life events and experiences. We most often held our meetings at a taqueria that served delicious food, making our meetings that much more enjoyable.

The meetings followed a basic format or series of steps that we refined over the first few meetings.

1. *Meeting facilitation.* I usually planned the meeting agenda and facilitated the meeting from the agenda, which sometimes included notes for some of the items listed below. For example, if we found one particular piece of literature interesting and relevant the month before, I reminded the group of its significance and raised ideas for continuing the discussion and its application to our emerging data.
2. *Individual research update.* Each of us started by reviewing our data collection and analysis over the past month; this helped us articulate out loud where we were in our individual focus and to hear updates from our colleagues about their research progress.
3. *Sharing of data snippet.* Each of us then shared a "data snippet"—an anecdote about the children, a piece of children's art, part of the children's conversation, a small array of photographs of the children at work and play, a sample of the children's writing and dictation—that we thought was interesting and illuminating for our project, and which we also wanted feedback on from the other group members. It was critical that we each had chosen the data snippet carefully and thought ahead of time about its potential significance to our focus and our project as a whole.
4. *Group feedback.* Either all four of us presented and then we did the group feedback, or sometimes we presented our data individually and then received responses. Our responses were designed to applaud our colleagues' data and yet at the same time suggest interpretive ideas and/or data collection/analysis strategies to further strengthen the direction of the research.
5. *Literature.* We discussed any book or article that we either had read on our own or had decided to read as a group. The grant provided us with money to buy books and to photocopy articles. We tried to

relate a particular piece of literature to our data snippets and to use the literature to understand the ongoing value of our data, data collection tools, and data analysis ideas.

6. *Planning.* We closed each meeting with ideas and plans for the next month—what each one of us would collect and analyze, and what we might do differently as a group at our next meeting.

*Component 2: Individual Research Focus.* We decided not to choose one single research focus because (1) our interests varied, (2) our teaching backgrounds were different, and (3) the curricular emphases and our professional roles at our four respective sites varied. Further, the decision to choose our own individual language/literacy focus motivated each of us to participate and invest in this project. Our individual focus was something we already knew about and had a passion for. Early in the project, we recognized one benefit of this variety of topics—we were learning about aspects of children's language and literacy learning that we were not familiar with, and we were learning about it from one another's data and analysis.

*Toddlers' First Words.* Evangeline worked with toddlers at a corporate daycare center. She looked at toddlers' first words and approximations of words to express themselves and communicate with one another and their caregivers. She chose two case study toddlers, Anne and Jake, whom she had known since they were 3 months old. Evangeline worked with her colleagues to collect data on Anne's and Jake's first words. They decided to observe the toddlers at play, during quiet times alone, and as they explored their environment. The caregivers also talked about which kinds of materials and objects to place in the environment. Evangeline found it most useful to collect data through "brief encounters" with the toddlers, since this data collection technique most effectively matched where the toddlers were developmentally (moving quickly and often without notice from one object, action, and person to another).

> For example, when I first began observing Jake, an inquisitive and outgoing child, he had just transitioned comfortably into the toddler room. At first, he said "Hi Da!" when he greeted me in the morning. A few weeks later, it was "Hi Dandin!" From here, his morning greeting progressed to "Hi Dandelin!" Finally, one month later, he greeted me with "Hi Vangelyn!"

To catch these "brief encounters" with toddlers' first words, Evangeline and the other caregivers placed clipboards with data collection sheets in different areas of the room. The clipboards even sparked the children's interest, as they too wanted to write on the boards. So Evangeline added small clipboards around the room for the children to scribble on. She found it a challenge at first to collect data on her fast-moving toddlers and their developmental needs.

> Doing teacher research and promoting reflective practices during the day with toddlers is challenging. Our toddlers could sense when we were not giving them our full attention. Making a conscious effort to carve out time each day to reflect on what we were doing was helpful. We found nap time the best time to gather for discussion and to write up the data we had collected.

The length of our project, 2 years, gave Evangeline the time to work through these particular challenges in collecting data from toddlers. In this instance, this extended time was a great advantage over a more short-term project. It also provided the rest of us with a 2-year developmental span to see and hear how much progress toddlers make in their language growth.

*Second Language Learning.* Norma, a veteran Spanish/English preschool educator, wanted to focus on how her preschoolers learned English. She was particularly interested in finding out if there was any sequence of steps or stages in their English language development, and what her role and the role of peers might be in this process. Norma also collected data on the children's use of Spanish—who spoke Spanish, with whom, where, and how? Norma selected two case study children, Maria and Araceli, whom Norma felt embodied and portrayed behaviors and language patterns she noticed in the majority of her children. Norma collected English and Spanish language data in informal social situations such as initiating play (the casita, outside play yard, block area) as well as during literacy activities such as book reading, storytelling, and dictation. This is similar to Ivy's project, where she collected both child-initiated and teacher-initiated data.

The case study data helped Norma "identify a developmental path for preschoolers as they learn a second language." Norma used an audiocassette recorder to record selected children's conversations and book readings in English and Spanish, took written notes of the children's interactions and language, and collected selected samples of their artwork, dictation, and projects. Norma discovered that a small notepad, kept in a pocket, worked well for her in writing down her observation notes. "When we first began our project, I wondered how I ever would have the time to jot down any notes. But over time, I learned to just put down the essence of an interaction or a conversation in English and/or Spanish." The rest of the group not only learned about children's second language learning from Norma's data, but also learned new ideas for data collection and analysis.

*Literacy Environment.* Manuel, a teacher on special assignment, worked with several preschool teachers to redesign their classroom environments for improved literacy learning. He also selected two case study children, Tammy and Arthur, two children learning English as a second language. Since Manuel's first professional development goal was to involve the teachers in the redesign, his data collection focused first on collaboration with the teachers. He recorded and took notes on his meetings with the individual teachers, focusing on their goals and ideas for the environmental redesign. They chose the classroom areas to change and gave their ideas for new materials and new arrangements.

> Breaking down the goals for the environmental changes was helpful. For example, we thought of specific changes to carry out: select age-appropriate children's books, coordinate small-group reading with the children, and encourage the concept of the teachers as role models for children to copy and emulate. We also established writing centers to support writing activity through a variety of materials, teacher encouragement of children's journals, and the use of clipboards for children to draw and dictate their experiences.

To see how the newly revamped environment helped the children's literacy involvement in one particular classroom, Manuel also collected data on how Tammy and Arthur participated in the new language and literacy centers. For instance, Tammy was a relatively quiet child with a strong interest in books. She became even more interested in books with the new library center, and in looking at the books she began to talk in Chinese and interact more with her peers. The books, then, served as a social "go between" for Tammy and also as a new way to maintain her Chinese socially with peers and expand her English through the books.

*Dictation Strategies.* I looked at the dictation strategies of two case study preschoolers, Larry and Mariella, with whom I worked in my position as part-time literacy teacher. I had worked at this preschool for 2 years before starting our collaborative teacher research project, and my three teacher research colleagues helped me see new dimensions to the children's literacy learning. For instance, Evangeline's data gave me new insights into important developmental links between toddlers' first words and the first dictated words and sentences of my preschoolers. Norma's work on second language learning helped me see the steps and stages that my student Mariella was going through in her dictation and how I could best support her. I also learned, from Manuel's work in redesigning literacy environments, about new books and materials that I could use to strengthen my children's dictation.

The longitudinal span of our project also allowed me to see the children's dictation learning over time. For example, I collected data on Mariella's dictation for 2 years, and in one 6-month span she strengthened her English language knowledge as well as the nature of the dictation task.

*September*—Mariella drew several human figures in her journal. For her dictation, I said several words and phrases in Spanish ("mi papá, mi hermana, dos amigos") that I thought might fit her drawings. Mariella nodded or shook her head for each possible dictated label.

*October*—I dictated, "I love ice cream," and wrote it down for Mariella. I then said, "I love . . . ," and asked Mariella for her favorite flavor. "Mango," she said.

*January*—Mariella dictated "My mommy. My daddy. Diana."

*February*—I asked questions and Mariella answered, and then I wrote down her answers. For example, I asked, "What do you want to be when you grow up?" "I want to be a doctor," she said.

This span shows how Mariella's English comprehension and production grew slowly, and how she and I worked together to scaffold the dictation activity based on what she drew, her English vocabulary, her knowledge of English syntactical constructions, and her personal interests and experiences.

If our group were to carry out the project again, we would consider the following modifications:

1. Rotate the facilitation of the monthly meetings. Each one of us in the group could plan and run the meetings on a rotating basis. This would foster a more diverse agenda and add multiple viewpoints and ideas for coordinating the meetings and the overall direction of our project.
2. Find alternative ways to view one another's sites. Possibly, we could have videotaped portions of our language and literacy activities at our respective sites. This at least would have provided a picture of our classrooms on an ongoing basis.
3. Make increased use of email. We could join an electronic discussion board where we could log in and respond to one another's comments and ideas. This would keep the discussion going between our monthly meetings and not commit us to any additional commute time.
4. Invite other ECE colleagues to join our monthly meetings. This hopefully would inspire these professionals to start their own collaborative teacher research groups, and also provide our small group with

outside feedback and responses on an ongoing basis. Ideally, we would invite educators with professional backgrounds and research interests similar to ours.


THE PROJECTS IN this chapter illustrate excellent ways to design and implement teacher research focused on children's project-based work and the integration of children's language and literacy learning. Depending on how experienced you are as a teacher researcher, and your own particular research interests, you may wish to emulate and modify one or more of these projects. For instance, if you are interested in the relationship between English language development and storytelling, look again at Mary's project. If you are interested in starting or joining a collaborative group, look again at the last project in this chapter.

### Suggested Teacher Research Activities

1. Try out a project as Michael and his children did. See if you can find an opening and a beginning for your project from children's interest in an object, material, or experience, as Michael's children did with one snail. Then proceed slowly, following and yet slightly guiding the children as the scope of the project expands. As the children converse, make drawings, use reference books, read and listen to stories, and participate in other activities in the project, begin your data collection. Try putting the data into folders at the beginning, simply to keep track, in an organized way, of the increasing amount of data. As Michael did, use a variety of tools to collect and analyze the data (e.g., audiotaped recordings of the children's conversations and emerging theories, children's drawings and representations of their found objects, photographs of key incidents and discoveries) and then begin, with the children's help, to mount selected data onto documentation panels. This will allow all of you to revisit the data, while at the same time seeing new directions for your project.

2. As Mary did, consider a teacher research project on storytelling. Again, like Mary, focus on one child, preferably a child learning English as a second or third language. Keep your data collection simple, reading and rereading a stable collection of books and stories, and document your own storytelling strategies and goals, as well as the child's emerging stories. Make sure to date all material so you can, as Mary did, compare and contrast the child's stories over time. You then can look for changes in English language development—

syntax (grammatical order and constructions), phonology (sounds), semantics (word meanings), storytelling style, patterned language, and so on.

3. Extend the storytelling project into a story dramatization project, or pursue only a drama project. As in Sivinee's project, choose only a few children's books to read, share, discuss, and act out with the children. As Sivinee did, track the following in your data collection (you can put this up on a large chart or mural paper in your classroom or wherever you work): children (Who are the children participating in the drama?), roles (Which roles from the stories do they choose?), choice (How do the children choose the roles?), entrance (How do the children enter the drama?), props (Which props do they choose and what is the effect?).

4. Think about ways to look at some of the same kinds of data that Ivy did in her project. For instance, look at a few particular areas of your classroom or ECE setting. Who is playing and working where? With whom? What materials are they using and how? What kinds of literacy learning and engagement are going on? To what extent is this engagement child-centered and child-initiated? Then consider your own role—what are you presently doing to "insert" teacher-directed literacy learning into what the children are already doing? Look at the effectiveness of this kind of instruction. For instance, are you seeing the wonderful kind of transfer that Ivy discovered in her project?

5. As Daniel, Evangeline, Norma, and Manuel did, form a collaborative teacher research group on selected aspects of children's language and literacy. Choose either an on-site collaboration, the easiest and most efficient to start with, or a cross-site collaboration, as I did with my three colleagues. If you choose an on-site collaboration, you may want to focus on one aspect of children's learning, such as the use of oral language to solve interactional conflicts with peers. You can turn this into a cross-age project, too, whereby the toddler teachers and the preschool teachers each collect their own data on their respective children. During the regular joint meetings, the toddler and preschool teachers can share and compare their data on their different age groups. As we did, also try reading articles and/or books related to your topic, and spend some time in your regular meetings discussing the relevance of this material to your project.

# CHAPTER 6

# Forms of Writing About and Disseminating Teacher Research

Dreaming and Gleaming

*I don't think I am a real poet yet,*
*even though I know how to imagine,*
*I still think that radishes should be green,*
*though the sky is blue.*

*Even though I know how to imagine,*
*sometimes my thoughts get confused,*
*though the sky is blue,*
*as a bee distracts me.*

*Sometimes my thoughts get confused,*
*like how the wind turns into a hurricane*
*as a bee distracts me,*
*making me something else.*

*Like how the wind turns into a hurricane*
*I still think that radishes should be green,*
*making me something else.*
*I don't think I am a real poet yet.*

Soñando y Brillando

*Yo no creo que soy una verdadera poeta,*
*aunque puedo imaginar,*

146

*pienso que los rábanos deberían ser verdes,*
*aunque el cielo es azul.*

*Aunque puedo imaginar,*
*a veces mis pensamientos se confunden,*
*aunque el cielo es azul,*
*cuando una abeja me distrae.*

*A veces mis pensamientos se confunden,*
*como el viento se convierte en huracán*
*cuando una abeja me distrae,*
*haciéndome algo diferente.*

*Como el viento se convierte en huracán*
*pienso que los rabanos deberían ser verdes,*
*haciéndome also diferente.*
*Yo no creo que soy una verdadera poeta.*

—Mehrnush Golriz, age 10


## Guiding Questions

1. What are traditional forms of writing in educational research? What are other current ways of using writing to represent teacher research?
2. How can we use narrative and stories to depict and analyze our teacher research?
3. What is the role of poetry in representing our teacher research ideas?
4. What are engaging ways to integrate writing, visuals, and art?
5. What are effective ways to represent our research for dissemination to colleagues and others?

"Sometimes my thoughts get confused/like how the wind turns into a hurricane/as a bee distracts me/making me something else." Mehrnush's observation is a lot like teacher research—we start looking one way in our research, then get sidetracked or a bit lost or find a new direction, and we momentarily seem to lose our "research bearings." And so our research often gets messier rather than neater as we get going. It is often only a bit later, when we sit down and begin ordering and thinking about the meaning of our material and data, that we find our bearings and a direction for our "data gems." In this process of making sense of our data—both as we collect our material and in our later reflections—writing plays a critical role in describing, analyzing, and disseminating our research.

Writing serves as a central way to disseminate our teacher research to multiple audiences at the same time—immediate caregiver and teacher colleagues, supervisors and administrators, children's families, local community members, and other early childhood professionals, researchers, and policymakers in the field. Writing records our research ideas and interpretations both for ourselves and for others, influencing our continuing teacher research and the thinking and research of others. There are a few efforts in the current early childhood field to more broadly disseminate teacher research. One such effort is "Voices of Practitioners," a column in "Beyond the Journal," an online publication of NAEYC (see http://www.journal.naeyc .org/btj/vp/ for examples of teacher research articles). The column publishes the work of early childhood teacher researchers and is particularly interested in original research that informs caregiving and teaching and has implications for the broader field.

## INNOVATIVE WAYS TO WRITE ABOUT TEACHER RESEARCH

Writing about educational research has taken a variety of forms or structures. One of the most long-standing forms involves a five-section or five-chapter format.

1. *Introduction.* What is the focus of your research? What are your research questions? What is your research rationale and the theoretical and research background for your study? How do you propose to find answers to your research questions?
2. *Research Methodology.* What is your study design? Is it qualitative or quantitative? What is your research site and who are the participants? What are your data collection methods? What are your data analysis methods? How valid is your study design and your research tools?
3. *Literature Review.* What does the educational research literature say about your research focus? What is the main body of knowledge on your topic? What do researchers agree on? Is there any disagreement? What are central ideas, issues, theories, patterns in the research literature? Where are the gaps and lack of knowledge and research? How does your study seek to add to this existing body of knowledge on your topic?
4. *Findings.* What are the most interesting and relevant findings from your study? What are the most telling patterns, correlations, discrepancies, trends, factors, strategies, characteristics? What visuals will you use to report your data?

5. *Discussion and Conclusion/Implications.* What are your most interesting findings, and why? How can you link these findings with the
   relevant literature you presented earlier? What do your data confirm
   and/or disprove from the literature? What does your study add in
   terms of new knowledge to the field? Based on your findings, and
   the relevant literature, what are your primary conclusions, and what
   are the implications for your particular area of research?

This format constitutes a strong tradition in educational research that is
widely recognized and accepted as a standard "product" for a research
project. There are variations to this structure, though, that are also effective
and that specifically promote the voices and needs of teacher researchers.

For instance, in working with early childhood teacher researchers at the
university level, Barbara and I have modified the traditional five-chapter
approach. Since the practitioners that we work with take a course on practitioner research as well as a course on narrative inquiry and memoir, their
write-ups incorporate ideas and strategies from these two courses. The practitioner research course emphasizes the idea that teachers are the ones who
know their practice best, and therefore teacher research projects (from data
collection to write-up to dissemination) begin with the day-to-day concerns
and ideas of teacher researchers, rather than gaps or holes in a particular
area of the research literature. The narrative inquiry and memoir course
emphasizes teacher researchers bringing in their memories of critical experiences and events from their personal and professional lives. The course also
highlights the value of narrative and poetry as powerful ways to describe
and interpret our work.

Teacher researchers seeking an expanded toolbox of skills and techniques
for writing up and representing their research can make use of the following:

*Personal Journals and Teaching Notebooks.* A personal journal/diary and
   also a professional teaching notebook or journal chronicle the moments and experiences of a busy work day. Write personal and professional reflections and responses on what you see and hear and
   feel and think as projects get underway and evolve. It is helpful to
   include photographs and other artifacts to enrich the observations,
   thoughts, and reflections. The journal can include more personal
   artifacts, while the teaching notebook includes artifacts from the
   early childhood setting.

   Jessica Fickle, featured in Chapter 4, remarks on the value of ongoing journal writing as a way of reflecting on her inquiry: "I use a
   daily teaching journal to talk to myself, talk myself through my
   projects and teaching, and to see what else I could be doing. I look

at it later, one week later and even one year later. I reread my material to keep myself in check, to make sure that I am doing what I wanted to do with my project and line of inquiry."

*Sketches and Art.* Chapter 2 discussed the important forms and functions of documentation panels as artistic, informative teacher research products and curricular extensions. Art also can be used effectively in other ways. For instance, make simple pencil sketches in teaching notebooks that both represent and help visualize the unfolding data. Keep a separate sketchbook or pad for drawing or using watercolors or other artistic media to represent what you see and observe. These art forms constitute a parallel track of data reflection, response, interpretation, and analysis to use later to complement what is written in words and connected text.

*Use Multiple Sections and Vary the Literature.* Try reconfiguring the traditional five-chapter format into several sections, some longer than others, and choose from an eclectic mix of novels, short stories, drama, expository text, educational research, curriculum materials, narrative, memoir, journalism, and poetry as your literature. In this way, fashion a structure to support your project focus, style of writing, personal experiences and professional life, and voice as a teacher researcher.

In writing up your research, you don't always need to have a "stand-alone" literature review; rather, you can integrate your data, analysis and interpretations, and literature within the *same* sections. While this may seem daunting at first, with practice and a sense of adventure, you can interweave data examples, your ideas and reflections, and relevant theory and practice from varied literature sources.

*Conscious Writing Strategies.* Create an expanding repertoire of writing strategies that you add to over time. Be conscious and deliberate about many of these strategies, and borrow, adapt, and mimic the strategies and techniques you like in what you read. Use these when you write up your teacher research projects. When you begin, you can use these strategies consciously and deliberately, and while this may feel awkward or cumbersome at first, over time they will become more a natural part of your toolbox of writing skills.

*Narratives and Stories.* Use stories to show and reflect upon what was learned over the course of a teacher research project. Just as stories are powerful lenses in working with children, so too do they help us render and relive a scene or an incident with a child, retell the evolution of our thinking and understanding over the course of a project, and encapsulate lessons learned from the research experience. Stories bring the reader into the here and now, into close proximity to children's voices and ideas and feelings, and pull the reader along as the story unfolds toward its conclusion. Teacher researchers note the value of stories for improving their writing:

"I believe that exposure to others' stories has helped me write better. I have become more creative and now I see myself as a storyteller."

"I see myself as a writer who needs to work on my craft. It is frightening to discover how quickly you lose your writing ability. I am excited about continuing on this path and improving my skills through stories."

"I feel like my stories initially come out flat as I try to tell *everything*. The challenge has been choosing what is most significant and stretching that out."

*Memoir and Memories.* Memories are powerful repositories of ideas, experiences, incidents, events, feelings, and thoughts. Memoir helps bridge the personal with the professional, linking the lives of teacher researchers with their children, families, and colleagues. Memoir is a way to relive and retell critical incidents and experiences that might be linked with certain elements of a teacher research project. It also personalizes and individualizes the research process as well as the write-up, enabling us to put our particular stamp on our work. As Jessica Fickle remarks, "It's a big risk to look at myself, but it's valuable for my own learning." Another teacher researcher comments, "I still don't see myself as a writer but I do feel a little more comfortable writing personal and professional memories."

*Poetry.* As early childhood professionals, who listen for children's first words and the sounds of children's early language, we are especially well suited to incorporate poetry into our teacher research. Poetry comes from the senses—the heart and the mind and the soul, as well as the ears and fingers and eyes and mouth. Poetry helps us observe and capture elements of our teacher research with sensitivity and feeling. We also can say things in poetry that we can't say as well in expository prose or even narrative. In poetry, we can come closer to the elemental sounds, rhythms, and movements of our work with children; at the same time, we can use poetry to stand back and render again and again what we are learning and struggling with in our teacher research. Teacher researchers note the value of poetry for improving their writing:

"The poetry writing brought back some of my enthusiasm for writing poems."

"I became more attuned to imagery and emotion and the power of words/language."

"I enjoy writing poetry and see myself continuing to write. Hopefully the more I do, the better I will be as a writer."

"I was surprised and pleased with some of the poems I wrote. A couple conveyed exactly what I wanted but I was frustrated that they didn't all come out as strongly."

## NARRATIVE INQUIRY—THE VALUE FOR TEACHER RESEARCH

In the framework of narrative inquiry (see especially the work of Clandinin & Connelly, 2000), which I draw on in the following discussion of its application to teacher research in early childhood, practitioners are seen as the knowledgeable "insider" experts on practice. Knowledge of what we do, whether it involves teaching reading or building a sense of community, owes a great deal to our practical knowledge as professionals working with children on a daily basis. This knowledge of practice also lends itself to reflection and inquiry, and one valuable way to do this is through narrative. Narrative is both a way of experiencing the world and a way of understanding and improving our work. We grow, then, as individuals and as professionals through the stories we live, experience, relate, tell, listen to, and write. Narrative helps us go beyond what may appear uninteresting or what does not stand out for us as practitioners; it helps us uncover underlying factors, ideas, feelings, characteristics, events, and experiences that influence how and why children act, think, and feel. As Ivy Ng, the preschool teacher researcher, put it, "When we collect and analyze data, we're telling stories. When we think about the topic of research, we're narrating events and problems that make us want to study and find solutions."

Narrative inquiry is a framework about the forms and functions of narrative in educational research and practice. Based in particular on the ideas of Clandinin and Connelly (2000), it can be seen as having two main aspects of direction for our teacher research: inward/outward and forward/backward. In the inward/outward relationship, the inward direction relates to our inner feelings and thoughts as practitioners, while the outward direction connects with our environment. In forward/backward, forward relates to our future lives, while backward connects to events and experiences in our past lives. In other words, when we teach and work with children, we experience this inward/outward and forward/backward direction—we think and feel *as* we experience events and experiences in our environment with children, and we do so consciously and subconsciously in connection with where we've come from and where we want to go as individuals and as professionals.

By collecting narratives of children at work and play, writing our own stories about the children, writing stories about ourselves, and in general utilizing narrative forms in writing up our teacher research, we can bring a new sophistication of understanding to our work. By going forward and backward and inward and outward through narrative (in our project design, data collection, data analysis, and writing and representation), we add dimensions of time and experience and knowledge to our evolving use of teacher research that strengthens our conceptual understanding and teaching practice.

Narrative inquiry also emphasizes different kinds of texts for reflective practitioners—field texts, interim texts, and research texts (Clandinin & Connelly, 2000). Field texts are the raw data closest to what we hear, see, and feel with children and adults with whom we work. This material might include children's dictations, oral stories, our conversations with children, artwork, dialogue in the playhouse, block constructions, or painted pictures. This is the basic stuff or artifacts of children's work, play, and socializing. Interim texts are texts that are a bit more removed from the action of the classroom or early childhood setting. These may include our reflections and observations in our notebooks or journals, conversations with colleagues, ideas and thoughts that we write down on scraps of paper, or photographs we take of the children and then attach a description or reflection to. Last, research texts are more formal oral, written, and electronic texts where we state, describe, and reflect on what we collected and what we've thought about and pondered. The research texts are those most likely to be shared with colleagues and disseminated.

Lukas Frei, a Head Start preschool teacher, carried out a teacher research project on the value of interactive reading for English learners (Frei, 2004). His project made use of field, interim, and research texts.

Field Text (excerpt from his fieldnotes)

Scene: 10/5, 10:00 a.m., on the rug area. Lukas is reading *New Shoes, Red Shoes* with two children, Parris (native English speaker) and Jennifer (English learner). The book is on Lukas's lap between the two children. The children then proceed to "read" (from memory and also repeating Lukas when he reads) the text. Parris first reads some text and puts her fingers on the correct words. Jennifer joins in and turns a page. Parris suggests that they take turns.

*PARRIS:* If I get two she (Jennifer) got to get two [pages]. If I get two she got to get two. (starts to read and then lets Jennifer read as it is her turn; Jennifer moves her finger along the words but does not actually say anything until she sees the pictures of the shoes)

*JENNIFER:* Purple, black, green, red (as she points to each shoe). You read this side (the left-side pages) and I'll read this (the right-side).

*PARRIS:* (disagreeing) I thought you were my friend. (She leaves. Jennifer then points to the text for Lukas to read, and she runs her fingers over the words as he reads to the end of the book. Parris then returns with a different book to read.)

## Interim Text (excerpt from his data free-write)

In this transcript, I am reading a book with Parris (native English speaker) and Jennifer (English learner), and each child is sitting beside me on a chair with the book on my lap. Parris initiates the turn-taking routine, stating, "If I get two she got to get two." In this way, Parris sets the rules for interactive story reading, rules that she has acquired over previous experiences, both with book reading and peer interaction. Parris views the activity as a collective activity, not something to do alone. She recognizes the value of social interaction in story reading.

Parris is good at following the text with her finger as the text is read aloud. She can remember the text phrases and "reread" it for herself by verbalizing the memorized text and running her finger over the words. She can't actually read the text phonetically, but she uses the strategy of imitation and memorization as a way to experience reading for herself the way she observes adults around her do.

## Research Text (excerpt from his final write-up)

When I was able to ask challenging questions that allowed Sherryl (another child) to produce thought-provoking responses, Sherryl would co-construct the knowledge with me. In my reading sessions with Parris and Jennifer, I read the text for Parris who would "read" it back for Jennifer. My role as the teacher was different with Parris and Jennifer together than with Sherryl alone. While I provided an important role for Parris and Jennifer as a mediator between the two during their turn-taking negotiations for the book *New Shoes, Red Shoes*, in retrospect I would have liked to have created and fostered more in-depth discussion as I did with Sherryl. This is definitely an area for me to grow in as a teacher and as a facilitator of discussion in the context of story readings. Gambrell and Mazzoni (1999) say that

English learners like Jennifer, who are in the beginning phase of their English language development, need to listen and talk about storybook pictures more than to read or imitate the actual text. This is because literacy development builds on language development, and so a solid oral language foundation needs to be created before venturing too deep into highly specific literacy skills. This foundation is built within the social interactions that require oral communication to exchange information and co-construct meaning. In this way, prior knowledge acts as a pillar for language growth.

Lukas's field text is an example of data captured directly from his classroom. Recorded on an audiocassette recorder, it's an immediate record of a small reading scene with two of his students. All he has to do is play it back, and Lukas can re-enact what happened. These data then become a more complete field text when Lukas transcribes them and puts them down on paper.

In turn, Lukas's interim text takes us a further step away from the raw data of the field text and begins a process of reflection and inquiry about what is going on in his data. He composed the interim text as a data freewrite, not doing any prethinking or preorganizing, but simply writing down his thoughts, observations, and reflections on the data captured in the field text.

Lukas's research text is his final and most formal representation of his field and interim texts. He integrates only essential and the most telling aspects of his field text and interim text into a cohesive and extended discussion. Lukas is able to compose his final write-up by relying on the richness of his already created field texts and interim texts; in effect, much of his observation and reflection has already been done. This frees Lukas to concentrate on integrating the two—the data and the reflections—and to add in relevant literature as he sees fit to support and extend his discussion. This circular movement of writing—from field to interim to research text, and back again—enriches the depth and breadth of writing about our teacher research.

## INTEGRATING POETRY, MEMOIR, AND STORIES

Poetry lends itself to writing down our smallest observations, moments, images, feelings, thoughts, and reflections. A poem easily fits into a pocket. Poems in teacher research may be used as analysis and reflection along the way in a project, or end up as part of a "finished" product like a documentation panel or an article. Poetry fits the essence of the early childhood world—young children's sensory experiences, small discoveries, powerful feelings, small insights and revelations. Poems also can be helpful for teachers whose first language is not English, allowing them more freedom to write without worrying too much about English syntax and expository text organization.

Alvina Cheah, a teaching assistant at a Jewish preschool, has research interests in examining her personal cultural and ethnic identity, which helps her understand and appreciate the identities of her children. In one project, Alvina found poetry a helpful way to capture her memories of growing up as a bicultural person and to link it to her evolving identity (Cheah, 2005).

### On the Question of Race

They ask me to write
down my race
And I think and think very seriously
and consider
writing down the truth
and have my answer read
I have a woman with dark hair
cooking over a hot stove
and humming an unknown tune
I have a man who tries to get me
to speak the language I once knew
I have a girl whose looks resemble me
her hair is dark brown as are her eyes
Inside of me.
I have a Pwa Pwa and Gon Gon
who drink tea and watch old movies that
feature flying monkeys and men with wigs
. . .
I have a small jade lion
facing the front door
so that no evil will enter
the house
I have people gathered around the table
eating rice from a bowl
using chopsticks
I have superstitions
in which the dragon is the most
fierce and powerful creature in the world
Inside of me.

. . .
I have movie heroes such as Bruce Lee and Jackie Chan
and legendary heroes like Mulan
I have many dialects,
Toisan, Cantonese, and Mandarin
Inside of me.
But I stop and simply write down
Chinese.

Alvina reflected on this and her other poems on culture and identity.

> I still don't really know culturally who I am or where I belong. Every
> time I begin to feel comfortable with either culture, something pulls
> me back to a sense of displacement. Like me, many second-generation
> Asian children are faced with the complicated issue of discovering
> who they are through the conflicting viewpoints of both cultures.
> Working in ECE and facing the struggles as well as reaping the
> benefits of growing up bicultural, I think it is very important for my
> preschoolers to learn at a young age about their different cultures and
> those of their peers. This will help influence the ways that my children
> form their self-concept.

Poetry helped Alvina express and communicate her internal reflections on
her bicultural identity with passion and conviction. This kind of poetic writing, over time, will enrich her other writing on her teacher research as it
develops a strong sense of voice and style.

Poetry also can be integrated with stories. Nathan Weber, a teacher of
toddlers at a private urban preschool, has research interests in how our personal and cultural roots influence our teaching philosophies and work with
children. In one set of stories and poems, Nathan explored how the environment of his early upbringing influenced his identity and educational philosophy as a preschool teacher (Weber, 2005)

Desert Trailhead

Our preschool would meet
at the trailhead.
Walking the worn narrow path.
Our lives intersecting
with cacti, creosote, desert sage.
Life of 4 year olds.
A desert inspection.

Plaques, etched with names,
very important names of
plants and trees.
Repeated. Walks. Repeated.
Exploring our world.
I could take you there
Today.
My bones know the way.
They could carry us back
across sand mountains that
whisper secrets about
sage scent winds.
I know my mind nests
quiet, desert-like.
hatchlings emerging
from incubated experiences
of where I grew up.

## The Story of Roh Shelduck and the
## Family Anatidae Tadorna Cristata (an excerpt)

*We almost forgot how we got to the desert, but Roh Shelduck used
the stars to write out a story.*

Our story begins on a pond in the Mojave Desert, California. You
may be asking yourself, "A pond in the desert?" Let me tell you
reader, there are many things in the desert that may seem unbeliev-
able. For example, in Death Valley, where temperatures reach 130
degrees Fahrenheit, lives the Devil's Hole Pupfish. It's a fish that
adapts itself to the most desolate and unforgiving environment and
has survived for 20,000 years. It withstands waters up to 112 degrees
Fahrenheit. So when I tell you our story begins on a pond in the
Mojave Desert, believe me when I tell you a family of shelducks lives
on the pond.

Roh, his sister, Tae, and their mother made a home on the north
end of the pond. They were a small part of the Shelduck family.
Surrounding the pond were over 100 families. They were content
living on their little desert oasis.

Now, a shelduck is like a duck, but is considered to be a type of
goose. So, Roh and his family were not the color of rubber ducks, or
of colorful Mallard ducks. They were the color of dry grass after a
desert heat wave: they were brown. Some said it was to fool Coyote.

Sometimes Roh even lost his own sister, Tae, in the desert camou-
flage. Roh heard the story, from his mother, about why they were
brown.

Nathan used poetry and stories as a new lens for reseeing and rehearing
important influences on his upbringing in the desert. He discovered through
this new kind of writing that the desert had a powerful influence on his personal identity, which in turn revealed to him the importance of the environment for his preschool teaching.

> I noticed that all my stories and poems came back to my early
> memories and how they related to the desert. I did hours of research
> for "The Story of Roh Shelduck," and tried to emulate mythological
> stories I had heard before. The story is meant to illustrate how, as a
> child, I imagined I got to my birthplace in the desert. I learned that
> poems and stories can bring larger issues into our relationship with
> readers. Memoir can give us an entry point into a conceptual
> question or research question. For example, my stories and poems
> based on my memories examine how certain environments can aid
> learning and our understanding of the world. They also show us
> how children's relationship with nature affects how they understand
> the world.

As Nathan reflects, poems and stories (whether fictitious or "real" or a mix-
ture of both) "bring larger issues into our relationship with readers." Poetry and narrative, then, broaden and deepen the power of our teacher
research—and the voices behind our research and thinking—for others who
form a larger audience. They help readers and listeners to pay attention
more closely, to open our ears and eyes wider to hear and see what we
describe and reflect on.

## USING STORIES, PHOTOGRAPHS, AND ARTWORK

Teacher research products also can integrate stories, photographs, and
artwork. These can be done via documentation panels, as presented in Chapter 2, and also in articles, papers, curriculum materials, multimedia, journals, and informal classroom and school displays. While this integration of
data can become more involved and a lengthier process than using only text,
it can produce aesthetically pleasing products that catch the eye and make
us want to "read" on.

## Binational Immigrant Families

Connie Jubb, a veteran English/Spanish primary grade teacher, is interested in the binational experiences of her children's families living both in the United States and Mexico. Aided by several small grants and a sabbatical from her school district, Connie made two extended trips to the rural pueblos of Mexico to meet and talk with families of her students. She also recorded stories of families in the U.S. city in which she works. Connie wanted to hear their stories of family life in Mexico and the United States—what families did together, their work, their experiences—and also to talk with family members about their cultural, familial, and immigrant experiences and perspectives. Connie produced several books (in English and Spanish) that integrated the families' stories, child and adult art, and photographs. The books were for teachers to use as curriculum materials. Connie notes, "In the thirty years that I have been teaching in bilingual schools, I have seen very few books that address the experiences of my students and their families living in two countries and two cultures. I wanted to find a way to write down these family histories and make them into books for use in the classroom."

Each of Connie's books is told from the point of view of a child in a family. For instance, *My Little Ranch in Mexico* (Jubb, 2003) is told from Uriel's perspective and voice, and he begins by introducing himself and his family.

> My name is Uriel and I am 7 years old. I live in a small apartment in a big city and even so I have a burro! Of course, I've only seen my burro in photos because it lives in Mexico with my grandparents. I've never been to the village but one day I plan to go there to see what it's like. Fortunately, I know my grandparents because they come to visit us here in Berkeley, California. My grandpa, Papa Juan, is really funny. When my brother and I come home from playing soccer and we tell him that we won the game he always says, "That couldn't be true because I didn't see it!"

Connie also added in information from stories told by other family members and put it in the book as told from the child's perspective. For example, Chapter 5, "How My Mother Taught My Grandfather to Read," is told from Uriel's point of view (even though he didn't originally tell the story).

> When my mother was 16 years old she signed up to become an adult literacy teacher in the village. The National Adult Education Institute organized the program. My grandfather remembers: "Gelo taught me how to read a little. Every day she would leave me my homework and

every evening I would show her—Look, I finished my homework! She would show me pictures of animals, like a burro, and I would read its name written underneath.

Connie arranged each book into several chapters that captured important elements and experiences of the families' life on both sides of the border, and which she knew children would be interested in. For instance, the chapters in Uriel's *My Little Ranch in Mexico* are: Chapter 1, "Uriel"; Chapter 2, "Papa Juan's Life"; Chapter 3, "My Grandparents Went Through Hard Times"; Chapter 4, "My Mom, the Cowgirl"; Chapter 5, "How My Mother Taught My Grandfather to Read"; and Chapter 6, "We Have Dreams for the Future."

Connie did not audiotape the conversations with the families or their stories; she did not want to take the time to learn how to use the tape recorder unobtrusively. Instead, she relied on writing down the material in notebooks. Connie recorded the families' stories directly in front of the family members, seated in their kitchen or living room, and often stopped as she wrote to ask clarifying questions. She did not prepare a set of questions for each family ahead of time.

> But I did think ahead of time about which questions I wanted to ask. As each interview started, each one took its own course; you realize when you do this, that you just scratch the surface, there are so many stories that these families have to tell. For example, in the first pueblo I went to, I visited four families. I called one family ahead of time. I got off the bus and the family was waiting for me. They wanted to feed me, it was around 9 p.m., and then the father just started in telling stories. He told me the history of the town and the family. I didn't have time to think; I just got my notebooks out and started writing down what he said as best I could.

After taking down the families' stories, Connie typed them up and also edited the language for clarity. On her second trip to Mexico, she took the typed versions back to the families and read them out loud. They then made the edits together. She asked the families, "Is this right?" "Does this belong?" "Anything else to add?" Sometimes, the families here in the United States didn't know about all of their parents' experiences in Mexico, so the grandparents would add in the missing information and events for them. Connie remembers that one family was so excited to add more information to their stories as they drove Connie back to the airport. "It was amazing how much they wanted to add," Connie recounts, "and I scribbled it all down while I was in the car."

After Connie asked the families on both sides of the border to edit the typed versions, she asked a bilingual editor friend to read through and make editing suggestions for all the stories. Her friend checked for accuracy in Spanish vocabulary, usage, and syntax. She also edited the stories, making them all shorter and more focused. Connie deleted some material and re-wrote certain sections, and feels that the editing greatly improved the accuracy and quality of the final books. Connie also translated two of the books into English on her own.

When Connie first envisioned the project, she thought the final products would be simple photocopies of the typed stories of the families. In the end, though, they became beautiful books pleasing to the eye, well-made to last, and integrated text, art, and photographs. For example, Figure 6.1 shows a page from *My Little Ranch in Mexico*.

A graphic artist friend of Connie's offered to do the layout for the books at a greatly reduced cost, and he arranged the material so that text, art, and photographs were well laid out and balanced. He also suggested that the children add paintings to the books, and so Connie asked several children to do paste paintings that eventually were added to the book. At least one parent also added her own drawings. "She wanted to revisit her childhood," Connie remembers, "and so she herself wanted to do the drawings for *My Little Ranch in Mexico*." As for the photographs, Connie took most of them (with a conventional camera, which was easier for her), and the families gave some photographs to Connie to use. The final books were professionally produced at a printer on high-quality paper, which Connie paid for through a small grant. She printed 35 copies of each of the seven books. In addition, Connie made an iMovie of her visits with the families in Mexico and gave each U.S. family a copy on a CD-ROM. Connie, aided by the technology teacher in her school district, added a soundtrack of ranchero music.

Connie has since used the books in her classroom, and other teachers also have used the books as curriculum materials. Connie found the project an invaluable experience that strengthened her identity as a reflective practitioner and extended her relationships with her children and their families.

> The project was a form of reflection, and has informed my work incredibly. When I now ask my parents where they are from, I feel such a strong connection with the families. I can now talk about a particular pueblo in Mexico. It helps me make connections every day with children and families. It has also helped me engage in a whole new kind of conversation with families beyond just how their child is doing in school. Doing this kind of project, involving oral histories, you have to establish trust and learn to ask questions that get more information and good stories. After a while, the people just came to

**Figure 6.1.** A page from *My Little Ranch in Mexico*.

always came in their best clothes, freshly bathed and with a pencil in their hand, ready to learn.

My mom felt proud of her students, like her own father, when they were able to read an entertaining story for the first time. My mom says that my grandfather was a good student because at times he corrected her math!

There was one older woman student, my mom recalls, who was very excited one day because she had written her fist letter! The letter was written to the governor of Jalisco, the state where Atemajac is located, thanking him for the adult literacy program in the villages. The woman wanted my mom to check her letter to make sure everything was correct. She was thrilled because she had written an entire page.

My mom remembers that everyone was very proud when they received their first diploma. "This is a time when you say to yourself, I have done something beautiful for the world," my mother told me.

me and told me stories. It became a two-way exchange that honored their experiences. We were sharing their experiences and sharing the commonality of the children that I teach. The experiences of these immigrant children, who are living as transnationals, are universal to many immigrant groups. We as teachers need to become more aware of our families' life experiences.

To further strengthen the project, Connie now sees several components to change:

- Take a third trip to Mexico to personally hand the families the final published books
- Do more editing on the text for greater clarity and succinctness
- Revisit certain stories and find out more information
- Rewrite the text to make it easier for younger children to read it
- Rewrite some stories to make into little guiding reading books for young children to read on their own
- Give monetary compensation to everyone who helped with the project

Several factors contributed to the high quality of the content and presentation in Connie's published books: long-term commitment to story collection and reflection, a careful editing process, enlisting others in the editing process, engaging the help of a graphic artist for layout and design, professional printing of the final product, and funding to pay for some of these services.

## Forming Bonds of Trust with Children

Jessica Fickle, highlighted in Chapter 4 for her project on toddler language, carried out another project on her children's attachment (Fickle, 2003). She collected and analyzed data from her teaching notebooks (4 years' worth) and from classroom observations (6 months' worth). Like Connie's books, Jessica's final product integrates expository text, entries from her teaching journal, personal and professional stories, poetry, art, and photographs. Jessica's writing during her data collection helped her compose her final product.

> I used a reflective journal to record my teaching day, and these recorded thoughts, plans, ideas, and events (both good, not so good, and in between) helped me "see" the day in a different light. I also was relieved and delighted to use poetry and drawings, all of which allowed me to question the events of the day in a thoughtful way. This appealed to me because I have difficulty writing down my ideas. This new way of writing allowed me more freedom to record and think about my day. The poetry also reflected my personal "voice." I could be an artist, a teacher, *and* a researcher.

Jessica also learned to see the value of stories as an overall way to frame and organize the poetry, drawings, and photographs from her project.

> I realized that I could express my thoughts about teaching in a
> personal way through stories. I began to practice my writing. My
> voice became stronger. I began to write story after story about the
> children in my class. I wanted my voice to be strong and interesting,
> and to express the importance of the teacher–child bond of trust. Each
> new story brought a new voice, a new passion, and new confidence in
> my writing.

Jessica organized her final written product into two main sections: personal
experiences and professional experiences. Both sections consist of Jessica's
journal entries, stories, poems, photographs, and her own drawings and
paintings. This was the real strength of her final product.

Jessica's photographs expanded her artistic talents and, like the art and
photographs in Connie's published books, made her final product a more
pleasing and sophisticated artifact of her inquiry and research.

> It is very hard for me to express my joy and love of teaching only in
> words. So I also took photographs for this project, as I always do
> anyway in the course of my teaching. I wait for the moment, a
> moment that my heart says, "There is that child." When I take
> photographs, write poetry, or paint as part of my projects, I have my
> heart in my hand and I use it in the process of creating something. I
> am an artist and the artist in me affects my teaching and my reflective
> work as a teacher researcher. Photography represents life and teach-
> ing, and I use these works of art to teach and learn both about the
> children and about myself.

Jessica emphasized the capturing of small moments with her children that
each told a story about trust and attachment.

> Each moment captures a different story. Sometimes these moments
> happened over and over again, like when Stanley put his shoes next to
> mine. Sometimes these same moments changed a little and sometimes
> I questioned the outcome of the moment. For example, one day
> Stanley was not listening to me during nap. He was upset because he
> could not go outside . . . he started to throw his blanket. . . . I asked,
> "Stanley, do you want me to move my shoes away from yours?"
> Stanley put down his arms and just looked at me. "No," he said
> quietly. "Well, then you need to listen to me. Put your mat back
> together and lie down." Stanley put his mat back together and lay
> down. After a few minutes I invited him back to his regular nap spot.
> While I lay on the floor next to Stanley, I wondered if I had stepped

over some line with what I had said. This moment had belonged to Stanley. . . . Each child wants to have a moment with me and me alone; each child deserves this time. When creating a place for children to explore such a moment, I create another layer of attachment.

Jessica used photographs to convey her children's attachment to beloved objects and activities in her classroom that fostered a sense of attachment, safety, and trust. Figure 6.2 shows an artistic photograph of a child at work on a puzzle. Rather than just a label, such as "Robin working on puzzle," Jessica wrote a poem from a child's point of view to add text to the photograph.

**Figure 6.2.** Jessica's poem/photograph.

---

*A Foundation of Trust*

With one layer I have something to hold when I am scared.
With two layers I have something to hide under when I am playing.
With three layers I have something to build when I am learning.
With four layers I have a something to pull on when I fall down.
With five layers I have something I can create to give to others.
And with all the layers I have a place to stand
when I am scared, playing, learning, creating, and giving.

The effect on the reader of the poem/photograph is like the experience of reading a good children's picture book, where text and picture tell different parts of the same story. They invite the reader to pay attention more deeply, pulling us in to listen to the child and marvel at her concentration and sense of comfort in this "frozen moment." Although only a short poem and a single photograph, it hints at Jessica's larger story of attachment and trust in her classroom, and ties us to the other text, photographs, and art in her final teacher research product.

## USING AUDIT TRAILS AS ANALYTICAL GRAPHICS

Pat Sullivan (2005), a veteran teacher of toddlers and preschoolers in her home childcare setting, carried out a teacher research project on critical literacy. This focus was an important part of Pat's curriculum and personal and professional commitment to social justice and activism. She was particularly interested in using audit trails (Vasquez, 2004) to strengthen her teacher research skills and knowledge of critical literacy.

Pat's project initially emerged from the children's interest in a U.S. presidential election.

> My house was a polling place for the last presidential election. I saw it as an opportunity for the children in my care to witness the voting process. What I had not anticipated, however, was the aftermath of the election when our predominately democratic population watched in disappointment as Bush was re-elected. Disappointment soon grew to fear when several of the children's families were faced with financial hardships due to federal funding cuts. As the war news got worse and more and more families were worried about another 4 years of Bush, the children in my care began to talk about what their parents were saying, and how the election affected their families.

Pat and her co-teacher audiotaped the children's conversations and then met to discuss how conversations, books, field trips, and activities could extend the children's interests and learning. One recording captured the children's understanding of the connections between the election and such social issues as race relations and power.

> *Scene*: 11/29/04. Tasha (co-teacher), Matthew (high school volunteer, Black/Italian, age 16), Ohana Shawnee, (age 4), and Jerusha (African/Hawaiian, age 4) are playing with doctor kits and performing medical

attention on the Care Bears. They spontaneously start talking about President Bush.

*OHANA:* My mom hates Bush.

*MATTHEW:* My mom doesn't like him too much either.

*JERUSHA:* Bush is a bad man. He doesn't like Brown people. I don't want him to be President.

*OHANA:* Kerry won.

*MATTHEW:* No, Kerry lost, Bush is still our president.

*OHANA:* He's a bad man. He needs to go to jail.

*JERUSHA:* I'm afraid of him. He wants to hurt the Brown people. I don't want to be Brown anymore.

*TASHA:* (teacher) I like being Brown and just because Bush doesn't like Brown people that doesn't mean I still can't like being Brown. You are a very pretty color brown. I like that we both are Brown together. I don't care if Bush doesn't like me. Do you like me?

*JERUSHA:* I like you.

*OHANA:* I like you too! I'm a pretty brown too!

*MATTHEW:* We don't care that Bush doesn't like us. We like each other!

The children continued this conversation over time, and Pat observed that both Jerusha and Ohana were afraid that Bush could hear them when they talked about him and would arrest them and send them to Iraq to be killed in the war. So Pat asked the children if they wanted to write to President Bush to discuss their fears. Jerusha told her a long story about how the president would trace the letter back to her and Ohana and send them to Iraq. The teachers thought it important for the children to become proactive rather than helpless and afraid, so they decided to write President Bush, but to send the letter from a post office not near the house and without signing their names. Jerusha and Ohana dictated the letter to Pat.

Dear President Bush,
    We want you to care for all the people, Black people, White people, grandmas, and everyone who needs help. We think everyone in the world should have a home and family that loves them. Nobody should be hungry and people should give them food. We want you to send the troops back to their homes.

In writing up this critical literacy project, and reporting on the children's conversations and this letter, Pat found it helpful to use the idea of an audit trail (Vasquez, 2004). An audit trail is a "public display of artifacts gathered by researchers that represents their thinking. An audit trail is meant to be visible not only to the people in a classroom community but others in the school community as well" (p. 3). The audit trail not only helped Pat reconstruct the events and discussions that she and her children engaged in, but allowed her to reflect on the power of critical literacy to transform children's thinking and action. Table 6.1 shows the first audit trail that captures the early stages of the children's critical literacy work.

Pat noticed that the children's interest in the president and themselves as children of color was connected with the children's developmental understanding of family identity and race. After examining her data on the children's conversations about bi/multiracial identity (such as what they liked and didn't like about their skin color and their hair), Pat created the Family Identity Audit Trail, as shown in Table 6.2.

The children's conversations with the teachers about the president, the treatment of people of color, and bi/multiracial children and identity sparked further discussion on who's American and who's not.

**Table 6.1.** President Bush Audit Trail Chart

| Issue(s) | Context | Curricular Engagements | Action(s) | Other Issues Generated |
|---|---|---|---|---|
| Bush is a scary president because he doesn't support the things low-income and Brown people need from their government | Bush administration is cutting federal funding for education, medical coverage for the poor and elderly, and forcing schools to close in low-income neighborhoods | Letter writing<br><br>Research on government at the federal, state, and local level<br><br>Research on the next election(s) | Letter to Bush, Pelosi, Feinstein, Newsom, and the school board urging that they protect the interests of children in school and their families, no matter what color they are<br><br>Letters to parents urging them to vote for candidates that will support children and the things that they need | Racism in America<br><br>Brown people are not real Americans |

**Table 6.2.** Family Identity Audit Trail Chart

| Issue(s) | Context | Curricular Engagements | Action(s) | Other Issues Generated |
|---|---|---|---|---|
| Biracial children and the problems of not looking like the parent they live with | Most of the children are biracial and are beginning to see the differences between themselves and their parents | Geography—using a globe and a map of the world<br><br>Research on the meaning of "family" | Pinpointed countries of origin for all the children<br><br>Developed family trees to show connections | Hair and hair care for African-American hair<br><br>Learning some Japanese, Spanish, Tagalog, and Shawnee words |

JULES: (to Jerusha) You're very dark.
JERUSHA: But I'm still a girl.
JULES: I'm an American.
PAT: Jerusha is an American, too.
JULES: But I'm all American.
JERUSHA: My dad is from Africa.

Table 6.3 shows the third audit trail that Pat created, on the children's interest in race and what it means to be American.

The audit trails helped Pat separate out key themes from the children's work on critical literacy (President Bush, race and identity, and what it means

**Table 6.3.** Who Is an American? Audit Trail Chart

| Issue(s) | Context | Curricular Engagements | Action(s) | Other Issues Generated |
|---|---|---|---|---|
| Who are Americans? | White people are real Americans and the rest have other countries they can go back to. | History of America<br><br>Development of a timeline<br><br>Define American citizenship | Read and watch movies about the history of America<br><br>Make a timeline that shows the events leading to now<br><br>Posters—I Am an American | Why don't White people have to call themselves White Americans? |

to be American). The audit trails also helped Pat see connections between her data (the children's conversations), the social and educational context, the curricular ideas, curricular activities, and issues for further study. The audit trails linked her most important and interesting data, displayed this information in organized visuals, provided graphics easily displayed in her home caregiver site, and effectively integrated the important data into her project write-up.

In writing intended primarily for ourselves—in our personal journal and professional notebooks—we explore the hows and the whys of our teacher research. This is like our prep work in the kitchen. The finished meal, ready to be served to guests, is the final write-up or other form of representation that serves as both closure and extension of our teacher research. It both affirms our voices and passion and extends our thinking and reflections for a wider audience of colleagues, researchers, parents, and policymakers. It is our public record and contribution to educational research and practitioner knowledge. From narratives to poems to art to photographs to audit trails, writing and other forms of artistic representation are critical for understanding our data and disseminating our teacher research.

### Suggested Teacher Research Activities

1. Reread the above section on Lukas's use of field texts, interim texts, and research texts in his project. As you undertake your own teacher research project, use this strategy to collect and analyze and write up your findings. For example, as Lukas did, record a short snippet of children's conversation and then transcribe it. Then, put the data "under your pillow," and later on look at it and do a free-write about it. Take no more than 15 minutes to write about the transcript—what you see, what it might mean to you and the children, how it fits into the focus of your project—and try to write without stopping and worrying about order and organization. Later on, when it comes time to write up your project more formally, then return to this data free-write (and others you do, too) and integrate it into your write-up. Try adding a reference to educational literature, as shown in the example from Lukas.

2. For practice at narrative and memoir thinking and writing, read sections or all of Vivian Paley's *Wally's Stories* (1981), and then look at pages 148–153. Look carefully at the dialogue, what the children say and what they believe, and also how Paley recasts this dialogue and presents it to us. The children are talking about Valentine's Day, what it is, and what it means to them. Write a short "reaction free-write"

about one of your childhood beliefs (Valentine's Day, the tooth fairy, Santa Claus, the moon or the sun, where babies come from, God, and so on). Write down your memory—What is it? What did you believe and feel? Then let this free-write of associated memories sit for a while, and later on turn it into a short story with characters, plot, setting, and so on. You can, of course, embellish and fictionalize your memories as you wish. Then conclude with a paragraph in which you reflect on the value of memory writing and story writing for observing and recording your memories of teaching.

3. Read parts or all of Susan Goldsmith Wooldridge's *Poemcrazy*, and then look at p. 11. Write a poem of a "pile of dozens of words," just as she does in the book, about a certain place or part of your early childhood environment. Consider some place that is special and that has had an influence on your educational philosophy, curriculum, way of relating to children, way of doing teacher research, and so on. Sit and observe the place first and then just start a free-poem or free pile of dozens of words that come to mind from your observation. Let the poem sit "under your pillow." Then later on reread it several times and circle those key words that indicate the positive power and influence of this special place. Then turn the poem over and write a paragraph reflection on how you might transfer some of these qualities to other areas of your environment.

4. Create an audit trail chart for your teacher research project, as Pat did in this chapter. Write "Issue(s), Context, Curricular Engagements, Action(s), and Other Issues Generated" across the top of your chart. Then as you collect data in your project, and begin to find important issues and topics you want to better understand, you may find it helpful to create more than one chart, as Pat did in her project. Begin filling in each chart as your project progresses and look for connections across elements in the chart. If certain elements are scarce, for example, "Curricular Engagements," then stop and reconsider how your data collection and analysis can be extended to your actual teaching curriculum. In your final teacher research write-up, refer to the audit trail charts as a source for your reflections.

## SUGGESTED RESOURCES

### Narrative and Stories

Abrahams, R. (1983). *African folktales: Traditional stories of the Black world*. New York: Pantheon.

Abrahams, R. (1985). *African-American folktales: Stories from Black traditions in the new world*. New York: Pantheon.

Applebee, A. N. (1978). *The child's concept of story: Ages two to seventeen*. Chicago: University of Chicago Press.

Champion, T. B. (2003). *Understanding storytelling among African American children: A journey from Africa to America*. Mahwah, NJ: Erlbaum.

Cruikshank, J. (1998). *The social life of stories: Narrative and knowledge in the Yukon territory*. Lincoln: University of Nebraska Press.

Dyson, A. H., & Genishi, C. (Eds.). (1994). *The need for story: Cultural diversity in classroom and community*. Urbana, IL: National Council of Teachers of English.

Eagan, K. (1986). *Teaching as storytelling: An alternative approach to teaching and curriculum in the elementary school*. Chicago: University of Chicago Press.

Eakin, P. J. (1999). *How our lives become stories: Making selves*. Ithaca, NY: Cornell University Press.

Engel, S. (1995). *The stories children tell*. New York: Freeman.

Isbell, R. T. (2002). Telling and retelling stories: Learning language and literacy. *Young Children, 57*(2), 26–30.

Jalongo, M. R., & Isenberg, J. (1995). *Teachers' stories: From personal narrative to professional insight*. San Francisco: Jossey-Bass.

Lee, C. (1991). Big picture talkers/words walking without masters: The instructional implications for ethnic voices for an expanded literacy. *Journal of Negro Education, 60*(3), 291–304.

Lee, C. (2001). Is October Brown Chinese? A cultural modeling activity system for underachieving students. *American Educational Research Journal, 38*(1), 97–141.

Lindfors, J. W. (1999). *Children's inquiry: Using language to make sense of the world*. New York: Teachers College Press.

Lyons, N., & LaBoskey, V. K. (Eds.) (2002). *Narrative inquiry in practice: Advancing the knowledge of teaching*. New York: Teachers College Press.

Miller, P., & Sperry, L. (1988). Early talk about the past: The origins of conversational stories of personal experience. *Journal of Child Language, 15*, 293–315.

Pagnucci, G. (2004). *Living the narrative life: Stories as a tool for meaning making*. Portsmouth, NH: Heinemann.

Paley, V. G. (1981). *Wally's stories*. Cambridge, MA: Harvard University Press.

Propp, V. (1968). *Morphology of the folktale*. Austin: University of Texas Press.

Ritchie, J., & Wilson, D. (2000). *Teacher narrative as critical inquiry: Rewriting the script*. New York: Teachers College Press.

Whaley, C. (2002). Meeting the diverse needs of children through story telling. *Young Children, 57*(2), 31–35.

## Memoir and Memory

Augenbraum, H., & Stavans, I. (1993). *Growing up Latino: Memoirs and stories*. Boston: Houghton Mifflin.

Carlson, L. (Ed.). (1995). *American eyes: New Asian-American short stories for young adults.* New York: Random House.

Conway, J. K. (1989). *The road from Coorain.* New York: Vintage.

Davis, L. (2000). *My sense of silence: Memoirs of a childhood with Deafness.* Urbana, IL: University of Illinois.

Dillard, A. (1986). *An American childhood.* New York: HarperCollins.

Howard, K. (Ed.). (1990). *Passages: An anthology of the southeast Asian refugee experience.* Fresno State University.

Kim, E. (2000). *Ten thousand sorrows: The extraordinary journey of a Korean war orphan.* New York: Doubleday.

Krupat, A., & Swann, B. (Eds.). (2000). *Here first: Autobiographical essays by Native American writers.* New York: The Modern Library.

Mathabane, M. (1986). *Kaffir boy.* New York: Touchstone.

McBride, J. (1996). *The color of water: A Black man's tribute to his White mother.* New York: Riverhead Books.

Meier, D. (1997). *Learning in small moments: Life in an urban classroom.* New York: Teachers College Press.

Pham, A. (1999). *Catfish and mandala: A two-wheeled voyage through the landscape and memory of Vietnam.* New York: Farrar, Straus, & Giroux.

Stepto, R. (1998). *Blue as the lake.* Boston: Beacon Press.

Ung, L. (2000). *First they killed my father: A daughter of Cambodia remembers.* New York: Perennial.

Walker, R. (2000). *Black, White, and Jewish.* New York: Riverhead Books.

Washington, M. H. (1991). *Memory of kin: Stories about family by Black writers.* New York: Random House.

## Poetry

Baca, J. S. (1986). *Black mesa poems.* New York: New Directions.

Carlson, L. (Ed.). (1994). *Cool salsa: Bilingual poems on growing up Latino in the United States.* New York: Henry Holt.

Jordan, J. (2000). *Soldier: A poet's childhood.* New York: Basic Books.

Kooser, K. (2005). *The poetry home repair kit.* Lincoln: University of Nebraska.

Nye, N. S. (2000). *Come with me: Poems for a journey.* New York: Greenwillow.

Nye, N. S. (2001). *Mint snowball.* Tallahasee, FL: Anhinga Press.

Silko, L. M. (1981). *Storyteller.* New York: Arcade.

Wooldridge, S. G. (1996). *Poemcrazy: Freeing your life with words.* New York: Three Rivers Press.

# CHAPTER 7

# Future Directions for Teacher Research in Early Childhood Education

*Because of teacher research I've flipped my whole philosophy about children and the goals of my teaching.*

—Julie Vazquez-Torres (preschool teacher)

*I'm more aware of myself with the children. I do talk out loud more in my head now. I am more aware of my teaching. I'm also not so hard on myself.*

—Jessica Fickle (toddler teacher)

## FORMS AND FUNCTIONS OF EARLY CHILDHOOD TEACHER RESEARCH

The theory and the examples of early childhood teacher research presented in this book are excellent conceptual and practical places to both start and extend our teacher research. The examples of real-life teacher research projects focus on critical aspects of caregiver and teacher lives in early childhood—children's nonverbal and verbal communication, friendships, games and play, and early literacy learning. These projects provide windows onto particular ways that teacher research can influence our conceptual understanding of how and why children learn and grow, as well as provide a window onto our professional learning and growth. In this latter sense, teacher research is a wonderful homegrown, grass-roots form of professional growth and practitioner knowledge. As Lilian Katz (personal communication, July 20, 2006) says about pursuing long-term projects, that they promote new "dispositions" and "a habit of mind" in intellectual ways, so too does teacher research.

175

In terms of the methodology of the projects, the following are critical aspects of carrying out effective and meaningful teacher research:

- project length (weeks, months, years)
- frequency of data gathering (hourly, daily, weekly)
- length of data-gathering sessions (moments, minutes, half hours, hours)
- children's ages (infant, toddler, preschool, primary)
- role of the teacher researcher (observer, participant, observer/ participant)
- data sources (children's nonverbal interactions, children's conversations, peer-to-peer interactions, adult-to-child interactions, whole group, focus children)
- data collection tools (written fieldnotes, audiocassette recorders, camcorders, reflective teaching journal, data collection sheet, survey, digital camera)
- data analysis ideas (themes, patterns, routines, culling through photographs, selecting audiotapes to transcribe)
- data representation (narrative description, reflective interpretation, internal reflection, charts, tables, transcripts, photographs)

We can add these to our teacher research toolbox, increasing our knowledge and understanding of the value (functions) of teacher research and the process (forms) of doing teacher research well.

## WHY DO TEACHER RESEARCH IN EARLY CHILDHOOD EDUCATION?

Teacher research is a pursuit, like any other that is meaningful and powerful, that takes time, energy, passion, collaboration, and patience. In this sense teacher research is an "add on" to the already overloaded responsibilities of educators in the field. And yet, with the appropriate cooperation and vision of early childhood administrators and policymakers, teacher research has the potential to help us make important changes in our educational lives and the early lives of the young children under our care. As practitioners, teacher research can help us

- redefine how we view our roles as educators
- rethink our educational philosophies
- become more reflective practitioners on our practice
- deepen our conceptual understanding of children's learning and development

- promote opportunities to discover new and improved teaching and caregiving practices
- provide opportunities to collaborate and dialogue with our colleagues
- take a critical stance toward "accepted" and status quo aspects of the profession and field
- improve our skills and talents as observers of and listeners with children
- slow down our teaching and caregiving schedules and pacing, challenging us to watch, listen, feel, and think about the small moments of our children's learning
- provide a "built-in" structure of ongoing professional development both for ourselves and for our colleagues
- extend our ideas, practices, and research findings to local colleagues as well as others in the field of early childhood
- improve our artistic talents in analyzing and representing our research data through art, photography, and writing
- develop our writing talents and skills through written analysis and dissemination of our teacher research
- find a new language and a new passion for working in the early childhood field that prevents teacher "burnout" and promotes a sense of discovery
- provide opportunities to invite children and families to become "co-researchers" in our teacher research, strengthening home–school connections and parent communication
- provide a more diverse range of opinions, ideas, and viewpoints within the field of early childhood educational research
- use research findings to press and advocate for policy changes within the field of early childhood at the local, state, national, and international levels

We are currently at an interesting juncture in the areas of teacher research and classroom teaching and caregiving. We have innovative models for teacher inquiry, such as the project-based learning from the innovative Reggio Emilia schools in Italy, the project approach, and the application of Howard Gardner's multiple intelligences theory. These frameworks, as well as others in early childhood, can be borrowed from to form our own ways of envisioning and doing teacher research. As we take from these innovative curriculum and philosophical movements, we need to take into account our local educational contexts—our own specific children, our families, colleagues, and communities —and fashion forms of teacher research that meet our needs and concerns. In this grass-roots, local effort, teacher research gathers a varied chorus of voices that speak for us as individual educators and as community members.

## WHERE DO WE GO FROM HERE?

What are fruitful new directions for teacher research in early childhood education in terms of the focus of our research? What can happen in terms of practitioners, administrators, families, teacher educators, policymakers, professional organizations?

### Toward an Early Childhood Teacher Research Agenda

There are several areas of children's learning and development, and also practitioner development and growth, that we can focus on in the near future.

- *Social Justice and Equity*: The project undertaken by Pat Sullivan in this book is an excellent example of a practitioner using teacher research to explore issues of social justice and equity in early childhood settings. Since early childhood is the foundation for young children's views and experiences with getting along with one another, and with understanding and taking a stance toward the world of relationships, a focus in teacher research on social justice will deepen our character/social curriculum. It also will help even young children—as Pat shows with her toddlers and preschoolers—become more aware and care deeply about justice and injustice in their immediate worlds. This new focus will help politicize and particularize our curriculum and our relationships with children and families.
- *Children's Cognitive Development*: Teacher researchers can draw upon the structure of developmental and brain-based approaches to further open our eyes to cognitive and social developmental discoveries in the field. An interesting avenue in this area is to see our children as co-researchers in our work, as we discover and learn in cognitively based ways. A renewed teacher research focus on cognition and brain-based work in the field can help us know children in deeper ways not necessarily captured in standard assessments. When we have a good grasp of the cognitive research literature, and have carried out our own teacher research projects on children's cognitive learning, we become wiser consumers and users of the checklist assessments found more and more commonly in early childhood centers across the country.
- *Children's Play*: An early childhood focus on children's play can help us return to one of the hallmarks of high-quality early childhood programs. As seen, for instance, in the teacher research projects undertaken by Julie Vazquez-Torres and Aaron Neimark, teacher research on play deepens our conceptual understanding (how and why children play) and practical applications (e.g., whether to intervene or not).

The decline of playhouses and dramatic play areas in primary grades, and the proliferation of assessments in preschools, combine to make less time and space for play for young children. Often, it is the little "stands" that we take in our centers and schools that help bring back a focus on play. Teacher research, in projects like Julie's and Aaron's and others profiled in Chapter 3, can help turn around the current de-emphasis on the centrality of play in early childhood.

- *Reflection, Knowledge, and Professional Growth*: As more and more states consider universal preschool, and also propose more advanced education and training for early childhood practitioners, teacher research can help with a focus on practitioner reflection and knowledge. It can help sharpen our senses—making our eyes and hearts and minds more sensitive and observant of children's learning (and lack of learning). Teacher research also can help elevate our conceptual understanding of how and why children learn best, and how and why we can make changes in our caregiving and teaching to accommodate and support our diverse children and families. To this end, then, early childhood teacher research projects—along with a focus on an area of learning such as math or science or play or friendships—also need to retain a reflective component. So in the beginning we should ask ourselves, "How do I hope this project will help me become a better observer, thinker, reflector of my children and of my own practice?" And during a project, "Am I reflecting and considering all the interesting angles and nuances of my data so far? What am I missing that I am not doing? What new directions can I go in that would be more fruitful?" And at the end of a project or series of projects, "Ah, I am finally done! No more transcribing and searching for patterns and gems in the data. Now I can ask, 'What did I learn? What would I do differently next time? How have I grown as a practitioner? How have I grown as a teacher researcher?'"

## The Role of Early Childhood Practitioners

*When I was growing up in Veracruz, we were not allowed to talk to each other. One time the teacher threw an eraser across the room to me and told me not to talk to my neighbor, my friend. It must be the opposite in education. You have to foster community and co-dependence. When we do project work and teacher research, we have to talk and collaborate. We have to coexist and work together. The more and more I learn about teaching and reflecting, the more I think that we have to co-depend and collaborate.*

—Michael Escamilla (preschool teacher)

There are several steps we can take to begin our teacher research work.

- Seek out teacher educators with whom you are familiar who are doing work in teacher research, and form a collaborative partnership in which you can seek and receive ongoing mentoring. This mentoring can be done face-to-face at a local institution, by correspondence, or online via email with teacher research mentors who are at a distance from your site.
- Form a teacher research group at your early childhood site and devise a collaborative structure (see the section in Chapter 5 on group collaboration in teacher research) that fits your needs and schedules.
- Undertake a small, short-term teacher research project on your own; use the examples of projects in this book and other resources as a guide to devising and implementing a "doable" and interesting project.
- Disseminate your teacher research work at your site, to local colleagues, at a conference, or on the internet, or submit it for publication to a journal or magazine, or as a book.
- Encourage your administrators, board of directors, and school board to learn more about the value of teacher research; advocate for professional development money and training as well as release time to carry out your teacher research.

## Administrators

*A school is a place of change. The children are like seeds and we are like the water and the sun. We must teach them to talk and communicate and think in new ways. I get frustrated when the administration wants change that only comes from above; change must start in the classroom.*

—Michael Escamilla

Site managers and directors, and other early childhood administrators can take on new roles in terms of promoting teacher research.

- Learn more about the value of teacher research as a form of ongoing, teacher-centered professional development.
- Bring in experienced teacher researchers to inform and educate your faculty and families about the benefits of teacher research.
- Devote a period of time in your faculty meetings for faculty to share and discuss their teacher research data collection and analysis.

- Encourage your faculty to form collaborative teacher research partnerships either within a certain age/grade level or across age/grade levels.
- Encourage practitioners to choose topics and areas of focus of their own interest; avoid imposing your interests or needs (assessments, standards, paperwork) on them.
- Advocate the use of narrative logs, anecdotal records, stories, and photographs rather than checklists for observing children's learning.
- Become involved in selected aspects of the data collection and analysis yourself; present your ongoing findings and speculate on their significance at your meetings.
- "Talk up" the value of your faculty's teacher research work with your families; put this aspect of the teachers' work in writing on your site's website, brochure, informational materials.

## Families

*I remember when some children saw a tiger butterfly in the garden; it was very unique and we knew it from a book. Several kids got together and we went to see the butterfly. I have a picture of the butterfly and the kids; I did not think that this was the beginning of a project. No, I thought that this was a finding, something unique, and I wanted to share the children's excitement with their parents. It was exciting for the children, and for me, and so it must be for the parents, too. Documenting and recording daily learning experiences like the butterfly discovery is not just for me; I am also thinking in terms of the parents, what I want the parents to know about their children.*

—Michael Escamilla

Families can become involved in a site's teacher research work in the following ways:

- If you are looking for an early childhood setting for your child, ask about the site's philosophy and interest in teacher research and other forms of reflective practice.
- If your child is already at a site that does not have an institutionalized form of teacher research, encourage the site director or principal or family care provider to begin work in teacher research.

- If your child's setting already is involved in some form of teacher research, talk with the administrators and the teachers and let them know you are interested in becoming involved; this involvement can range from putting up documentation panels to co-collecting data.
- Carry out your own research at home or in your community (community center, Saturday language/culture school, religious school); take some ideas for teacher research projects from this book and adapt them to fit your needs and interests.

## Teacher Educators

*How can we sustain teacher research when we are not in a teacher education program?*
                                                —Ann Ewbank (teacher educator)

Early childhood teacher educators can play a critical role in promoting teacher research out in the field.

- Whether at the A.A., B.A., M.A., or Ph.D. level in early childhood, create specific courses on teacher research—this will help promote a new generation of early childhood professionals knowledgeable and passionate about teacher research.
- In survey courses on educational research, include attention to the forms and functions of teacher research.
- In courses on early childhood curriculum and children's development, connect observing and assessing children's learning with the critical aspects of reflection, inquiry, and teacher research.
- When assigning papers in a range of courses, expose and encourage students to other forms of writing beside the traditional five-chapter format, and encourage students to use poetry, stories, photography, and art as effective means of representing project findings, ideas, and implications.
- Encourage students to make use of and cite a varied collection of written material in addition to published educational research—this can include short stories, novels, memoir, poetry, and journalism (some of this material can be in a language other than English, with a translation provided).
- Invite students and graduates to present their teacher research work at regional, national, and international conferences.
- Invite students and graduates to publish their teacher research findings.
- Create and serve as mentors to local networks of teacher researchers meeting and collaborating on their shared teacher research.

## Policymakers

*Teacher research is about challenging knowledge that's out there, and at the same time understanding our practice.*
—Mary Klehr (teacher researcher)

Policymakers in early childhood—at the local, state, and national levels—can exert tremendous positive influence for teacher research to become embedded in early childhood practice.

- Advocate for education codes, legislation, and local governance of early childhood education to include funding for and training in teacher research.
- In the creation and improvement of universal preschool at the local and state levels, earmark specific money for training and inservice on teacher research.
- Explicitly include the value of teacher research for fostering teacher inquiry and improving educational practice in policy documents and task force reports.
- Draft policy that allows and encourages early childhood administrators to provide inservice training in teacher research, and for teacher research to be used as a legitimate form of additional observation and assessment.
- Draft policy that links the potential for teacher research for educators working with children 0–5 and those working with children in the primary grades.

## Professional Organizations

Early childhood professional organizations like Zero to Three and the National Association for the Education of Young Children also can play even more important roles in promoting teacher research.

- Include teacher research as a key component for an early childhood site to gain accreditation from NAEYC.
- Devote specific strands and area emphases to teacher research in a professional organization's national and local conferences and professional/leadership institutes.
- Include keynote speakers who will speak on the value of teacher research for the early childhood field.

- Include as a regular feature or highlight the contributions and experiences of teacher researchers in an organization's publications and website.
- Provide a small stipend or grant to interested teacher researchers to fund their own research projects.

THESE ARE ALL important suggestions for possible future directions for teacher research in early childhood. Almost any combination of action steps from these groups of early childhood stakeholders will help promote teacher research. It is important, though, for us not to wait for others to start—we need to advocate now for a place for teacher research in our work and in the early childhood field. Let's pause and think about its potential to change our roles as educators, deepen our understanding of our children, and improve our teaching and caregiving practices. We wish you well in your teacher research and are pleased that this book is one of the stepping stones on your personal and professional journey.

# References

Abu El-Haj, T. R. (2003). Practicing for equity from the standpoint of the particular: Exploring the work of one urban teacher network. *Teachers College Record, 105*, 817–832.

Alipio, V. A. (2004). *The perspectives of international teachers in U.S. early childhood settings*. Unpublished masters field study, San Francisco State University, San Francisco.

Alvarado, K. M. (2006). *Embracing your fears: Exploring science with children*. Unpublished masters field study, San Francisco State University, San Francisco.

Arnett, J. (1989). Caregivers in day-care centers: Does training matter? *Journal of Applied Developmental Psychology, 10*, 541–552.

Ashton-Warner, S. (1963). *Teacher*. London: Virago.

Atwell, N. (1987). *In the middle: Writing, reading, & learning with adolescents*. Upper Montclair, NJ: Boyton Cook.

Ballenger, C. (1999). *Teaching other people's children: Literacy and learning in a bilingual classroom*. New York: Teachers College Press.

Bredekamp, S., & Copple, C. (1997). (Eds.). *Developmentally appropriate practice in early childhood programs* (Rev. ed.). Washington, DC: National Association for the Education of Young Children.

Brookline Teacher Research Seminar. (2003). *Regarding children's words: Teacher research and language and literacy*. New York: Teachers College Press.

Brown, M. W. (1947). *Goodnight moon*. New York: HarperCollins.

Bullough, R., & Pinnegar, S. (2001). Guidelines for quality in autobiographical forms of self-study research. *Educational Researcher, 30*(3), 13–21.

Burnaford, G., Fischer, J., & Hobson, D. (Eds.). (2001). *Teachers doing research: The power of action through inquiry* (2nd ed.). Hillsdale, NJ: Erlbaum.

Cadwell, L. B. (1997). *Bringing Reggio Emilia home: An innovative approach to early childhood education*. New York: Teachers College Press.

Calkins, L. M. (1986). *The art of teaching writing*. Portsmouth, NH: Heinemann.

Carr, W., & Kemmis, S. (1986). *Becoming critical*. London: Falmer Press.

Cheah, A. (2005). *Culture clash*. Unpublished paper, San Francisco State University.

Cheng, A. M. Z. (2004). *First language maintenance of Chinese American children*. Unpublished masters field study, San Francisco State University, San Francisco.

Chock, E. (Ed.) (1981). *Small kid time Hawaii*. Honolulu, HI: Bamboo Ridge Press.

Clandinin, D. J., & Connelly, F. M. (2000). *Narrative inquiry: Experience and story in qualitative research*. San Francisco: Jossey-Bass.

Cochran-Smith, M., & Lytle, S. (1993). *Inside/outside: Teacher research and knowledge*. New York: Teachers College Press.

Cochran-Smith, M., & Lytle, S. (1999). The teacher research movement: A decade later. *Educational Researcher, 28*(7), 15–25.

Collier, J. (1945). United States Indian Administration as a laboratory of ethnic relations. *Social Research, 12,* 265–303.

Committee for Children (2002). *Second Step: A violence prevention curriculum. Preschool/kindergarten-grade 5.* Seattle, WA: Author.

Cooke, B. (2002). *A foundation correspondence on action research: Ronald Lippitt and John Collier.* Institute for Development Policy and Management. Working Paper No. 6/2002. Retrieved January 11, 2005, from http://www.sed.manchester .ac.uk/idpm/publications/wp/mid/mid_wp06.htm

Corsaro, W. (1985). *Friendship and peer culture in the early years.* Norwood, NJ: Ablex.

Day, J. M. (2003). *Culturally responsive teaching and the emergent writing of African American kindergartners.* Unpublished masters field study, San Francisco State University, San Francisco.

DeVries, R., & Kolhberg, L. (1987). *Programs of early education: The constructivist view.* New York: Longman.

Dewey, J. (1902). *The child and the curriculum.* Chicago: University of Chicago Press.

Dewey, J. (1938). *Experience and education.* New York: Macmillan.

Duckworth, E. (1996). *"The having of wonderful ideas" and other essays on teaching and learning* (2nd ed.). New York: Teachers College Press.

Edwards, C., Gandini, L., & Forman, G. (Eds.). (1998). *The hundred languages of children: The Reggio Emilia approach to early childhood education* (2nd ed.). Greenwich, CT: Ablex.

Elliott, J. (1991). *Action research for educational change.* Philadelphia: Open University Press.

Emig, J. (1971). *The composing process of twelfth graders* (Research Report No. 13). Urbana, IL: National Council of Teachers of English.

Escamilla, M. (2004). A dialogue with the shadows. *Young Children, 59*(2), 96–100.

Espiritu, E., Meier, D. R., Villazana-Price, N., & Wong, M. K. (2002). Promoting teacher research in early childhood: A collaborative project on children's language and literacy learning. *Young Children, 57*(5), 71–79.

Fickle, J. (2003). *A foundation of trust: A memoir of a toddler teacher.* Unpublished masters field study, San Francisco State University.

Fisher, A. M. (2004). *The challenges of children's first language maintenance in an urban preschool.* Unpublished masters field study, San Francisco State University, San Francisco.

Foley, L. (2003). *Course project for cognitive development.* Unpublished paper, San Francisco State University, San Francisco.

Frei, L. (2004). *Promoting interactive story reading with preschool English learners.* Unpublished masters field study, San Francisco State University.

Gambrell, L., & Mazzoni, L. (1999). Emergent literacy: What research reveals about learning to read. In C. Seefeldt (Ed.), *The early childhood curriculum: Current findings in theory and practice* (3rd ed., pp. 80–105). New York: Teachers College Press.

Gandini, L., & Goldhaber, J. (2001). Two reflections about documentation. In L. Gandini & C. P. Edwards (Eds.), *Bambini: The Italian approach to infant/toddler care* (pp. 124–145). New York: Teachers College Press.

Goswami, D., & Stillman, P. R. (1987). *Reclaiming the classroom: Teacher research as an agency for change.* Portsmouth, NH: Heinemann.

Grant, G. (2001, Spring). Distorting Dewey: Progressive ideals, lost in translation. *Education Next.* Retrieved August 9, 2006, from http://www.educationnext.org/2001sp/71.html

Graves, D. H. (1983). *Writing: Teachers and children at work.* Portsmouth, NH: Heinemann.

Greene, C. (2003). *Rethinking the meaning of staff development: Research as a permanent learning strategy.* Unpublished masters field study, San Francisco State University, San Francisco.

Grinberg, J. G. A. (2002). "I had never been exposed to teaching like that": Progressive teacher education at Bank Street during the 1930s. *Teachers College Record, 104*(7), 1422–1460.

Hamilton, M. L., & Pinnegar, S. (2000). On the threshold of a new century: Trustworthiness, integrity and self-study in teacher education. *Journal of Teacher Education, 51*(3), 234–240.

Hamilton, M., & Weiss, M. (1990). *Children tell stories: A teaching guide.* New York: Richard C. Owen.

Hankins, K. (1998). From cacophony to symphony: Memoir in teacher research. In B. S. Bisplinghoff & J. Allen (Eds.), *Engaging teachers: Creating teaching and researching relationships* (pp. 13–25). Portsmouth, NH: Heinemann.

Helm, J. H., Beneke, S., & Steinheimer, K. (1998). *Windows on learning: Documenting young children's work.* New York: Teachers College Press.

Himley, M. (Ed.) (with Carini, P. F.). (2000). *From another angle: Children's strengths and school standards: The Prospect Center's descriptive review of the child.* New York: Teachers College Press.

Hohmann, M., & Weikart, D. P. (1995). *Educating young children: Active learning processes for preschool and childcare programs.* Ypsilanti, MI: High/Scope Press.

hooks, b. (1994). *Teaching to transgress: Education as the practice of freedom.* New York: Routledge.

Hubbard, R. S., & Power, B. M. (2003). *The art of classroom inquiry: A handbook for teacher researchers* (Rev. ed.). Portsmouth, NH: Heinemann.

Jubb, C. (with Medina, U., Moreno de Medina, A., Moreno Meza, J., & del Refugio Frias, M.). (2003). *My little ranch in Mexico.* Berkeley, CA: Design Action/Inkworks Press.

Jue, C. (2005). *Adapting a scripted language arts program for first grade English language learners.* Unpublished masters field study, San Francisco State University, San Francisco.

Kamii, C. (1982). *Number in preschool and kindergarten: Educational implications of Piaget's theory.* Washington, DC: National Association for the Education of Young Children.

Kamii, C. (1989). *Young children continue to reinvent arithmetic—2nd grade: implications of Piaget's theory*. New York: Teachers College Press.

Kamii, C., & Housman, L. B. (1999). *Young children continue to reinvent arithmetic—1st grade: Implications of Piaget's theory* (2nd ed.). New York: Teachers College Press.

Kasperzyk, A. (2005). *Environments and the art of teaching: How does a teacher's past environment from childhood affect her role in the environment she currently teaches?* Unpublished paper, San Francisco State University, San Francisco.

Katz, L. G., & Chard, S. C. (1989). *Engaging children's minds: The project approach.* Greenwich, CT: Ablex.

Katz, L. G., & Chard, S. C. (1996). *The contribution of documentation to the quality of early childhood education*, EDO-PS-96-2, pp. 1–5. Retrieved May 1, 2006 from the Clearinghouse on Early Education and Parenting Web site: http:// ceep.crc .uiuc.edu

LaBoskey, V. K. (2004). The methodology of self-study and its theoretical underpinnings. In J. J. Loughran, M. L. Hamilton, V. K. LaBoskey, & T. Russell (Eds.), *International handbook of self-study of teaching and teacher education practices* (pp. 817–869). Dordrecht, The Netherlands: Kluwer Academic.

Lagemann, E. C. (2000). *An elusive science: The troubling history of educational research.* Chicago: University of Chicago Press.

Latif, R. (2005). *I'm not ready.* Unpublished paper, San Francisco State University, San Francisco.

Latif, R. (2006). *Creating a relationship of trust: A personal journey of a teacher.* Unpublished masters field study, San Francisco State University, San Francisco.

Lee, S. (2003). *Leadership development: Mentoring relationship model.* Unpublished masters field study, San Francisco State University, San Francisco.

Lewin, G., & Lewin, K. (1942). Democracy and the school. *Understanding the Child, 10,* 7–11.

Lewin, K. (1938). Experiments on autocratic and democratic principles. *Social Frontier, 4,* 316–319.

Lewin, K. (1946). Action research and minority problems. *Journal of Social Issues, 2*(4), 34–36.

Lewin, K. (1948). *Resolving social conflicts.* New York: HarperCollins.

Lewis, C. C., & Tsuchida, I. (1998, Winter). A lesson is like a swiftly flowing river: How research lessons improve Japanese education. *American Educator,* pp. 12–17, 50–53.

Lin, M. (2004). *Storytelling: The story of one child.* Unpublished paper, San Francisco State University.

Lopez, K. (2005). *The role of language in the infant–caregiver reciprocal relationship.* Unpublished masters field study, San Francisco State University.

Loughran, J., & Northfield, J. (1998). A framework for the development of self-study practices. In M. L. Hamilton (Ed.), *Reconceptualizing teacher practice: Self-study in teacher education.* London: Falmer Press.

Lyons, N., & LaBoskey, V. K. (Eds.). (2002). *Narrative inquiry in practice: Advancing the knowledge of teaching.* New York: Teacher College Press.

Markevich, A. (2006). *The impact of play on young children's learning of mathematical concepts*. Unpublished masters field study, San Francisco State University, San Francisco.

McGaughey, L. (2001). *Young children's approaches to computers: A comparison of two settings*. Unpublished masters field study, San Francisco State University, San Francisco.

McNiff, J., Lomax, P., & Whitehead, J. (1996). *You and your action research project*. New York: Routledge.

Meier, D. R. (2000). *Scribble scrabble: Learning to read and write with diverse children, families, and teachers*. New York: Teachers College Press.

Meisels, S. J., Jablon, J. R., Marsden, D. B., Dichtelmiller, M. L., Dorfman, A. B., & Steele, D. M. (1994). *An overview: The work sampling system*. Ann Arbor, MI: Rebus Planning Associates.

Miles-Banta, L. (2004). *Building community among five-year-olds*. Unpublished masters field study, San Francisco State University, San Francisco.

Neimark, A. (2005). *Do you want to see something goofy? Peer culture in the preschool yard*. Unpublished masters field study, San Francisco State University.

Ng, I. (2006). *Learning to balance skills and meaning in a preschool literacy curriculum*. Unpublished masters field study, San Francisco State University.

Noffke, S. E., & Stevenson, R. E. (Eds.). (1995). *Educational action research: Becoming practically critical*. New York: Teachers College Press.

Noffke, S. E., & Zeichner, K. M. (1987, April). *Action research and teacher thinking: The first phase of the action research on action research projects at the University of Wisconsin–Madison*. Paper presented at the annual meeting of the American Educational Research Association, Washington, DC.

Olsen, C. (2001). *Adult learners' response toward constructivist strategies in an ECE teacher training program*. Unpublished masters field study, San Francisco State University, San Francisco.

Paley, V. G. (1981). *Wally's stories*. Cambridge, MA: Harvard University Press.

Paley, V. G. (1984). *Boys and girls: Superheroes in the doll corner*. Cambridge, MA: Harvard University Press.

Paley, V. (1988). *Bad guys don't have birthdays: Fantasy play at four*. Cambridge, MA: Harvard University Press.

Paley, V. (1990). *The boy who would be a helicopter*. Cambridge, MA: Harvard University Press.

Paras-Frei, J. (2004). *Togetherness and community for toddlers in early childhood education*. Unpublished masters field study, San Francisco State University, San Francisco.

Piaget, J. (1950). *The psychology of intelligence*. New York: Harcourt Brace.

Piaget, J., & Inhelder, B. (1969). *The psychology of the child*. New York: Basic Books.

Richardson, C. (2001). *Caregiver responsiveness and the quality of infant-caregiver attachment in child care*. Unpublished masters field study, San Francisco State University, San Francisco.

Richardson, D. (2002). *Second Step® and social/emotional learning among African*

*American and Latino children.* Unpublished masters field study, San Francisco State University, San Francisco.

Schön, D. (1983). *The reflective practitioner: How professionals think in action.* New York: Basic Books.

Shyu, J. T. (2005). *Book reading with infants: How caregivers promote language development for infants.* Unpublished paper, San Francisco State University, San Francisco.

Soulé, J. M. (2003). *Marble tracks project.* Unpublished paper, San Francisco State University, San Francisco.

Soulé, J. M. (2004). *The early childhood classroom environment: How children use play spaces.* Unpublished masters field study, San Francisco State University, San Francisco.

Stackwood (Swanegan), S. (2001). *Developing a curriculum on character education for primary students.* Unpublished masters field study, San Francisco State University, San Francisco.

Stenhouse, L. (1981). What counts as research? *British Journal of Educational Studies, 29*(2), 103–114.

Stevenson, S. (2003). *Understanding and improving teacher retention in early childhood programs.* Unpublished masters field study, San Francisco State University, San Francisco.

Stribling, S., & Kraus, S. (in press). Balancing meaning and mechanics in the writing of first-grade children. *Beyond the Journal,* Young Children. http://www.journal.naeyc.org/btj/vp/

Sullivan, P. (2005). *Critical literacy with preschoolers.* Unpublished paper, San Francisco State University, San Francisco.

Tanner, L. (1997). *Dewey's laboratory school: Lessons for today.* New York: Teachers College Press.

Thrupp, M. (2005). *The shark boy: Use of strong interests in play.* Unpublished masters field study, San Francisco State University, San Francisco.

Tidwell, D. (2006). Nodal moments as a context for meaning. In D. L. Tidwell & L. M. Fitzgerald (Eds.), *Self-study and diversity* (pp. 267–286). Rotterdam, The Netherlands: SensePublishers.

Traiprakong, S. (2004). *Promoting story dramatization in preschool.* Unpublished masters field study, San Francisco State University, San Francisco.

Vasquez, V. M. (2004). *Negotiating critical literacies with young children.* Mahwah, NJ: Erlbaum.

Vasquez-Torres, J. (2004). *Preschool children's fantasy play in a Montessori environment.* Unpublished masters field study, San Francisco State University.

Vecchi, V. (1998). The role of the Atelierista: An interview with Lella Gandini. In C. Edwards, L. Gandini, & G. Forman (Eds.), *The hundred languages of children: Advanced reflections on the Reggio Emilia approach to early childhood education* (2nd ed., pp. 139–148). Greenwich, CT: Ablex.

Vygotsky, L. S. (1978). *Mind in society: The development of higher psychological processes.* Cambridge, MA: Harvard University Press.

Vygotsky, L. S. (1986). *Thought and language.* Boston, MA: MIT Press.

Waddell, P., McDaniel, M., & Einstein, G. (1988). Illustrations as adjuncts to prose: A text appropriate processing approach. *Journal of Educational Psychology, 80*(4), 457–464.

Waters, E., & Deane, K. (1985). Defining and assessing individual differences in attachment relationships: Q-methodology and the organization of behavior in infancy and childhood. In I. Bretherton & E. Waters (Eds.), *Growing points of attachment theory and research* (pp. 41–65). Chicago: Monographs for the Society of Research in Child Development.

Weber, N. (2005). *Growing up in the Mojave desert*. Unpublished paper, San Francisco State University.

*Word from the (415): Poems and stories by youth of San Francisco*. (1996). San Francisco: WritersCorps Books.

# Index

# About the Authors

**Daniel Meier** is an Associate Professor of Elementary Education at San Francisco State University. His teaching and research interests are children's first and second language and literacy learning, teacher research, and narrative inquiry and memoir. He is the author of *Learning in Small Moments—Life in an Urban Classroom*, *Scribble Scrabble—Learning to Read and Write*, and *The Young Child's Memory for Words—Developing First and Second Language and Literacy*. All of the books are published by Teachers College Press. He also serves, with Barbara Henderson, as co-editor of "Voices of Practitioners," an online feature of NAEYC's *Young Children* journal.

**Barbara Henderson** is an Associate Professor in the Department of Elementary Education at San Francisco State University. She received her Ph.D. in Education from Stanford University in 1996, her Multiple Subjects teaching credential at San Francisco State University, and her B.A. from Haverford College. At Stanford, she was awarded a Spencer Foundation fellowship, which in part funded her dissertation work. Her dissertation was a teacher research study on early literacy, focusing on how diverse children in an urban public school setting develop voice as authors. Her more recent work has been self-study research of her teacher education practice, especially ways of teaching the methodology and practices of teacher research. At San Francisco State University, Barbara works with elementary teacher credential students and with students pursuing Master of Arts in Education degrees with a concentration in Early Childhood Education. Her courses address cognitive, social-emotional, and physical development and learning in cultural contexts, and teacher research. Previously Barbara taught children at the elementary and preschool levels.